THE

NUCLEAR
SPHINX
of TEHRAN

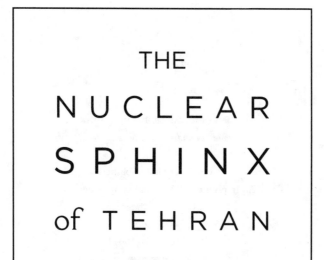

THE
NUCLEAR
SPHINX
of TEHRAN

MAHMOUD
AHMADINEJAD
AND THE STATE
OF IRAN

YOSSI MELMAN and MEIR JAVEDANFAR

CARROLL & GRAF PUBLISHERS
NEW YORK

THE NUCLEAR SPHINX OF TEHRAN
Mahmoud Ahmadinejad and the State of Iran

Carroll & Graf Publishers
An Imprint of Avalon Publishing Group Inc.
245 West 17th Street
11th Floor
New York, NY 10011

AVALON
publishing group incorporated

Copyright © 2007 by Yossi Melman and Meir Javedanfar

First Carroll & Graf edition 2007

ISBN-13: 978-0-78671-887-0
ISBN-10: 0-7867-1887-0

9 8 7 6 5 4 3 2 1

Interior design by *Maria E. Torres*

Printed in the United States of America
Distributed by Publishers Group West

Contents

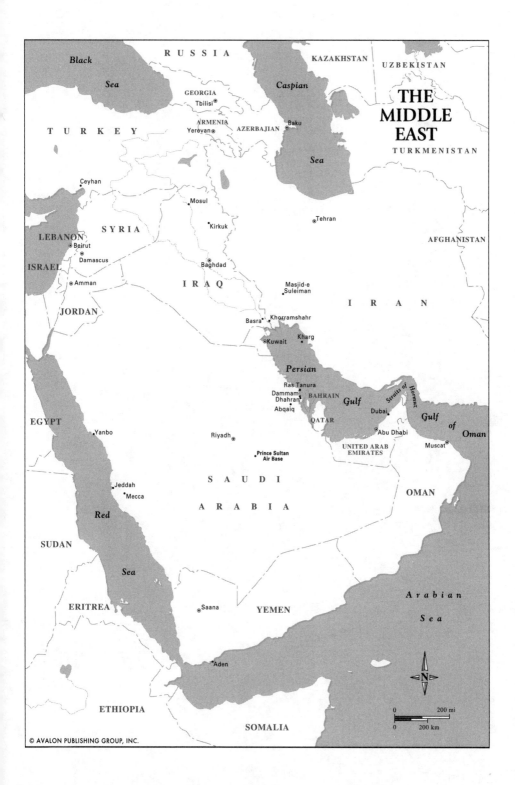

Acknowledgments

THIS BOOK OWES its birth to the intellectual generosity of many people who shared with us their insights and thoughts about Iran and its nuclear program. We interviewed many dozens of sources. Very few of them agreed to be named. Most demanded anonymity. These are civil servants, scientists, IAEA officials, intelligence operatives, military personnel, and other experts in their respective fields. Among these were many Iranians inside and outside Iran. During the research for this book we had to walk a tightrope between maintaining our integrity as investigative journalists and analysts, and our obligation to the safety of our sources. We had to honor and protect their readiness to speak to us.

The world perceives Iran as a closely monitored society, a country ruled by an iron fist. There are elements of truth in this description. However, Iran is a multifaceted and intriguing society. Within its Islamic boundaries there is sufficient room for vivid discussions and diversity.

These debates have increased since Mahmoud Ahmadinejad was elected president in the summer of 2005. His inflammatory rhetoric has turned into a grave source of concern for most of the international community. The fear is growing that in the near future he who called to wipe Israel off the map may have his finger on the nuclear button. However, many Iranians are also worried that their president's words are leading to further isolation of their country. Because of these developments, 2007 and 2008 may become a historic junction, not only for Iran, Israel, and the whole of the Middle East, but also to the entire world.

We are grateful to our agent Linda Langton, who laboriously pushed this project to see the light of the day. She deserves our deep gratitude. We thank Adelaide Docx, the assistant editor, for her painstaking work, and Walter Bode, our editor, for his meticulous professionalism.

Last but not least, we owe a great debt to our families who supported us.

Yossi Melman dedicates this book to Billie, Yotam, and Daria and to his parents who passed away and can't be with him today to read it.

Meir Javedanfar dedicates this book to his parents and brother, to Mr. Nethanel (Navid) Toobian, and to Mr. Bayat, his high school history teacher in Iran, the beloved land of his birth.

Prologue: The Funeral

"MY DAD WAS an ironmonger," said Mahmoud Ahmadinejad, in Tehran Radio's studio 4, during a preelection interview. "He worked very hard so I could go to the University of Science and Technology and study civil engineering. But in 1993 Father passed away due to an accident."[1]

A year later Mahmoud Ahmadinejad, president of the Islamic Republic of Iran, helped lower his father's coffin into the grave. Ahmad Ahmadinejad died in 2006 from heart complications, not in an accident in 1993 as his son had claimed in 2005. No one is quite sure why Ahmadinejad told such a palpable lie so publicly. Perhaps he thought he could shield his family from the public spotlight. Or perhaps he was trying to hide something.

He was not, however, trying to hide his father, at whose graveside he showed deep grief and full respect alongside his brothers and sisters. Mahmoud Ahmadinejad had visited his father frequently during Ahmad's illness and, in November 2005, canceled a planned visit to Tunisia because of his father's ill health.[2]

The funeral of Ahmad Ahmadinejad offers a glimpse into the mysterious life and beliefs of his son, the president of Iran, one of the most influential leaders in the international arena. From beginning to end, the ceremony was carried out in strict Islamic fashion. Everyone in the large crowd of mourners, including Mahmoud Ahmadinejad, wore black, the color of mourning in Shiite Islam. Members of the public and government officials filled Narmak mosque. They prayed and afterward beat their chests rhythmically to the sound of drums. This is similar to the rituals of Ashura, the

Shiite tradition dating back to the death of Imam Hussein, the third Shiite imam.[3]

Ahmad was a popular figure in his community and a deeply religious man. Legend has it that he prayed every day of his last thirty years in Narmak mosque.[4] His family in his native Aradan province told visitors that he had refused to eat at the table of people who did not pay Zakat (Muslim alms). According to relatives, when he sold his house in Tehran for approximately $55,000, he donated half to charity.[5]

After Ahmad's grave was covered in flowers, Mahmoud Ahmadinejad thanked the mourners and offered them a story about his father. He told them how his father had been a devoted follower of the martyred Imam Hussein, contributing money to the Ashura ceremony each year—save one, when he was having financial difficulty and genuinely could not afford to help. He felt so guilty about this that he became exhausted and started having nightmares. Then one night he dreamed that someone came to him and said, "Don't worry, Ashura has its own master. It will look after itself." The next day he ran into a friend in the bazaar. Upon learning of his predicament, the friend immediately offered to lend him money.[6] Ahmad's dream had come true.

For seven days after his father's death, Mahmoud Ahmadinejad did not smile once for the cameras. His lips cracked open only at the sight of a group of visitors whose profession had given him many happy memories: the Iranian national football team.

The year that elapsed between the announcement about the fictitious death of father and the real one, the emotional funeral, and the sudden change of mood in front of his heroes—perfectly exemplifies the enigmatic nature of the Nuclear Sphinx of Tehran.

CHAPTER ONE

Faith and Family

ON OCTOBER 28, 1956, Seyyede Khanom Saborjhian gave birth to her fourth child, a boy named Mahmoud, during a difficult time for the Saborjhian household. Ahmad, Mahmoud's father, was struggling to make ends meet with the income from his barbershop in the village of Aradan, near the Alborz Mountains, four and a half hours from Tehran by car.[1] Both Ahmad and Seyyede Khanom were born and brought up there, and at the time of Mahmoud's birth they lived in a rented house on Hemat Abad Avenue, near the Hosseiniye where villagers gathered to mourn the martyrdom of Imam Hussein, the third Shiite imam.[2]

Ahmad Saborjhian's barbershop turned out to be his second business failure, following a grocery store that proved unprofitable.[3] By 1957, on the advice of Seyyede Khanom's brother, the family decided to follow him to the nation's capital.[4] Moving to Tehran was very common in those days for poor people in search of economic opportunities. The family settled in the Pamanar neighborhood, an impoverished district in southern Tehran near the main city bazaar.[5]

Ahmad Saborjhian initially made a living teaching the Koran, but his meager income necessitated yet another career change, his fourth in two

1

years.[6] His decision to become a blacksmith proved a wise one, however, for in the late 1950s Tehran was experiencing a construction boom largely fueled by the migration of hundreds of thousands of rural folk, and blacksmiths were in demand. As Saborjhian had done, such migrants usually settled in the poorer sections of southern Tehran, turning some neighborhoods into temporary shantytowns with no running water or electricity.

Lacking sufficient funds to establish his own business, Saborjhian entered into a partnership, opening a shop in the Narmak neighborhood, close to the Narmak Jame mosque where he regularly prayed.[7] The family later moved to this neighborhood.

Soon after the family's move to the big city, Ahmad Saborjhian made what might have been a difficult decision for him—he changed his name. In Iran in the early 1900s, most people had been instructed to adopt surnames, a custom not widely practiced in rural areas before then, and many chose names related to their profession or their native region. "Saborjhian" originates from the occupation of thread painting, a skill used in weaving carpets, suggesting that Ahmad's ancestors were employed in that industry. In Iran carpet weaving is associated with the countryside and sweatshops employing children as young as twelve, who were and still are paid next to nothing. Therefore the name might have aroused disdain among Tehranis, many of whom called migrants from the country *dehati,* a derogatory term for "peasant." The change of surname meant disconnecting from the family, from its heritage and roots.

The new surname, Ahmadinejad, very cleverly incorporated references to Ahmad and Seyyede Khanom's background and strong religious beliefs. *Ahmad,* or righteous, is one of the many names of the Prophet Muhammad. Also, by reflecting his own first name in his surname, Ahmad ensured that all future Ahmadinejads would remember the name of their forefather, who had sacrificed his past by moving to Tehran to better his descendants' lives. The second part of the name, *nejad,* means "a race of people," so the two words conjoined signify "from the race of Prophet Muhammad."

Seyyede Khanom's family are in fact direct descendents of the Prophet Muhammad. Seyyede is an honorific title, the feminine form of Seyyed (which her father carried) and one of the titles used in the Shiite world to distinguish those who have a direct bloodline to the Holy Prophet. In her native Aradan, she was called Seyyede out of respect for her father. Many locals don't even know what her real name was.[8] In Tehran Seyyede Khanom gave birth to another three children, bringing the total to seven: four girls and three boys. Mahmoud, barely one year old at the time of the move, attended the Saadi school for his junior schooling and then the Daneshmand high school, situated in the Narmak neighborhood where he grew up.[9] The young Ahmadinejad was known as an intelligent, studious, and dutiful child. He woke up early in the morning to review his notes for the upcoming school day, in sharp contrast to many other children in Iran. Tardiness at school was so common there that, in the 1980s, national television produced an entire fifty-part program to teach children how to arrive at school on time. The mother of a friend called Ahmadinejad Mahmoudy the good boy and told her son that Mahmoud would "make sure you won't be led astray."[10] As a schoolboy, this son of a former Koran teacher was excluded from Koran lessons for being too young. Showing the determination and stubbornness that would later be so evident, Ahmadinejad insisted, "No, no, I know how to read the Koran."[11]

Ahmadinejad's aspirations and determination made him a successful student well into his high school years. According to classmate Nasser Hadian, he finished as the best student in many subjects in high school, English included.[12] And after his friends and fellow congregants at the mosque asked him to lead extra classes in subjects such as mathematics. Since then Ahmadinejad developed a passion for teaching.[13]

He was similarly committed to his family, even in high school. When Mahmoud realized that his father was having financial problems, he took a job at a neighbor's workshop, where he ran the metal press used to produce parts for air conditioners.[14] At times Ahmadinejad's devotion to his family has proved so intense that it made him embarrassingly blind to convention and protocol. For example, he once took his father to meet Iran's Supreme Leader, Ali Khamenei. Despite his limited education (only six years of junior high school), Ahmad Ahmadinejad liked to write poetry, a skill that in Iran is associated with high levels of education and artistic talent.[15] To read poems in public, especially before distinguished guests, is an honor usually reserved for those who have high literary qualifications. Nonetheless, during the meeting Ahmad recited poems in praise of Khamenei and the late Ayatollah Khomeini.[16] Mahmoud was unfazed.

Ahmadinejad was equally dedicated to his religion—understandably so, given his family background. His mother was renowned in their native Aradan for her piousness; in gatherings she would not sit next to men who were unrelated or unknown to her. Ahmadinejad's religious upbringing did have an impact on his anti-U.S. views. His father often took the young Mahmoud to the mosque where, among other topics, the influence of the United States on Iran was severely criticized.[17] After finishing school in 1974, Ahmadinejad decided to take the university entrance exam, known to be the most competitive test in Iran's entire educational system. Those students who can afford it enroll in expensive preparatory classes for the Concours, as it is called, using the French word. Ahmadinejad was not one of those students.[18] Nonetheless, he had good grades, was determined to succeed, and most important, knew that without a university degree he would have little chance of breaking out of the poverty that had trapped his parents and friends. Furthermore, not taking the opportunity to improve his future would have been to flout the very sacrifice his parents had made by coming to Tehran seventeen years earlier.

The exam puts enormous psychological pressure on students. Some show symptoms of nervous breakdown; others get sick before, during, and after taking it. In some extreme cases it has even led to suicide. Ahmadinejad was so ambitious and self-assured that he predicted he would achieve one of the top ten places in the country. In 1975 he sat the Concours exams with approximately 150,000 other students. In the middle of the exam, his nose suddenly started to bleed. His nerves had finally caught up with him. Undeterred, Ahmadinejad cleaned himself up and continued. Despite the upset, his score was the 132nd highest. It wasn't the top ten place that he had originally predicted, nevertheless, this score was very respectable, as it placed him in the top 1 percent of all those taking the exam in Iran.[19]

Ahmadinejad's good grades would have enabled him to attend any university. He was accepted by a number of them, including the prestigious Amir Kabir University. He chose in 1975, to attend the University of Science and Technology because it was close to his house in Narmak. He enrolled in a civil engineering course, a logical choice for the son of an ironmonger who had long worked on building sites. The construction industry, which had enabled Mahmoud's father to feed seven children, was still booming. A civil engineer could provide an even better life for his own family. Furthermore, there is less prejudice in the construction sector than in other professions, since the majority of workers are from the countryside. Ahmadinejad, a man with strong rural roots, would fit in with the workers, thus increasing his chances for success.

The second half of the 1970s were exciting and tense years; the shah's regime was beginning to show its first cracks. Mahmoud became politically active and had several channels of expression open to him. Coming from a poor family, he could have easily joined the student branch of the communist Toodeh Party, to which many young people with underprivileged backgrounds belonged. He might have been tempted to join the MEK (Mujahedeen Khalq—People's Mujahedeen movement) because of its insistent call for justice and equality. He could even have been tempted to join SAVAK. An acronym for Sazemane Ettelaat va Amniyate Keshvar (the National Organization for Intelligence and Security), SAVAK was the shah's feared and hated omnipotent security service.

Ahmadinejad chose to stay true to the religious convictions his parents had instilled in him. He first became one of the founders and an active member of the Islamic Student Union. At the time, it was said in Iran that the bright young urban students joined the MEK whereas the Islamic groups with slower, more parochial students joined Islamic groups, such as Ahmadinejad's Islamic Students Union. It seems that Ahmadinejad's excellence in class was an exception among the Muslim student hard-liners who were battling the shah's reign. He later joined another prominent Islamic student society, Daftare Tahkim va Vahdat—the Office for Strengthening and Unity (OSU). Its main aim was to support cooperation between university and religious students in activities against the shah. The head of this organization was Ayatollah Seyyed Muhammad Beheshti, Ayatollah Khomeini's right-hand man. He created the revolutionary council, which brought together many anti-shah organizations, the OSU among them.

In addition to his OSU activities, Ahmadinejad was involved in the publication and distribution of *Jeegh va Daad* (Scream and Shout), a religious student magazine. This was dangerous. Ahmadinejad could have been arrested, either by the police or by one of the feared secret services, for disseminating anti-shah information. On a number of occasions members of the magazine staff got into fistfights with rival Marxist students outside the university gates.

In the prerevolutionary days, members of the student Islamic society were at the forefront of the demonstrations and attacks against the shah. Many were arrested and tortured. The harrowing stories of torment meted out by SAVAK were the stuff of nightmares for both young revolutionaries and their families, who were sometimes also tortured as a result of their child's activities. Electrocution, beatings of the genitalia, and hot irons applied to prisoners' backs were popular methods practiced by SAVAK, leaving many prisoners scarred for life—if they survived at all. These horror stories sent antigovernment activists and their families, such as the Ahmadinejads, into hiding. Fearing that they would be easily found in their native Semnan province, the family took refuge with close friends in the Golestan province, north of Tehran.[20] Mahmoud disappeared, too, but only for a short time, returning to Tehran before Imam Khomeini's return from exile in February 1979.

By 1979 Ahmadinejad's anti-shah activities had raised his standing in the OSU.[21] Senior revolutionary figures took notice and sent him to Lebanon to meet with Lebanese Shiite militias.[22] This might have been Ahmadinejad's first and only trip abroad before he was elected president twenty-six years later.[23] The trip that intrigues most observers, however, is one that would have taken him only to the other side of Tehran. Unfortunately, it is near impossible to establish whether Ahmadinejad crossed the barbed wire outside the U.S. embassy compound in Tehran when it was seized by his fellow student colleagues in September 1979.

In 2005 an opposition Iranian Web site, Iran Focus, published what it said were pictures of Ahmadinejad accompanying an American hostage after the embassy takeover.[24] According to its reports, Ahmadinejad was involved in the planning stages of the attack.[25] The Arabic television network Al Jazeera has reported that he was in favor of attacking the U.S. and Soviet embassies simultaneously.[26] A number of former hostages claim that they indeed saw Ahmadinejad.[27]

On the other hand, the president's aide, Meisan Rowhani, denies that Ahmadinejad was involved in the actual capture of the U.S. embassy. "He thought that if we did that, the world would swallow us,"[28] said Rowhani. Ahmadinejad dropped his opposition to the attack after he heard that Ayatollah Khomeini supported it. To date, neither the CIA nor Israeli intelligence nor the British MI6 secret intelligence service have been able to determine with "relative certainty" whether Ahmadinejad was involved in the taking of U.S. hostages in 1979.[29]

The other major event in Ahmadinejad's life as a student was meeting his future wife, who was also studying at the University of Science and Technology. In 1980, when Mahmoud was twenty-four, the couple married on the university grounds.[30] She subsequently received her mechanical engineering degree and went on to earn a master's degree in education from the same university. She then became a lecturer there, remaining until her husband's election in 2005.[31]

Public appearances by Mrs. Ahmadinejad have been rare. No one saw her during the presidential campaign. No reference was made to her in Ahmadinejad's biography in the presidential campaign literature. The world caught the first glimpse of Mrs. Ahmadinejad on March 2, 2006, when she accompanied her husband on an official trip to Malaysia. Dressed in a black chador, she appeared next to her husband in a number of official photos. She never uttered a word in front of the cameras.

Husband and wife both believe in a simple and puritanical lifestyle. According to an Iranian blogger, when Ahmadinejad was mayor of Tehran a family friend went to the Ahmadinejads' house to apply for a permit. When he rang the bell, Mrs. Ahmadinejad opened the door and the visitor presented her with a box of chocolates along with a letter explaining why he wished to apply for the permit. Mrs. Ahmadinejad told him, "I am going to take either the letter or the box of chocolates; the choice is yours. We are not used to taking presents for doing our job, and if we wanted to accept such presents our lifestyle would not be simple. Instead we would have a more luxurious lifestyle."[32] Until very recently the couple and their three children lived in a three-bedroom home on 82nd Plaza in Narmak, built in 1965.[33]

When elected president, Ahmadinejad vowed not to be a "palace dweller," adamantly asserting that he would continue living in his house. However, for reasons of security the Ahmadinejads moved not long after the election to the presidential residence on Pastor Street in Tehran. Even after moving, though, they maintained a spartan lifestyle. "There weren't even sofas in the living room," noted a recent visitor. The family still owns their old house in Narmak, which is now the president's public relations office. Some of their furniture remains there.[34]

Ahmadinejad was also forced to stop driving his thirty-year-old Peugeot, which has no air-conditioning, for security reasons.[35] These days he is driven everywhere in a jeep, which doesn't stop him from reaching out through the sunroof to collect request letters from the public. On a visit to the Golestan province in March 2006, he received 135,000 letters, the majority of which were passed to his delegation, but he has also been seen on numerous occasions with his hands full of them.[36]

Mrs. Ahmadinejad's cooking seems to particularly please Mahmoud. Tehran is not short of restaurants and the Tehran municipal building has its own canteen. However, during his tenure as mayor of Tehran, Ahmadinejad was famed for taking home-cooked lunches to work every day. While on his first official visit as president to the United Nations in New York in 2005, a *Time* magazine reporter asked Ahmadinejad if he still brought his lunch to work in a bag. "That continues," he replied, adding, "Is there a problem with that? What's wrong if you want to eat the food that your wife has cooked?"[37]

The Ahmadinejads have three children together, a daughter and two sons. Their daughter is an engineer like her father, having completed her electrical engineering degree in 2006. She married in 2005 and will likely make Ahmadinejad a grandfather in due course.

Their second child, Mahdi, went to his father's alma mater. On August 14, 2005, Mahdi was elected a chairman of the Islamic Students Union's central committee, again following in the footsteps of his father.[38] It has been reported, though, that in November 2005 Mahdi Ahmadinejad was removed from his post for "not fulfilling his commitments and lack of commitment to the organization's regulations."[39] In 2006 a local newspaper in northern Iran reported that Ahmadinejad had chosen a bride for Mahdi from Iran's Mazandaran province, a region whose women are renowned for their beauty.[40] So far there has been no further news about the wedding.

Being the president's son does have its disadvantages. Many people come to Mahdi with their financial problems, hoping he will get his father to help. One particularly distasteful instance occurred at the mourning ceremony for Mahdi's grandfather Ahmad at the Narmak mosque. Thirty minutes into the ceremony, Mahdi stepped into the garden and was immediately confronted by a young man. Ignoring the fact that Mahdi was mourning the recent loss of his grandfather in a holy place, the young man beseeched him to ask his father for help with a $21,000 debt. Mahdi politely listened, and then reentered the mosque.[41]

The Ahmadinejads also have a teenage son, Ali Reza. He completed high school in 2005. In 2006, Ali Reza followed his mother's footsteps, by taking a degree course in mechanical engineering, but in Amir Kabir University, and not the University of Science and Technology. During the 2005 presidential elections Ali Reza accompanied his father on a number of campaign trips to southern Tehran. He is a quiet and shy teenager with a huge appetite for the Internet. On at least on one occasion Ahmadinejad has bemoaned the large Internet phone bills that Ali Reza had incurred.

In the early days following the revolution, Ahmadinejad and his comrades focused on assisting the regime with its plans to turn the country into a strict Islamic state. Within a year, however, another dramatic event changed the direction of Iran and of Ahmadinejad's life. In September 1980 Saddam Hussein's Iraqi forces invaded Iran. Ahmadinejad's election autobiography says that as soon as the war broke out, he rushed to the western region of the country. The Farsi wording—*dar fa'aliyat'haye poshtibani mantaghe talash kard*—translates as "he took part in supportive activities in the region" (the west of Iran). The expression *fa'aliyat'haye poshtibani,* or "supportive activities," is used in times of war to describe logistical support that assists the combat forces operating on the front line.

We are forced to guess the kind of support Ahmadinejad provided, though, as his own election Web site, Mardomyar.com, did not give exact dates for his activities immediately after the outbreak of the conflict. It says only that during the 1360 decade of the Iranian calendar (1981–91) he served the people of Maku, Khoy, and the Kurdistan province for a total of six years.[42] The Iranian opposition has leveled many accusations at him in regard to this period, some charging that he made the details deliberately ambiguous to hide his alleged involvement in the execution of political prisoners at the notorious Evin prison.[43] This prison is where SAVAK brutally tortured and executed the regime's opponents. After the revolution Khomeini's judicial officials turned the prison into their own chamber of horrors, where unlimited pain and death was inflicted on anyone deemed antirevolutionary.

A newly discovered interview that Ahmadinejad gave to Iran Radio as part of his election campaign sheds some light on this matter. In it Ahmadinejad states that during the first four years of the war, he was deputy governor and then governor of the cities of Maku and Khoy. For the next two years he served as a construction consultant to the governor of the Kurdistan province.[44]

The question remains why his election biography fails to mention exactly when he served as a bureaucrat. Why doesn't it say that in the first six years of war Ahmadinejad worked in an office? Is it because such an acknowledgment would have damaged his image as a revolutionary patriot? Perhaps he didn't want people to know he was sitting behind a desk while others were getting killed at the front. There is further confusion over the start date of his military service. According to his election biography, "In the Persian calendar year of 1365 [1986], Ahmadinejad voluntarily joined the Islamic Revolutionary Guard Corp (IRGC)." However, in the same Iran Radio interview Ahmadinejad specifically said that during 1365 (1986), "I was working as an advisor in the Kurdistan region." During the same radio interview Ahmadinejad said that in the years after 1366–1367 [1987 and 1988], "I was in charge of engineering duties at the sixth brigade of the IRGC."

So was Ahmadinejad lying in saying he joined the war in 1986, when in reality he only enlisted in 1987? Another fact in his election biography makes the 1986 date questionable: he claims to have received his master's degree that same year. Surely it is impossible to have completed a master's while fighting in the war. It is far more probable that he studied for his MS while an advisor in the Kurdistan province in 1986 and only upon its completion a year later did he join the on IRGC. In other words, it is likely that Ahmadinejad only served one year and eight months, from 1987 until the end of the war in August 1988, and that his extension of this time years later was an attempt to improve his revolutionary credentials.

During the war Ahmadinejad was based at the IRGC's Ramezan Garrison in western Iran. According to his election biography, he served with a special unit of the IRGC and after completing a training program in the Ramezan garrison, he took part in Special Forces attacks in the Kirkuk area of northern Iraq.[45]

It has also been alleged that during his stint in the Ramezan garrison, Ahmadinejad was part of al-Quds brigade, which runs the IRGC's foreign special operations. This unit was, and continues to be, behind the murder of Iranian dissidents in a number of European cities, including Berlin, Rome, and Vienna. It is also reportedly in charge of training and maintaining links with terrorist groups around the world, such as Hezbollah in Lebanon. What seems certain about this period is that during his service with the IRGC, Ahmadinejad was in charge of the engineering tasks of the IRGC's sixth brigade and served in the war office responsible for Iran's western provinces.[46]

According to Iranian opposition sources, it was while in the Ramezan garrison that Ahmadinejad met General Aziz Jaafari, a.k.a. Muhammad Jaafar Sahraroudi, the IRGC commander who led an assassination team in Vienna.[47]

On July 13, 1989, three bodies riddled with bullets were found in a small apartment in Vienna. They were Abdul Rahman Ghasemlou, the secretary-general of the Democratic Party of Iranian Kurdistan (PDKI), his associate Abdullah Ghadrazar, and their Iraqi friend Professor Fadel Rasul.[48] The flat belonged to an Austrian who allowed these representatives of Iranian Kurds to use it for clandestine meetings with a secret Iranian delegation. The two groups were ostensibly seeking an end to the hostilities between Kurdish separatist militants and the Islamic regime in Tehran.

The night before, the three had arrived at the apartment for the third such meeting with the Iranian group—led by General Muhammad Shahroudi from the IRGC, an aide named Haji Mostafavi, and a third person, Amir Bozorgian, who was introduced as their bodyguard.[49] In the first two meetings the Iranians seemed sincere in their intentions to reach an agreement. In reality, their goal was to gain the Kurds' confidence in order to eliminate them.

A fourth person has been alleged to have been present at this fatal meeting: Mahmoud Ahmadinejad, then a colonel in the IRGC and now president of the Islamic Republic of Iran.

After the bodies were discovered, the Austrian police arrested General Shahroudi at the local hospital, where he had been taken for minor injuries suffered during the altercation in the flat, and the supposed bodyguard, Bozorgian. The two denied any connection to the killings, claiming that all six men had been attacked by strangers. The socialist government of Chancellor Franz Vranitzky quickly accepted the explanation, although it was full of holes. The Austrian police concluded that no other Iranians had been involved in the incident.

Shahroudi was subsequently put on the first plane to Tehran. Bozorgian, actually an officer in Iran's ministry of intelligence and probably the assassin, managed to leave Austria a few days thereafter. Four years later he was involved in the assassination in Rome of an ex–Iranian diplomat who had defected to the opposition MEK movement. He is currently on Interpol's Wanted Fugitives list.

However, new evidence uncovered by an Iranian journalist who shared it with an Austrian member of Parliament (the Austrian parliamantarian refused to name him for the journalist's safety) showed that two Iranian assassination teams were in Vienna at the time of the murders. One operated at the apartment where the meeting took place and the other was a backup team, which was alleged to have been headed by Ahmadinejad. "In contrast to the first hit team," says Dr. Peter Pilz, leader of the Austrian Green Party and a member of the Austrian Parliament, "which traveled on a tourist visa and posed as innocent visitors, [Ahmadinejad] arrived in Austria on a diplomatic passport. His mission was to provide the weapons for the assassinations, which he was carrying in a diplomatically sealed bag."[50] After handing over the weapons, Pilz alleges, Ahmadinejad waited near the apartment with a pistol. If the first team did not succeed, he would finish the job.[51]

Ahmadinejad's participation in that operation has been denied by the Iranian government. This has been further complicated by the fact that no solid evidence has been presented to the public to prove his participation. Although it may be almost impossible to substantiate the facts of this story, it nonetheless embodies the enigma that is Mahmoud Ahmadinejad.

However, what has been stated openly in public is that Ahmadinejad's claims that he was a brave commando are dubious. "He was neither courageous nor was he a leader," said Hamid Reza Jalaeipour, a governor under Ayatollah Khomeini who appointed Ahmadinejad his deputy in the 1980s. "He was hardly ever at the battlefront. He was afraid."[52]

After the war Ahmadinejad went back to the University of Science and Technology to teach. He also joined the university's scientific board, which primarily decided on scientific projects for the school and determined the curriculum for scientific courses. In the five years following the war Ahmadinejad held two posts, the first being advisor to the Islamic culture and guidance ministry. He entered the ministry after the future president, Muhammad Khatami, who was dismissed because his policies were too moderate for extreme conservatives. Ahmadinejad fit the profile the conservatives were looking for, and he was appointed because of his dedication rather than any training or experience for the job.

In 1993 he advanced up the political ladder, to governor-general of a newly established province, Ardebil. Sandwiched between the Caspian Sea, the independent republic of Azerbaijan, and Iran's own eastern Azerbaijan province, Ardebil is a rural and mountainous region most known for Ali Daei, the country's famous footballer, and the former captain of the national team. Ahmadinejad seems to have been as dedicated an administrator as he was a student. He was named an exemplary governor-general for three consecutive years in his four-year term, though he had served fewer years and had weaker political connections in Tehran than the competition.[53] His abilities were severely tested when an earthquake measuring 5.5 on the Richter scale struck Ardebil on February 18, 1997, killing 1,100 people and injuring 2,600. Ahmadinejad oversaw the reconstruction of 7,500 housing units within nine months. This success underscored Ahmadinejad's managerial and administrative skills, especially in times of crisis, as well as his concern for people.[54]

That same year Ahmadinejad's career as governor-general came to an abrupt end when Khatami was elected president. Immediately after taking office, Khatami purged the government of many radical and conservative government officials, Ahmadinejad among them. With no job and little future in government, he returned to Tehran to complete his PhD and teach at the University of Science and Technology.

Ahmadinejad said he was popular with the students. "I never did roll call in the mornings. Sometimes students from other classes would come to my lectures," he told reporters.[55] He also said that his love of football, which he played with his students, was a factor in his popularity.[56] While teaching at the university he joined a team and took part in a number of tournaments. He is said to be very adept at controlling the ball and outmaneuvering opponents through nimble footwork at high speed.[57]

It is said in Iran that if football were a religion, it would come in a close second to Islam, and certainly Ahmadinejad's devotion to the game plays a part in his political career. In February 2006 he made an unannounced visit to the training camp of Iran's national team at the Azadi stadium where, dressed in a team uniform, he showed off his talent on the pitch. Before leaving for the 2006 World Cup in Germany, the national team players came to see Ahmadinejad and presented him with his own Iranian football jersey, bearing the number 24 and *Ahmadinejad* on the back. Nearly every Iranian schoolchild dreams of such an honor.

In contrast to Ahmadinejad's own rosy depiction of his time as a lecturer, others speak of his problems in adjusting to university life. Certainly he showed no inhibitions about his political views and no fear of academic reprisals, even during the reformist era. For example, it is said that Ahmadinejad used to wear a kaffiyeh, a black-and-white scarf worn by the ultraconservative Basij people's militia forces, an offshoot of the IRGC. Ahmadinejad's kaffiyeh branded him an ultraconservative—and proud of it. The Basij were a popular militia wing of the Islamic Revolutionary Guards, many of whom had been treated by the regime as cannon fodder.[58]

Ahmadinejad never gave up his political ambitions. While teaching, he became a member of various conservative movements—the Society of Islamic Engineers, for one—and rejoined his old friends at the group he had founded, the OSU. Eventually he settled on his next attempt at political office: mayor of Tehran.

Ahmadinejad ran for mayor as the candidate of a coalition named the Abadegarane Iran-e-Islami, or Developers of Islamic Iran. Known as Abadegaran, it is a neoconservative coalition with strong links to the establishment. Its membership is mostly made up of second-generation revolutionaries who fought in the war and are critical of traditional conservatives. The group's main goal is to reconcile the original values of the Islamic revolution with the country's current realities.[59]

Ahmadinejad, one of eight candidates in the race, did not need to campaign strenuously; voter apathy more or less handed victory to him. Tehranis had become dissatisfied with the infighting and inefficiency of the reformists of Khatami's coalition, who were then running the city.[60] On election day in spring of 2003, only 12 percent of eligible voters turned up at the polls, and those 12 percent were mostly underprivileged and highly religious. They had heard about Ahmadinejad's conservative and religious values in sermons at the mosques and from the Basij. They chose him because he was devout, a local from a low-income neighborhood, and disliked by the corrupt establishment. Even his PhD in traffic management proved an advantage. One of the most congested and polluted cities in the world, Tehran was in dire need of a professional traffic engineer.[61]

Ahmadinejad's two years as mayor were relatively successful. Tehranis admired him for acting quickly to resolve problems, in sharp contrast to the previous administration. (According to a popular local saying, politics and driving are the same in Tehran—they both move at one kilometer per hour.) As well as being admired for his speed and decisiveness, Ahmadinejad was prized within the administration for his ability to seek compromise and consensus among his managers.

Ahmadinejad continued to teach part-time at the university, at least in part because he had decided to live off his teacher's wages rather than accept the mayoral salary. "I have my income from teaching at university," he responded to reporters who questioned the decision. "Why should I receive [the mayor's salary]? I work for the government and I get wages," he continued, referring to his university pay. "Thank God it's enough. My wife also earns."[62]

In 2003 the mayor's salary was $2,000 a month, with another $2,000 monthly for living expenses. Ahmadinejad worked unpaid for twenty-four months, forfeiting the equivalent of $100,000 and much more via kickbacks. Ahmadinejad proudly pointed out that the money "stayed in the bank account of Tehran city. It's not going anywhere. It's expended on Tehran."[63]

Ahmadinejad then added, "The point of view and perceptions of authority should change. Managers should live with the people. A manager should not have a lifestyle that doesn't allow him to have an understanding of people's sufferings."[64] On a number of occasions during his tenure Ahmadinejad reportedly donned the orange uniform of a street cleaner, one of the lowliest positions in Iranian society, to show solidarity with them. In one well-publicized instance he was said to have exited his own car and helped clear a blockage in an open sewer.[65]

Ahmadinejad was known as a devoted mayor who worked hard, putting in long hours. He must be the only mayor of Tehran who never took a holiday. Despite the power and responsibility that came with his new office, Ahmadinejad stayed true to his conservative political and religious ideologies. He turned cultural centers into prayer halls, especially during the holy month of Ramadan. One of his most controversial acts was the decision to allocate separate elevators in the town hall for men and women, in accordance with strict Islamic laws. The reformists depicted him as a religious zealot, but they were too weak to force him to rescind the policy.

Another significant step he took was to bury the newly found remains of Iranian soldiers, casualties of the Iraqi invasion, in the squares of southern Tehran. In commemorating his lost comrades, Ahmadinejad was reminding the people of Tehran that they owed their freedom to those young men who went to fight against Saddam Hussein. Some residents objected, saying that the program was simply an opportunity for ultraconservatives to symbolically broaden their reach in Tehran and that the burial sites were eyesores. Nevertheless, in March 2006 Basij students at Sharif University of Tehran forced the interment of unknown soldiers on university grounds despite opposition from more than 82 percent of the students, many of whom formed human chains in an attempt to stop the burials, to no avail.

A much more popular decision, from both an aesthetic and a cultural viewpoint, was commemorating Iranian victims of Iraq's chemical attacks by unveiling plaques to their memory. Iranians consider Iraq's use of chemical weapons against their soldiers and citizens a crime against humanity that must be remembered.

This sense of abandonment by the international community and helplessness against Iraq's chemical attacks left a deep scar on the psyche of Iranians. It convinced many that when it came to Iran's defense, no one could be trusted except Iranians themselves. According to an Iranian war veteran, "We Iranians want to say 'Never again' to such attacks against our people. With the international organizations such as the UN being so [pro-Western] and weak, realistically the only way we can ensure that weapons of mass destruction are not used against us is by having them. Especially a nuclear bomb—with that kind of weapon in our arsenal, no one will ever dare gas us again."[66]

When Ahmadinejad's official performance report was released, on April 20, 2005, he was still in office, but that month he declared his candidacy for president. The report cited major increases in public transportation (bus fleets grew by 112 percent and rail lines and tracks were expanded), garbage recycling (up more than 2000 percent in a span of two years), and fire services.[67] Ahmadinejad's positive contributions as mayor won him external as well as internal praise. He was short-listed in an international mayoral competition, along with another sixty-five mayors, only nine of whom were from Asia.[68]

In addition to his duties as mayor, Ahmadinejad also became the manager of the *Hamshahri* newspaper, the official mouthpiece of the city government. He turned the paper into a conservative daily that reflected the opinion of the Abadegaran coalition, to which he belonged.[69] Ahmadinejad cut an authoritative figure at the newspaper, very much in charge. Some staff left for this reason, while others were fired by Ahmadinejad, including the editor in chief (for not supporting his candidacy) and even his replacement (who was dismissed a week before the June 2005 elections). He also dismissed another reporter because she dared pose a question about the country's security services, a taboo subject in Iran.[70]

Samane Ghadrkhan, a journalist based in Tehran, noted that by the end of his tenure as mayor, Ahmadinejad had made a number of enemies. "When his term started, the organization as one was behind Ahmadinejad," he said. "By the time he left, it was split in two, with half opposed to him." Ghadrkhan also criticized the mayor's performance, noting that "although Ahmadinejad fulfilled many of his promises, he failed in others. The biggest failure was his promise to pave all of Tehran's roads with asphalt in forty-five days. He didn't even get close to fulfilling this promise. His conservative points of view also led to alienation of many within the town hall."[71] Ghasem Khorami, another Tehran-based reporter, complained that Ahmadinejad "turned the city into a hotbed for conservatives, using it to surround himself with people who backed him."[72]

Ahmadinejad's biggest critics have been, predictably, the reformists. They questioned his own honesty and attacked him for granting contracts to inept cronies and former IRGC comrades who wasted the city's money on poorly planned projects. One such case is the construction of a monorail line in central Tehran that was to run from Sadeghiye Square to Tehran's Mehrabad International Airport. Because of insufficient planning and the absence of any feasibility study of the route, $10 million was spent on the project, with very little construction to show for it.[73]

Another example involves $2 million paid for lighting to be installed in Tehran's streets for religious festivals. After the contract was signed, the supplier wrote Ahmadinejad saying that the amount agreed upon was insufficient; another $1 million was then doled out. Subsequent investigations show that the contract was nothing more than a phantom agreement; the money was paid, but no work was carried out.[74]

In April 2005 Ahmadinejad declared his candidacy for the presidency of the Islamic Republic of Iran. He campaigned right up until two days before the first round of elections on June 17, 2005. (Ahmadinejad's campaign, and the reasons for his election, will be discussed in chapter 2.) Although viewed as an outsider, Ahmadinejad nevertheless managed to win 19.5 percent of the vote in the first round, while former president Hashemi Rafsanjani, the pragmatists favorite, won 21 percent.[75]

These were astonishing results. Rafsanjani, the son of a pistachio merchant who became a cleric, was a close ally of Khomeini's and one of the most powerful and wealthy politicians in the country. That now he barely beat Mahmoud Ahmadinejad, a candidate who had received neither serious national nor international attention, was shocking. The CIA, Mossad, and MI6 panicked. They had little idea who this man was and why he was so popular. With no single candidate gaining more than half the vote, the election went into a second round, in accordance with Iran's electoral laws. The result on June 24 brought about an even bigger shock: Ahmadinejad won 62 percent of the votes and Rafsanjani only 36 percent.[76]

CHAPTER TWO

Vote for the Unknown

AHMADINEJAD HELD HIS first election rally, a relatively modest affair, in the Haftome Tir hall in southern Tehran on May 27, 2005. He talked about the chief issues of his campaign: corruption, lack of justice, unemployment, and the deterioration of the economy.[1] These were popular and substantive topics that drew many people to his rallies.

Although he claimed during the elections that he did not represent any particular group, he was known to be a member of a number of conservative political factions.[2] Chief among them was Abadegarane Iran-e-Islami (known as Abadegaran), the coalition Ahmadinejad represented in the mayoral elections of 2003. A neoconservative coalition, the Abadegaran is critical of traditional conservatives and works to reconcile the original values of the Islamic revolution with Iran's current realities.[3]

Ahmadinejad was also a member of Jame'eye Isargarane Enqhelabe Eslami (the Islamic Revolution Devotees Society, or Isargaran). Members of the Isargaran are veterans of the Iran-Iraq war, including some disabled, freed prisoners of war, family members of those killed, and people who were involved in the revolution against the monarchy.[4]

Both coalitions belong to a conservative umbrella organization called Osulgarayan (meaning People of Principle), which counts among its other factions the Islamic Society of Teachers and the Islamic Society of Engineers. All these organizations are well established in Iranian politics and could have assisted Ahmadinejad with his campaign. However, instead of supporting him fellow conservatives tried to convince him to not run at all. After a strong intervention and vetting by the Guardian Council eight candidates remained in the race. Out of the eight presidential candidates, four were conservatives in the Osulgarayan faction: Muhammad Bagher Ghalibaf, a former general of the IRGC air force and a former National Police commissioner; Ali Larijani, an Iraqi-born former minister in Rafsanjani's cabinet and head of the Islamic Republic of Iran Broadcasting (IRIB); Mohsen Rezai, a former commander of the IRGC and a war hero; and Ahmadinejad.[5] Of those four, Ahmadinejad and Mohsen Rezai were expected to win the fewest votes.[6] So the two higher-visibility conservative candidates, Ghalibaf and Larijani, attempted to persuade Ahmadinejad and Rezai to withdraw.

Their first and foremost concern was that Ahmadinejad would take votes away from other, better-known conservatives. This was a genuine worry, as they were facing a formidable challenge from the nonconservative, pragmatist-reformist camp headed by former president Ayatollah Hashemi Rafsanjani and Mostafa Moeen (the only real reformist candidate), who were expected to do well at the ballot box. Mehdi Karrubi, a former speaker of the parliament who was considered a moderate conservative and the most independent candidate, was also a challenge to both camps. This was also because he formerly headed one of the powerful Bonyads (charity foundations), which enabled him to gather millions of dollars at his disposal. The eighth candidate was Mohsen Mehralizadeh, a former governor of Khorassan province who was loosely affiliated with the reformist-pragmatist camp.

While overtly the request that Ahmadinejad would leave the race was a matter of strategy for the conservative faction as a whole, personal vendettas also came into play. The Isargaran faction had already chosen Ghalibaf as their candidate. Even though Ahmadinejad was one of the founders of the organization, Isargaran passed him over because of his allegiance to Abade-garan in the 2003 Tehran mayoral elections.[7] Ahmadinejad had turned his back on Isargaran once, and now the group was returning the favor.

Publicly, the campaign to stop Ahmadinejad from nominating himself started five months prior to his first election rally, when his opposition started a rumor that Ahmadinejad had "exited the list of presidential candidates." Ahmadinejad neither denied nor acknowledged this report, but he was frustrated by the struggle and spoke openly about the conspiracy to force him to pull out of the race.[8] At one rally soon after his nomination, he declared, "They said to me, 'No one has heard of you, you won't win votes.'" Ahmadinejad's response, in his typically dry wit, was "I told them, 'If no one has heard of me, then don't worry—if I lose, no one will notice.'" The crowd erupted in applause.[9]

Ahmadinejad wasn't always so witty. Just before the first round of presidential voting on May 30, 2005, he announced that he would publicly name those who were pressuring him.[10] Although he didn't do so, it was a clear warning shot to his enemies.

Initially, the prospect for the conservatives seemed bleak. The pragmatist Rafsanjani was favored to win the highest number of votes, followed by Moeen, the reformist candidate. The conservatives were expected to come in third at best. Polls published three days before the election showed Rafsanjani leading with 22 percent.[11] However, the conservatives were in surprisingly strong positions. Ghalibaf was second with 20 percent and Mayor Ahmadinejad third at 15 percent. The reformist candidate, Moeen, came in fourth at 10 percent, and the other candidates polled in the single digits.[12]

The pressure on Ahmadinejad to withdraw subsided. On June 16, a day before the election, Rezai decided to drop out of the race. Though he may have done so because of his alliance and friendship with Rafsanjani, Rezai's withdrawal took the heat off Ahmadinejad.[13] The polls also showed that Ahmadinejad had a chance to win and, in fact, that he was more popular than some established conservatives, such as Larijani. Ironically, the political life of the most notorious anti-Western president was saved by a purely Western concept: polling.

Ahmadinejad 's sudden success resulted from a number of factors, notably his declaration of war on corruption. One of the main reasons the Iranian people revolted against the monarchy in 1979 was corruption. In 2005, despite many promises, history was repeating itself. The country had become corrupt again, unbearably so for many Iranians. What was most offensive was that senior officials were largely responsible. These religious people, who had preached of a pure and just government under Islam, had become some of the biggest plunderers of Iran's wealth. So much so that corruption was looked upon no longer as a crime but as an essential technique to survive . . . and then to get rich.

The most destructive consequence of corruption and mismanagement wasn't just the loss of money; it was the loss of funds for social investment, for the population's basic needs. Daily life in Iran, especially in Tehran, is now far worse than it was under the shah.

- Traffic in Tehran is like nothing you have ever known. It takes hours and hours and hours to get anywhere, at about an hour and fifteen minutes per mile.[14]
- If you take a deep breath in Tehran, your lungs will sample some of the foulest air in the world.[15] On some days the level of air pollution is so high that schools are closed.[16]
- Noise pollution in Tehran is twice the level deemed safe by international health organizations.[17]
- Crime is increasing. Between 2001 and 2006 the number of illegal weapons entering the country increased by 1000 percent, to 27,300 firearms.[18]
- Iran is now one of the least safe countries in the world for air travel.[19] The country is unable to buy new Airbus and Boeing aircraft, partly because of the U.S.-imposed embargo but also partly because of the venality of Iranian officials. Instead of buying newer

versions of Russian-made aircraft to modernize the airplane fleet, corrupt officials used the country's money to buy the cheapest and most outdated planes. They then pocketed the rest of the cash allocated for aircraft purchases. The result has been crashes and unnecessary deaths.

- The bureaucracy has worsened. A simple task these days requires endless forms to be filed, as well as a dose of *zir-mizi* (money under the table).[20]
- The country's medical services are falling apart, and a growing number of patients are dying at the hands of overworked doctors.[21]
- There are estimated to be hundreds of thousands of prostitutes, most coming from poor urban families.

A famous Tehrani anecdote says that if you ever wanted to travel in time, you could do it in one day, by first visiting northern Tehran and then going to the city's southern side. Parts of northern Tehran look almost like a modern European neighborhood. Beautiful houses and apartments with modern cars parked outside line the streets. The shops offer the latest Western high technology and clothes. The streets are relatively clean.

In contrast, parts of southern Tehran bear a striking resemblance to an underdeveloped third-world city. The neighborhoods are crowded with old, small, run-down brick houses. In some cases many families share one house. The streets are dirty. The shops offer nothing but basic necessities. Many people live in abject poverty.

At the time of the election, the people of Iran were furious about the extent of corruption in Iran and its devastating consequences. And a figure perceived by some to be one of the biggest practitioners of corruption, Ayatollah Rafsanjani, was running for president.

Born in 1934 in the village of Bahreman, Ali Akbar Hashemi Bahremani Rafsanjani was born into a relatively wealthy pistachio-trading family. At the age of fourteen he went to seminary school in Qom, where one of his teachers was Ayatollah Khomeini. Despite the anti-Western sentiments of the revolution in which he later participated, Rafsanjani traveled extensively in the West and the Far East in the 1960s and 1970s. Among his destinations were Japan and the United States, where he visited twenty states.[22]

Following the Islamic revolution, Rafsanjani was first appointed speaker of the Majlis (parliament) and later its president, a post he held for eight years. Rafsanjani is credited with getting the country's economy back on its feet after the devastating Iran-Iraq war. Afterward he was appointed chairman of the Expediency Council, an advisory body to the Supreme Leader, at the time Grand Ayatollah Seyyed Ali Khamenei. Immediately after the revolution, the position of Supreme Leader was introduced to make clear that power rests with the clergy, not the politicians. It was tailor-made for Khomeini, who was admired, respected, and accepted by the revolution's supporters as a religious and a political authority. Upon his death in 1989 he was replaced by Khamenei, despite his inferior religious background and moral authority. All crucial and strategic decisions, including the nuclear project, are concentrated in his hands.[23]

Despite Rafsanjani's success in the first round of the elections, he made mistakes during the campaign that drove people to Ahmadinejad. For instance, one Rafsanjani election rally in Tehran featured attractive women in Islamic dress Rollerblading with Rafsanjani stickers all over them. As the girls handed out the stickers and posed with Rafsanjani posters, the stickers placed on their manteau-covered bodies attracted the attention both of drivers and photographers.[24] In Iran Rollerblades are considered luxury goods worn by wealthy and spoiled youth from northern Tehran. To buy even a low-quality pair costs seventy dollars, about a third of a civil servant's monthly salary. As much as some voters—especially the male ones—enjoyed Rafsanjani's female campaigners, many voters, the majority of whom are have-nots, found the show of wealth distasteful. Rafsanjani seemed unaware how offensive such scenes can be.

These scenes were especially damaging because some people felt that Rafsanjani had become a multimillionaire through corruption and coercion.

Despite his modern image, Rafsanjani wasn't a reformist. He made it clear that he had no intention of giving more freedom to the citizens of Iran. "When the shah gave us freedom, we drove him out of the country. We shall not repeat this mistake," Rafsanjani declared in a 1995 interview with the German daily *Frankfurter Rundschau*.[25] In fact, Rafsanjani's brutality against those who stood up to his practices is legendary. In some cases, those who did not cooperate were thrown in jail and tortured.[26] Many in Iran assumed that Rafsanjani's talk of economic progress was aimed primarily at lining his own pockets.

According to other reports, Rafsanjani is the proprietor of numerous business and properties in Iran, Europe, and Canada. Opposition sources maintain that Mahan Air, which flies to England and Germany, belongs to him. Daewoo automobiles manufactured in Iran are also part of Rafsanjani's business empire.[27]

It didn't help that Rafsanjani's son Mehdi was linked with an embarrassing public scandal. According to investigations by the Norwegian government, Mehdi was associated with a registered company in London that received a down payment of $5.2 million for "consulting services" as part of a $15 million deal with the Norwegian company Statoil.[28]

Mehdi's greed has distanced Rafsanjani from the social hopes and ideals of the Islamic revolution and turned the masses against him, his family, and his cronies. According to some reformists, Rafsanjani had also made enemies among the reformists. "In 1997, after the reformist Ayatollah Khatami replaced Rafsanjani as president, many reformists blamed the economic mess on Rafsanjani. They didn't *like* him, either," said Ali K., a former reformist journalist in Iran. [29] The conservatives disliked him even more. Some, in fact, detested him and considered him opposed to Velayete Faghih, the supremacy of the Islamic jurist consul.[30]

Rafsanjani's practices, and the widespread hatred in Iran for corruption, provided Ahmadinejad with his battle cry. He used a focused, multifaceted approach to reach as many people as possible. First and foremost were the poor, whose sheer ranks made them vital to victory. Officially, the number of

those living under the poverty line is 17 million, 25 percent of the population.[31] However, according to opposition sources, 90 percent of the population lives in poverty, about 61 million individuals.[32]

Because he was once one of them, Ahmadinejad could have used his own
experience to reach out to the poor. However, Ahmadinejad had left the mis-
eries of absolute poverty behind years ago. These days he had no problem
finding housing or feeding his children. So he needed to define the problems
the poor were facing, and where was he going to reach them?

Luckily for Ahmadinejad, the answers to both questions proved relatively
easy. The example of Tahere Khanom provides an explanation.

At six o'clock in the morning, Tahere Khanom's alarm clock starts
beeping. It's the beginning of a long day for this sixty-year-old woman, the
sole breadwinner for her family of ten in south Tehran. Her husband and
sons cannot find jobs. Reaching her work—cleaning the houses of the
wealthy—takes six hours and involves two buses and two shared taxis. On
the way she sees billboards advertising expensive designer watches and
luxury goods she couldn't even dream of buying.[33] She openly admitted that
her life is getting worse economically and asserted equally frankly that she
doesn't trust promises made by politicians. Nevertheless she wanted to vote
in the presidential election because she believed that it is her "religious
duty."[34]

The words *religious duty* were key to Ahmadinejad's outreach strategy to
the poor. Many of the poor are also religious and visit their mosque regularly, for social as well as religious purposes. Many mosques have social clubs
where people can discuss their problems. Members of the mosque also visit
the sick and the needy in their neighborhood. When banks turn down the
loan requests of poor applicants (which is in the majority of cases), they have
two choices left—their family and the local mosque. In many cases the
mosque is their only option, since their relatives suffer from similar financial
problems.

Another important reason the poor visit the mosque is because the government is not satisfying their needs. Instead of becoming a religious country

that promotes the values of justice and equality as taught by Islam, Iran has become more secular than many dared to imagine, largely as a result of corruption. The poor, many of whom took part in the revolution so that Iran could become a just country according to the laws of Islam, can only go back to the mosque, as the state has failed them. There, many keep alive their dream of returning to the glory days of Islam under Ayatollah Khomeini. As part of his presidential campaign, Ahmadinejad visited mosque after mosque.

In the mosques, he said openly what many Iranians and other candidates were afraid to say: that the current regime is fully responsible for its own failures. "We need a government that bases its laws and plans on Islam's thinking and laws. Unfortunately, despite the efforts of the past twenty-five years, we are still facing problems of corruption, poverty, and racism, and an increase in moral, organizational, and political corruption," said Ahmadinejad at the Imam Hassan Asgari mosque in the holy city of Qom.[35] Ahmadinejad's use of Islam as the blueprint for society was aimed at attracting the maximum attention of the religious crowd.

As time wore on, the ferocity of Ahmadinejad's speeches increased. Two weeks before the first round of elections, Ahmadinejad called for a new "third revolution" which, "like the first revolution [in 1979] and the second revolution [the takeover of the U.S. embassy], will rely on the rule of Velayate Faghih. It will present the purest, bravest, and most popular regime to the entire world."[36] While he didn't call for a coup d'état outright, Ahmadinejad's strong language showed the audience and fellow candidates that he was serious. To the poor his attacks meant "I am not afraid to say what has been on your mind for years."[37] To the Basijis they meant "I am with you. I have your militant spirit. I am not a shrinking violet who is just going to say nice things;[38] I am ready to take on the revolution's corrupt and elitist class who for years has been undermining you."[39]

As popular as Ahmadinejad's messages were with the audiences in mosques, he still couldn't get the word out to rural areas, where the majority of poor lived. Ahmadinejad did not have the time or the money to travel throughout the country. And the popular media in the countryside is sparse—Internet access is limited and Ahmadinejad couldn't rely on the Islamic Republic Broadcasting organization, which he complained was not treating him fairly.[40]

The most viable way to achieve his goal was to use the Basijis, who often agreed with Ahmadinejad's ideology and point of view. The group had one of the largest networks in the country, reaching into the most rural areas of Iran. Ahmadinejad was in the right position to tap into the power of the Basijis. Since the beginning of the revolution, the Basijis were treated by the regime as cannon fodder.

This was most evident during the Iran-Iraq war, during which Iran faced acute shortages in mine-clearing equipment. The task of sweeping the mines laid by the Iraqis was assigned to the IRGC. Initially the IRGC used donkeys and cows, but when the animals saw other animals getting blown to pieces, they got scared and ran away.[41]

The IRGC then decided the best way to fulfill its task was to use humans. Nothing could rival a human mind that has been infused with a powerful religious ideology. The IRGC's top echelon did not want to turn its own soldiers into human mine-sweeping machines because it would create havoc and turn the rank and file against them. So they held recruitment campaigns in the rural areas and small urban centers instead.

How do you convince a human being to sacrifice his life? The IRGC, in its indoctrination, drew lessons from the death of Imam Hussein. The future Basijis were told that they were fighting the same just battle as Hussein had and that their martyrdom would bring the same result: eternal life in splendor in the afterworld.[42]

In small towns and cities families were asked to send their children to the Basij for the sake of Islam. Many families, too poor or illiterate to know better, gave their children to the IRGC soldiers. The young Basijis were sent to training camps where the IRGC would turn them into sacrificial sheep. They were told that by becoming martyrs they would ascend to heaven. After their indoctrination, some of the poor Basiji soldiers were given plastic keys (made in Taiwan) that, they were told, would open the gates of heaven so they could enter and enjoy their magnificent afterlife.[43]

The Basijis obliged faithfully because they were believers. They ran in waves over the mines and were slaughtered. IRGC soldiers watched from a distance, and as soon as the Basijis were blown up and the mines were cleared, they launched their attacks. Even some Iraqi soldiers found the senseless deaths too much to bear. "You can shoot down the first wave and then the second," said an Iraqi soldier who witnessed the Basiji waves. "But at some point the corpses are piling up in front of you, and all you want to do is scream and throw away your weapon. Those are human beings, after all!"[44]

The IRGC still didn't care. The commanders' callousness and despicable cynicism reached a peak when they decided it wasn't enough that these Basijis were giving up their lives for them—they no longer wanted to bother themselves with the task of collecting their flesh and bones, which scattered over a large area.

To solve that problem the IRGC gave blankets to the Basijis, who were now told that instead of walking, they were to roll onto the mines wrapped in the blankets. That way, when they blew up the body parts would not spread so far.[45]

During the Iraq war, Ahmadinejad was himself an IRGC officer. It is not known how he reacted toward the Basijis. After the war, however, Ahmadinejad befriended them—he even started working with their organization—and proudly wore a kaffiyeh at the university. When he decided to run for president, he displayed his Basiji credentials at the top of his election Web site.[46] And after his victory, Ahmadinejad didn't forget his Basiji friends. He has worn his kaffiyeh in the Majlis on a number of occasions.

For the first time in nearly sixteen years, the Basijis had found a politician who openly identified with them, who was talking in a language they understood and saying things they wanted to hear. In return for Ahmadinejad's loyalty, the Basijis flocked to mosques and Islamic social centers to spread the word about the as-yet-unknown candidate Mahmoud Ahmadinejad. Where

Ahmadinejad couldn't go, Basijis went instead and urged the local imam to ask worshippers to vote for Ahmadinejad.

The Basijis put Ahmadinejad ahead of Rafsanjani, who never visited any of the provinces nor advertised in any villages.[47] It also put him ahead of other IRGC candidates such as Larijani and Ghalibaf because there are more Basijis than IRGC.[48] The Basij had received substantial financial and political backing from Ayatollah Khamenei since his rise to power in 1989. Moreover, IRGC support was split between Larijani and Ghalibaf, which meant fewer votes for each candidate and increased Ahmadinejad's lead.

Now that Ahmadinejad had secured a strong foothold with the religious poor and the Basijis, he turned to city dwellers. After all, many of them had suffered from the consequences of corruption.

On June 13, eleven days before the election, Ahmadinejad made a campaign stop in Esfahan. With its striking minarets and witty people, Esfahan is referred to as *nesfe jahan* (half the world) by locals. Ask any Esfahani why and he will tell you with bursting pride, "It's because Esfahan has everything, from breathtaking nature to amazing architecture. Once you have seen Esfahan, it's equivalent to seeing half the world."[49] Ahmadinejad must have felt that half the world had descended on him as he arrived at the city's Seyyed mosque. There some 25,000 elated people were waiting for him, despite a three-hour delay due to technical difficulties in his flight.

As the mayor of Tehran pushed forward in the Seyyed mosque, surrounded by his bodyguards, the eager crowd became more excited, frantic, and finally unstoppable. They pushed forward; Ahmadinejad's bodyguards struggled to push them back.[50] It took Ahmadinejad and his entourage a half hour to proceed 300 feet to the podium. When he finally reached it, the podium was almost knocked over by the surging crowd.[51]

During his campaign Ahmadinejad spent many hours praising *shahids*[52] (martyrs). The first victim of his campaign, however, did not choose to die; he simply stood no chance against the crowd. Behnam Karimian, an Ahmadinejad campaign official in Esfahan, left behind a widow, with whom he had lived for only one month.[53] His death created Ahmadinejad's own shahid. Behnam was buried the next day in a funeral attended by thousands and his flag-draped coffin was carried to his grave.[54] Ahmadinejad wasn't present.[55]

Nonetheless, the tragedy didn't affect the campaign. Ahmadinejad's next target was the young, and his first success among them again came from the poor, who had either already heard of him or belonged to Basiji city branches. Many such youngsters used their computer skills to spread the word about Ahmadinejad in major cities. A popular method was setting up pro-Ahmadinejad blogs.[56] Some of the bloggers gave Ahmadinejad the nickname of Dr. Tractor because in Iran a tractor is synonymous with construction, a sign of progress.

Other young supporters used text-messaging on cell phones to get people to vote for Ahmadinejad. This campaign lasted until two days before the elections. The plans drawn up by Ahmadinejad's supporters called for 300,000 of his allies to each send SMS messages to five people, encouraging them to vote for Ahmadinejad. The message also asked the recipient to forward it to five friends.[57]

As sizable as the group of young people was, though, Ahmadinejad still needed to find a way of delivering his message more broadly in the cities, which held more than 65 percent of the population. To do that, Ahmadinejad appeared in a very clever TV spot filmed at his house. The camera focused on Ali Reza, Ahmadinejad's then seventeen-year-old son, standing in the hallway of his house.

The interviewer asked him, "So where is your swimming pool?" Ali Reza pointed outside to a backyard far too small for a pool and said, "See for yourself."[58]

"So where is your sauna?" asked the interviewer.

To Ali Reza Ahmadinejad it seemed such a ridiculous question that he didn't even bother answering. He just shrugged.

The interviewer filmed Ali Reza Ahmadinejad in their living room, beside the desk he shares with his father in his parent's house.[59]

This was the opening scene from Ahmadinejad's election film. The next scene began by showing chandeliers, a marble staircase, and a view through

French windows that looked out on a sauna and a swimming pool. This was the house of Malek Madani, Ahmadinejad's predecessor as mayor. Everyone knew that Ahmadinejad could have had such things as mayor, but he had not even taken a mayoral salary.[60] The man who had warned he wanted to "cut off the hand of corruption" first needed to show evidence that he wasn't a hypocrite.[61]

Over soundtracks from the movie *Spy Game* and Oliver Stone's *Alexander the Great* (no royalties were paid because Iran has no copyright laws), Ahmadinejad spoke: "I ask the officials, 'Why are you living in such palaces?' 'Because we need to maintain the prestige of the country,' they tell me. Where do they get this [referring to the palace]? This is not according to Islam."[62] "They" were the previous government of Ayatollah Khatami and his predecessor Ayatollah Rafsanjani, who was now running for another term.[63] Everyone, including Ahmadinejad, probably though they knew the answer to the question. By embezzling $450 million from banks.[64] By running multibillion-dollar government foundations called *bonyads* that are not audited, don't pay taxes or customs, and are not restricted by quotas.[65] By forcing businesses to "donate money for Islamic causes," which in most cases makes its way into the deep and greedy pockets of state officials.

Ahmadinejad's election ad was in direct contrast to Ghalibaf's, which showed him flying an Airbus (he is a pilot), and to Rafsanjani's as well, in which the candidate talked about exercising when he had the chance. Neither of the ads was relevant to the life of Iranian people. Ahmadinejad's simple house, on the other hand, looked a lot like theirs.

As the election date neared, the exchanges between Rafsanjani and Ahmadinejad became more strained. In fact, Ahmadinejad sacked Mohsen Rafsanjani, his competitor's son, who had held a position at Tehran municipality. Why? Mohsen didn't show up at work for two weeks because he wanted to take time off to assist in his father's campaign. Ahmadinejad, as mayor of Tehran and ultimately Mohsen's boss, decided that he deserved to be fired for this. It was a bold move, as Rafsanjani was a powerful politician with many allies. He could have exacted a costly revenge.

The ninth presidential election in Iran's history took place on June 17, 2005. Of the 47 million people eligible to vote, approximately 29 million (62 percent) cast ballots.[66] A sizable part of the 38 percent who stayed away did so as a protest against the regime.[67] When the results of the first round of election were announced, Iran's citizens were as shocked and surprised as its politicians. Rafsanjani had won. Mahmoud Ahmadinejad had surprisingly come in second. Karrubi was third with 17.24%, while Mostafa Moeen, the reformist candidate, was fourth with 13.93%. Ghalibaf followed closely with 13.85%. Ali Larijani was sixth with 5.83%, and Mohsen Mehralizadeh came last with only 4.38%.

People gasped. Analysts were at a loss. The results were so unexpected that television stations in Los Angeles representing the expatriate Iranian communities and opposition groups called them a farce. This opinion was echoed by a number of politicians inside Iran who had been with the regime since the beginning of the revolution. Ahmadinejad himself seemed shocked at the results; his campaign team had not even prepared a podium for him to speak from in response to the results.[68]

"Some centers of power are violating the law and are trying to get more votes for a particular person with the help of the Guardian Council," proclaimed Ayatollah Karrubi, a well-known, respectful ayatollah, a senior government member, and one of the presidential candidates. Although he did better than expected in receiving the third-highest number of votes, Karrubi was dismayed by the fact that Ahmadinejad had bested him. Karrubi filed a long list of anomalies and clear cases of manipulations of the election system.[69] His complaints didn't get him anywhere. After the elections, Karrubi resigned in protest from his post as secretary-general of the Jame'e Roohaniyoone Mobarez (Association of Combatant Clerics).[70]

Because none of the candidates had won more than half the votes, as Iranian election law dictates, a runoff would be held between the two candidates with the most votes: Rafsanjani and Ahmadinejad. The date was set for June 24, one week later.

Behind the scenes, Rafsanjani was so infuriated that he wanted to leave the race. To him, Ahmadinejad had won because the authorities had stuffed the ballot box in his favor. This was not the first time that such an accusation had been leveled. Ex-officials have openly admitted to changing election results.[71] According to Robert Tait, the London *Guardian* reporter who was in Tehran during the elections, the complaints of fraud were "also backed up by an interior ministry poll inspector who spoke to the *Guardian* but did not want to be named."[72]

When Ayatollah Khamenei heard of Rafsanjani's intention to drop out of the race, he sent him a stern warning that he should participate in the second round.[73] Rafsanjani accepted, mostly out of fear. He knew that his withdrawal would look bad for Khamenei and the government. Such an act would also provide a huge boost to Iranian opposition movements, which had labeled the presidential elections undemocratic and a sham. In turn, Khamenei and other conservative elements in the regime would seek to settle scores with him. This meant that Rafsanjani would probably lose his political posts and business interests. However, Rafsanjani also decided to stay because he expected that his open complaint would result in fair treatment, thus leading to victory.[74] He expected to widen his lead over Ahmadinejad because he was the top candidate and had more money at his disposal for electioneering.

Rafsanjani's campaign turned nasty—or negative, as Americans say. His team decided to humiliate Ahmadinejad by likening the contest to a struggle between a mouse and a lion. Rafsanjani let it be known that he saw it as an insult that he'd even have to compete with a "commoner" such as Ahmadinejad.[75]

As if that weren't enough, Rafsanjani financed a smear campaign against Ahmadinejad. Rumors circulated that if Ahmadinejad came to power, he would create patrol groups to arrest young people not dressed in strict Islamic attire.[76] "Ahmadinejad will prevent men from wearing short sleeves," said one anti-Ahmadinejad message, which with others was also spread through leaflets and SMS messages.[77] This tactic caused great concern in the Ahmadinejad camp, since losing the youth vote could have been devastating to Ahmadinejad. As a result, Ahmadinejad dedicated a substantial part of his television appearance during the second round of campaigning to emphasizing that his government would focus on the economy and people's welfare, "not what hairstyle young people have,"[78] as he put it.

On Friday, June 24, according to government figures, 28 million Iranians—60 percent of eligible voters—cast their ballots. The results proved that Iran is indeed a country full of political surprises. Ahmadinejad won with 62 percent, a wide margin over Rafsanjani's 36 percent.

Not surprisingly, accusations of vote tampering did not die down; many had expected Rafsanjani to win and Ahmadinejad's support had increased astonishingly. Fraudulent or not, the results of the second round were set. The Guardian Council, which Khamanei influences, made a pretense of investigating the results and declared Ahmadinejad the winner.

The mouse had roared and the lion was soundly defeated.

Even a year after the elections, Rafsanjani's supporters point to "invisible hands" changing the election results.[79] At the very least, the Basij was illegally helping Ahmadinejad, since according to the Iranian constitution the armed forces are not supposed to intervene directly in elections. Who gave the Basij permission to use the military's cars, fuel, and time to send members around the country electioneering for Ahmadinejad? It had to be Khamenei. What Rafsanjani didn't know was that the fate of the ninth presidential election of the Islamic Republic of Iran was partially sealed almost two years before its actual date.

The process began with the first gulf war in 2003. Until then, military forces of the United States were no closer than 3,000 miles away, in Europe. There were some U.S. Navy ships in the Persian Gulf, but they posed no threat to the regime. However, when George W. Bush sent troops to invade Iraq, danger came uncomfortably close. The Americans and their NATO allies, primarily the British, were already stationed in Afghanistan. Now they were in Iraq. Memories of 1953 flooded the minds of Iranians, when the Brits and Americans overthrew the democratically elected regime of Muhammad Mossadegh because he had nationalized Iran's oil. Rumors of an imminent U.S. attack against Iran abounded.

In the spring of 2003 Khamenei, feeling threatened, decided to try and reach out to the Americans. His plan called for "comprehensive negotiations to resolve bilateral differences" between the two countries. Khamenei's proposal acknowledged that Iran would address concerns about its weapons programs and its support for anti-Israeli terrorist organizations.[80]

What did Iran get in return for reaching out to the United States? Nothing. The Bush administration did not respond. In fact, they shot the messenger. The poor Swiss embassy, which represents U.S. interests in Iran, was criticized for conveying the message.[81]

The Americans were too cocky to sit down and negotiate with the ayatollah's regime, and they did not hide their disinterest in dealing with them. The prevailing spirit of the neoconservatives in the Bush administration was that once Iraq was calmed, they might move to attack Iran.

Realizing this, Khamenei believed he had to respond aggressively. Where diplomacy had failed, he hoped confrontation would succeed. Khamenei embarked on a two-tier strategy to strengthen the defenses of his regime. He tried to deter the Americans from attacking by strangling them with their success. His first tactic was to undermine American chances of success in Iraq. Initially the Shiites, who constitute the majority in Iraq, supported American forces. Khamenei moved to ensure that they were under Iran's influence by dispatching 10,000 IRGC-trained soldiers to Iraq. These soldiers could be called into battle at any time.[82] Khamenei also strengthened Iran's political influence in Iraq by working with a number of high-ranking Shiite politicians who had lived in Iran for many years. These politicians became invaluable to U.S. plans for democracy in Iraq.[83]

Khamenei then called on yet another ally in Iraq, Jalal Talebani, the head of the Patriotic Union of Kurdistan. Talebani has had a political and military working relationship with the Islamic Republic since 1983. In 2004 he became Iraq's president, further strengthening Iran's influence in the country.[84]

Internally, things were coming to a head. The reformists were not to be trusted. They called for more freedom, which Khamenei did not support. He preferred to keep the levers of power strictly to himself. The reformists also wanted to improve relations with the West. Khamenei had tried once and failed; that was enough for now.

As the elections neared, Khamenei found himself in a dilemma as to which side to support. Rafsanjani was viewed by many as being corrupt; if he won, much of the hard-earned oil money would be lost to him and his corrupt allies. It would also lead to more poverty and contempt for the regime by the poor. Moreover, Rafsanjani, because of his business interests, favored relations with the West. Therefore it would be very likely that he would confront Khamenei.

Rafsanjani had embarrassed Khamenei before. In the late 1990s Rafsanjani's daughter printed a New Year's message from Farah Diba, the shah's wife, in her magazine, *Zan*.[85] This infuriated the conservative wing of Iranian politics, Khamenei among them. Rafsanjani's reputedly corrupt practices during his presidency had also angered Khamenei, but he didn't dare confront Rafsanjani at the time, for two reasons. First, there were allegations that Khamenei himself is corrupt and his cronies are no less so. Second, Rafsanjani was mainly focused on rebuilding the country and attracting foreign investment. Oil prices were low and Iran desperately needed money for construction, and Khamenei didn't want to rock the boat. In 2005, with the price of oil high, Khamenei felt secure enough to deny Rafsanjani the chance to become president.

Why didn't Khamenei support Ghalibaf or Larijani, the other conservative candidates who were ideologically close to him? Why instead support Ahmadinejad? Ghalibaf and Larijani both presented problems for Khamenei. Ghalibaf was tainted by a letter he had written to Khamenei asking him to brutally put down the student demonstrations of the late 1990s, which were demanding more freedom for the Iranian people.[86] If that letter were revealed in the campaign, it could seriously hurt Ghalibaf's chances and perhaps open the way for a more reformist candidate. Khamenei wanted the election to reverse the country's direction and ensure a solid victory for a conservative candidate.

As Khamenei saw it, Larijani, during his tenure as the head of Iran

Broadcasting, had brought in hard-liners who wanted more conservative proregime programs. In addition, Larijani was an Iraqi. Iran is not yet ready to have an Iraqi-born president. The wounds from the eight-year war have not yet healed completely. Khamenei wanted a solid candidate to swing the pendulum.

Ahmadinejad, on the other hand, seemed incorrupt, did not suffer from a shady past, and enjoyed the support of the Basij to a degree that none of the other candidates did. He also opposed improving relations with the United States.[87] Most important, he would be subservient to Khamenei. As a former Majlis member put it, Ahmadinejad "will be nothing but a presidential secretary to the Supreme Leader."[88]

CHAPTER THREE

A Messianic Vision

AS HE ADDRESSED the world leaders gathered for the annual United Nations General Assembly meeting in September 2005, Mahmoud Ahmadinejad believed that God had made him his messenger. The president of Iran said that a colleague later told him, "When you began with the words *In the name of God,* I saw a celestial light come and surround you and protect you." Ahmadinejad agreed. "I felt it myself, too," he replied. "Suddenly the atmosphere changed." The world leaders and participants "all sat there," he continued, "and for the duration of the twenty-seven or twenty-eight minutes, they did not even blink. I am not exaggerating. I looked up and I saw them. They were transfixed. It was as if a hand was holding them."[1] To Ahmadinejad, God had laid his hand on the heads of the participants to ensure that they would listen to the words of God's envoy— himself.

Upon his return from New York, the president met with Ayatollah Amoli at his home in Qom, a holy city strongly connected to the revolution and its founder, Ayatollah Khomeini. Ahmadinejad deeply admires Amoli, a senior cleric, and wanted to share with him the story of his first trip abroad, especially those special moments. As the two sat on the carpeted floor surrounded by a few aides, one of the aides filmed the conversation for the sake of history with a handheld video camera.

To the embarrassment of the president, the tape reached the hands of some of his political rivals and was placed on the Internet. They wanted the Iranian people and the world to see him as prey to dangerous hallucinations. Ahmadinejad is the first Muslim leader who has prayed for the hastening of the return of the Shiite Messiah, known as the Mahdi, at the UN General Assembly, an act that reinforced his conviction that he was carrying God's words and acting on behalf of the Messiah.[2] The story of the Messiah is shared by all three monotheistic religions. Christianity, Judaism, and Islam have different perceptions of the Messiah rooted in different traditions and historical background. Yet there is at least one common denominator: in all the religions, the coming of the Messiah is associated with colossal war. Talk of the Messiah's coming frequently surfaces during times of hardship and desperation. In Iran the Messiah was prominently discussed during the war with Iraq, especially at the front. There had been reports of the Messiah's appearance by soldiers who were brainwashed. Reza Behrouzi was one of these soldiers. A teenager recruited to fight in the front, he recalled having visions of the Mahdi as a man on a white horse wearing traditional Arabic dress. According to Reza, everyone wanted to run toward the horseman, but he drove them away. "Don't come to me!" he shouted. "Charge into battle against the infidels! Revenge the death of our Imam Hussein and strike down the descendant of Yazid!" As the figure disappeared, the soldiers cried, "Oh, Mahdi, where are you?" They threw themselves on their knees and prayed and wailed. When the figure appeared again, they got to their feet. Those whose strength was not yet exhausted charged enemy lines.[3]

It is one thing for a desperate young soldier to imagine such a scene in the heat of battle. When a head of state, an educated man, claims to experience supernatural events, the repercussions are much more serious. Never before had an Iranian leader so publicly acknowledged his messianic belief. With Ahmadinejad's election, this formerly taboo subject has become part of the central ideology of one of the most influential leaders of the world, with frightening implications.

The Mahdi, named Muhammad at birth, was born in A.D. 868, 255 years after the start of the Islamic calendar, in the city of Samara, Iraq. He was the son of Imam Hasan Askari, the eleventh Shiite imam, and Narjes, who is believed to have Iranian heritage. Some Shiite accounts describe the Mahdi's face as like a shining star, with a black mole on his right cheek. He has many titles, including the Twelfth Imam, the Lost Imam, Montazer (awaiting), Hojjat (Authoritative source), and Saheb Al Zaman (owner of time). He disappeared at the age of five.

His period of absence is divided in two parts, the first of which lasted for sixty-nine years. During this time, four people represented the Mahdi on earth. Upon the death of the last representative, the second and longer period of his absence started, and it continues until today. Many Shiites await his return. There are a number of conflicting accounts about what will signal the Mahdi's imminent return. The Ayandeye Roshan (Bright Future) Institute, based in the Qom, specializes in theological research about the Mahdi. It points to at least five "distinct signs" that need to happen before the Mahdi appears. The first is the rise of a fighter from Yemen called the Yamani, who attacks the enemies of Islam.

The second sign is the rise of an anti-Mahdi militant leader named Osman Ben Anbase, who will also be known as Sofiani. He will be joined by another anti-Mahdi militant called Dajal, whom many Muslims clerics have compared to the Antichrist. The uprising of Sofiani will precede the reappearance of the Mahdi in Mecca by exactly six months. These two forces, known as the forces of evil, will occupy Syria and Jordan and advance from there. The forces of good in this battle will be led by a man from Khorasan, a province in Iran, and the opponents will meet for an epic battle near the city of Kufa, in the Shiite heartland of southern Iraq.

The third distinct sign will be voices from the sky. The most distinct voice will be that of the Angel Gabriel, who will call the faithful to gather around the Mahdi. The fourth sign will entail the destruction of Sofiani's army. The fifth and final sign is the death of a holy man by the name of Muhammad bin Hassan, called Nafse Zakiye, or the pure soul. Fifteen days after he is killed, the Mahdi will appear in Mecca.

The Mahdi will appoint Jesus Christ as his deputy. People will recognize the Mahdi because there will be an angel above his head shouting, "This is the Mahdi. Follow him." The Mahdi will be wearing a ring that belonged to King Solomon and will hold the wooden stick that Moses held when he parted the Red Sea. His army of 313 will grow into 10,000, fifty of whom will be women.[4]

There are also signs considered to be indications, though not certain indications, of the Mahdi's return. Such signs include the inability to distinguish between men and women due to cross-dressing, and the death of 80 percent of the world's population in a massive war.

According to the Bright Future Institute, no one can force the return of the Mahdi, not even the Mahdi himself. The only power that can decree his return is God. Accordingly, Muslims should develop the capability of *entezar*, meaning the ability to patiently wait for the Mahdi's return.[5] Anyone claiming to be the Mahdi without the aforementioned signs is a liar.[6]

In the eighteenth century a Muslim religious leader by the name of Baha'allah claimed that he was the Mahdi; he and his supporters have been condemned as heretics by mainstream Shia, which is why the Baha'i minority is persecuted in Iran. Many Baha'is were killed by the revolutionary authorities after the 1979 revolution. However, not all Shiite factions agree about the signs indicating the Mahdi's return. The Koran itself refers not to any particular signs but only to general signs, such as war and great injustice in the world.[7] Details about the Mahdi—his appearance, how many soldiers will accompany him, the size of the war that will precede his return, and whether or not anyone can speed his return—are based purely on the interpretation of words and teachings, called hadith, of Prophet Muhammad and of Shiism's twelve Imams. Over the course of time, a number of collections of hadith have been compiled and consequently a number of different schools of thought have arisen about the Mahdi.[8]

One school is led by a radical Shiite religious leader named Ayatollah Muhammad Taghi Mesbah Yazdi. Nicknamed Professor Crocodile because *Mesbah* rhymes with *Temsah*, Farsi for "crocodile," he believes that although no one can force the return of the Mahdi, Muslims should strive to hasten it. Extremist messianic groups adhere to this precept, which is known as *taajil*.[9] One of Mesbah Yazdi's closest allies and friends is Mahmoud Ahmadinejad, and their close ideological fraternity has become an important fixture on Iran's current political landscape. The combination of a radical political leader and his extremist spiritual mentor who believe strongly in the Mahdi and the need to accelerate his arrival is a source of great concern to many Iranians and the international community.

Both under the shah and after the revolution, messianic Iranians (whose ranks Mesbah Yazdi later joined) tried to infiltrate the higher echelons of political factions, the government, and the military to find allies to help quicken the return of the Mahdi. Since gaining prominence among such messianics in the late 1970s, Mesbah Yazdi has worked under the cover of the Hojjatieh society, which was organized during the reign of the shah, ostensibly to fight Iran's "heretical" Baha'i community.[10] The Hojjatieh initially resisted supporting the revolutionary movement of Ayatollah Khomeini because it feared losing its hard-earned influence. To Mesbah Yazdi, Khomeini was an obstacle.

On their side, Khomeini's followers found Hojjatieh's stance self-interested and opportunistic. However, once the Hojjatieh realized that Khomeini's revolutionaries were gaining the upper hand, it immediately switched to supporting the revolution. After the Khomeini forces took power, the Hojjatieh became more revolutionary than the revolutionaries and tried again to recruit senior army and government officials.[11] In 1983 Ayatollah Khomeini disbanded the organization, whose ideology he called very dangerous—this from a man whose own revolution in 1979 was viewed as fanatical and dangerous to global stability.[12] Khomeini may well have seen the Hojjatieh for what it really was: an opportunistic messianic cult without scruples or loyalty. To have such an organization operating freely in his government could have been like nurturing a Judas in his bosom.

By then an important figure in Hojjatieh, Mesbah Yazdi moved to Qom, where he headed two religious institutions in which he continued preaching his message: the Haghani school and the Ayatollah Khomeini Institute. In the lobby of the institute, the members have posted a board displaying the number of days since the Mahdi disappeared.[13] Slowly, through building alliances, Mesbah Yazdi worked his way back into positions of power. Four of his former students and allies—Muhammad Rayshahri, Ali Fallahian, Ali Younessi, and Ali Akbar Mohseni Ejehi,the current minister—have been ministers of Intelligence and Security, a powerful position in both the cabinet and the Supreme National Security Council. Another prominent member is Akbar Velayati, Iran's former foreign minister, who is an advisor to the Supreme Leader. All of them are helping to increase the influence of Mesbah Yazdi and his messianic dreams in Iranian politics.

But Yazdi's golden opportunity to position himself as one of the most influential religious leaders of the country arrived with Ahmadinejad's entry into the presidential race. Yazdi issued a fatwa (religious decree) calling for all the faithful to consider it their Islamic duty to vote for Ahmadinejad. After the election, he claimed that Ahmadinejad became president only because of the Mahdi's direct assistance.[14] Soon the newly elected president declared his goal was to "establish an advanced, powerful, and exemplary society, so that it becomes a blueprint for the people of the world and thus ultimately serves as a platform for the reappearance of the Mahdi."[15] Ahmadinejad doesn't want to wait for the Mahdi—he wants to hasten his arrival.

While mayor of Tehran, Ahmadinejad had a costly city plan prepared for the arrival of the Mahdi, which included the route the Mahdi would take through the city.[16] After he was elected president, Ahmadinejad made an urgent visit to Jamkaran mosque near Qom, one of the main mosques associated with the Mahdi. Legend has it that the mosque was built after the Mahdi asked a local righteous man in a dream to do so. The mosque also has a well in which the public throws pieces of paper with their wishes in the hope that the Mahdi would answer them. After his visit Ahmadinejad substantially increased funding for the mosque's refurbishment. There are also reports that plans are being made for the construction of a direct train link from Tehran to Jamkaran mosque.[17]

Meanwhile Mesbah Yazdi's plan to infiltrate the government has advanced. Ahmadinejad named Mustafa Pour-Mohhamadi and Gholam Hossein Ejehi, former students of Mesbah Yazdi's, to the sensitive posts of interior minister and information minister. Both ministries have dominant positions in the cabinet, in the parliament, and on the Supreme National Security Council, giving their directors the opportunity to gain more allies and to manipulate sensitive intelligence information for their radical goals.

But Mesbah Yazdi's most powerful ally in Ahmadinejad's government is a relatively unknown official who shies away from publicity. He is Mojtaba Samare Hashemi, Ahmadinejad's confidant and most senior advisor. One of the most notable signs of Ahmadinejad's admiration for Samare is that he prays behind him, a sign of respect Ahmadinejad shows to very few people. Samare has unprecedented power over Ahmadinejad's policies and his mood. At times it seems the Iranian president is captivated by his advisor. With two words and a nod Samare convinced Ahmadinejad to change a decision 180 degrees in full public view. This remarkable incident occurred at the UN in September 2006. Gil Tamary, an Israeli reporter for Israel's Channel 10 news, boldly attended Ahmadinejad's press conference and asked him a question.

Ahmadinejad—a man who has declared his hatred for everything Israeli and "Zionist," especially "the Zionist-controlled media"—smiled nervously, not knowing what to do. Israel and Israelis are considered as the enemies of Iran and there can be no dialogue with them, so in accordance with twenty-seven years of Islamic Republic tradition, Ahmadinejad refused to answer Tamary. While stating his refusal in front of the packed room he looked to his immediate left, where Samare was sitting. Samare nodded and whispered to Ahmadinejad, "Answer it." Ahmadinejad instantly spent a full minute answering to Tamary's question. History was made.

Samare—or Brother Samare, as Ahmadinejad likes to call him—also believes strongly in the need to hasten the Mahdi's return. A former student of Mesbah Yazdi's, Samare is so devoted to his mentor that a photo of Yazdi hangs in his office instead of the nearly obligatory photo of Ayatollah Khomeini or Khamenei. This is a provocative step, yet Samare was willing to risk his political career for Yazdi.

Samare is an extreme Islamic ideologue. He first made his mark as an IRGC intelligence agent in Iran's Kurdistan district during the Iran-Iraq war. The IRGC's intelligence unit was closely associated with al-Quds brigade, of which Ahmadinejad was a member. Only the most ideological and fanatic followers of the regime were allowed to join the IRGC's intelligence unit. After the war Samare's beliefs and his connections landed him a job at Iran's foreign ministry, which at the time was being run by another of Mesbah Yazdi's follower, Ali Akbar Velayati. There he was reputed to be an unusually brutal instructor of young diplomats. He would lock his trainees in the basement of the ministry and indoctrinate them about how to act and think in accordance with the teachings of the Islamic Republic. In another class he famously trained students in obtaining information by threats and by sex.

He also taught diplomats how to identify potential traitors, colleagues who might be deviating toward foreign ideology. "The psychology of the infidels," as he called it, was recognizable by the "lines on a diplomat's trousers, his shoes and his smile." If, for example, a diplomat wore shoes with laces, it showed he was not dedicated to praying because he had chosen cumbersome shoes that were hard to remove. To Samare, smiling at strangers is a Western idea, a sign of weakness and a wish to appease. Samare was so ruthless that he had his former trainees followed abroad, sending members of his team to Iranian embassies to spy on them to ensure they did not "deviate." If diplomats were found to be straying from the party line, Samare would see that they were dismissed, no matter how senior their position.

In the late 1990s Samare left his position at the ministry of foreign affairs to assist in the election campaigns of conservatives in city elections. It was there that Mesbah Yazdi connected him with Ahmadinejad, and the two started working together. Samare subsequently and worked with Mayor Ahmadinejad as his advisor and brought him under his spell. According to people who worked there, Ahmadinejad was an ill-tempered manager unless he was with Samare. At those times, he never shouted or argued; he never even raised his voice. He just listened, as an apprentice would to his master.

Their special relationship has continued into Ahmadinejad's presidency.[18] Samare is feared among the ministers, whom he observes the way he watched over his trainees in the basement. Every day a minister, even a senior one, is called into Samare's office for "talks." Samare grills them about their performance and that of their subordinates. Ministers loathe these sessions. Samare intervened so much in the internal affairs of Pour-Muhammadi's interior ministry that he threatened to resign. After a number of Iranian ministers complained about Samare to Ayatollah Khamenei, Samare made Ahmadinejad issue a new directive saying that all ministers have to report to Samare before they meet with Khamenei, and then to debrief him afterward.[19]

Samare's grip on Ahmadinejad stems also from Mesbah Yazdi's direct orders. Mesbah Yazdi instructed Ahmadinejad to consider Samare his personal guide in messianic matters. Samare, far more messianic than Ahmadinejad, is in charge of most of Ahmadinejad's messianic projects, such as the Jamkaran shrine. Samare believes that his and Ahmadinejad's messianic policies should have a bigger say in all of Iran's policies, including the selection of the next Supreme Leader. Talking in public about replacing Khamenei is unheard of, but since Khamenei's prostate cancer is an open secret, political factions are talking in private about his succession.

The next Supreme Leader will be chosen by the Assembly of Experts, eighty-six clerical politicians, all male. In the days before the December 2006 election of the Assembly of Experts, Ahmadinejad dispatched Samare to the ministry of interior, where he was supposedly to ensure that the rules of the selection process were followed. But in fact he was there to disqualify as many reformist candidates as possible so that only the hard-liners, especially Mesbah Yazdi's messianic supporters, would be chosen. Before the candidates for the Assembly are selected they were referred to a committee of senior legal and religious experts called the Guardian Council, which has the final say in their approval.

Samare's culling of the reformist candidates was so rigorous that former president Khatami, who had hoped that his reformist camp would regain some of its power, admitted defeat before the elections took place. Even conservative members of the Guardian Council feared that the next Assembly of Experts would be populated mainly by messianic zealots. They retaliated by rejecting many of Samare's candidates, Mesbah Yazdi's son among them.[20]

Ahmadinejad and Samare also want to spread the power of the messianic faction into the nuclear program. In 2006, Ahmadinejad dispatched Samare abroad, first to France and later secretly to Japan to conduct backdoor negotiations about Iran's nuclear program. Such behavior infuriates Ali Larijani, the head of Iran's Supreme National Security Council, who considers himself the sole negotiator of nuclear issues with foreign countries. On the other hand, the Ahmadinejad/Samare messianic camp is supported by Gholam Reza Aghazadeh, the head of the Atomic Energy Organization of Iran (AEOI). A scientist by profession, Aghazadeh was the minister of oil after the revolution and was moved to AEOI in the latter half of the 1990s. He proved himself to be a much stronger administrator than Reza Amrollahi, whom he replaced, and turned the nearly defunct organization into the vanguard of Iran's nuclear ambitions.

Meanwhile, to ensure that Mesbah Yazdi's message would reach the public at maximum volume, Ahmadinejad increased government funding for his institution by 1000 percent, to $3.5 million.[21] Outside his cabinet Ahmadinejad also surrounds himself with fellow messianic believers, such as Ayatollah Meshkini, a very senior politician, and the former head of the Assembly of Experts. Shortly before Ahmadinejad's election Meshkini claimed that the Mahdi had personally signed the list of newly elected parliament members because he was happy with the government's Islamic direction.[22]

Messianic fervor seems to be spreading. Conservatives are also starting to speak of the Mahdi. After Ahmadinejad's appearance at the UN, Ali Davani, an important figure in the powerful Ansar Hezbollah political organization and a close Ahmadinejad ally, publicly declared that the UN speech was "one of the signs indicating the appearance of the Mahdi."[23]

To Mahmoud Ahmadinejad, the Mahdi's return will do much more than bring "justice and peace."[24] It will also turn the entire world into an Islamic republic. By hastening the return of the Mahdi, Ahmadinejad may also be angling for a senior position in the Mahdi's global Islamic government. In 2005 at a meeting hosted by the Islamic Society of Engineers, Ahmadinejad publicly stated, "During different periods of the revolution, we felt that a hand and a force is above the people of Iran. Holy prophets came to lay the groundwork for the realization of God's promise. This promise was the establishment of a global Islamic government, with the assistance of the Mahdi."[25]

This is a fearsome thought. In the twenty-first century, when a majority of countries try to honor national boundaries and respect cultural and religious differences, the leader of 70 million people wants his ideology to prevail over the entire world. Ironically this president, who has lambasted colonialism and expansionism in other countries, wants to do the same through religion. The danger of his ambitions becomes more evident the closer Iran comes to having a nuclear device.

Nor is Ahmadinejad a man given to half-measures. He is ready to give up his life for the sake of the revolution, as his religious belief demands.[26] To Ahmadinejad, shahadat (martyrdom) can be his part of the journey to spiritual perfection and should be pursued by all Muslims until the day the Mahdi arrives.[27] Ayatollah Khomeini is a major influence on this part of his ideology.[28] According to Khomeini, life is worthless and death is the beginning of genuine existence. "The natural world," he explained in October 1980, "is the lowest element, the scum of creation. What is decisive is the beyond: the divine world. That is eternal." This latter world is accessible to martyrs.[29] The other major influence is the slaying of Imam Hussein, the son of Imam Ali, in the seventh century. Hussein's murderer, Yazid, surrounded Imam Hussein and his seventy-two soldiers with his army of four thousand. Nonetheless, Imam Hussein fought on because he believed in the sanctity of his cause. In the heat of battle Hussein fell off his horse and his enemies cut off his head from behind, then held it up for all to see. Shiites believe this was a cowardly way to kill a man, and for many of them this battle represents the struggle between good and evil.

Hussein, the third Shiite imam, is also known as Seyyed Alshohada, the Lord of the Martyrs. To commemorate the martyrdom of Imam Hussein, Shiite mourners gather every year for ten days (in the month known as Moharram) to recount his story at mosques. The congregants are told how Imam Hussein was killed fighting the hated and corrupt Yazid, whose father, Moaviye, had attacked Imam Ali and usurped the reins of Islam from him. Imam Hussein's goal was to return Islam to the just and godly regime that it had been under his father, when its values were divine and in accordance to the Koran's teachings as preached by Prophet Muhammad. Imam Hussein's martyrdom is used to teach all Shiites that dying for Islam is holy and ensures a place in heaven.[30]

The story of Imam Hussein is the basis of Iranian religious education and tradition, so the concept of shahadat is deeply rooted in religious people's hearts. Ahmadinejad's father was a follower of Imam Hussein's teachings and his house was near a Hosseiniye, where people gathered to mourn the martyrdom of Imam Hussein. His father even had dreamed about his duties for the ceremonies commemorating Imam Hussein's martyrdom. He taught the importance of shahadat to his son from a very early age.

To Ahmadinejad, the revolution of 1979 was the continuation of Imam Hussein's struggle against heretics and evildoers. Anyone who confronts the revolutionary government must be fought as Imam Hussein fought Yazid. If there are no wars today, those who wish to become martyrs should not worry because there will be opportunities in the future.[31] This means that if pushed, he would welcome a war to defend his country and would perceive it as a battle between good and evil, exactly as he sees the battle that took place between Imam Hussein and Yazid. Ahmadinejad's promise that Iran's enemies await a "fate nothing short of destruction" flows inevitably from his ideology.[32]

Among those "enemies," none has been more a target for threats of destruction and annihilation than Israel. Ahmadinejad has stated on numerous occasions that Israel is an artificial Western invention created to cause division and havoc in the Middle East's Muslim countries.[33] Its founders, he maintains, managed to hugely exaggerate the "myth" of the Holocaust and use it as a tool to embarrass the German people, win international sympathy, and establish an illegal entity in what was Palestine.[34] Since then, the "Zionist entity" has managed to survive only through the support of imperialist forces such as the United States and Great Britain, and through the murder and expulsion of Palestinians from their lands.[35]

Ahmadinejad is also a strong believer in conspiracy theories. He viewed the Danish cartoons that mocked Prophet Muhammad—and touched off disturbances around the Muslim world in 2005—as a Zionist-inspired plot against Islam. In retaliation, his administration sponsored a Holocaust cartoon competition and a conference in December 2006 hosting a range of Holocaust deniers from all over the world. The cartoons tried to show that either the Holocaust did not happen or was exploited by Israel to enhance its interests at the expense of Palestinians.

Ahmadinejad has made it clear that in his opinion Israel has no right to exist, and he further describes it as a weak tree that will be uprooted by one storm. On several occasions he has said that Israel must be wiped off the face of the earth and it is only a question of time until that happens.[36]

Ahmadinejad hates Israel because he is a religious Muslim first and foremost, and a nationalist second. During the reign of the shah, many nationalistic Iranians supported Israel because they too consider themselves non-Arabs and Israel was a natural ally in their quest to stop Arab hegemony in the region. As far back as 1889 the Iranian king Naser'edin Shah suggested the idea of creating a state for the Jews, to the wealthy Jewish financier Baron Nathan Rothschild.[37] After the creation of Israel in 1948, the two countries worked together closely until 1979 when the shah was deposed. Since then all such contact ended.

Ahmadinejad has taken the religious viewpoint to the extreme. He is angered at not only Israel's illegal occupation of Arab land but also the Israeli government's secular nature.[38] Ironically, Ahmadinejad might have had more tolerance for Israel had it adopted a democratic theocracy, one controlled by scripture and religious authorities. It infuriates him that Israel does not follow a strictly religious system of governance, as Iran does. Ahmadinejad constantly accuses Israel of distancing itself from God, mocks its "liberalist" democracy, and sees it as a sacrilegious state, the "standard-bearer of Satan on earth."[39] Therefore, anyone who fights against Israel is fighting for God, and anyone who dies in the process is a martyr who will go to heaven.[40]

Ahmadinejad also considers Israel's supporters satanic, none more so than the United States. Although he does not hate the USA as deeply as he does Israel, his hostility started when he was six. Barely able to read, he managed to decipher a newspaper article that reported on privileges the shah had awarded American citizens in Iran, notably immunity from Iranian judicial prosecution, thus enabling them to commit crimes without being punished. Many Iranians, including Ahmadinejad's family, were infuriated by this policy, which they described as capitulation. To them it symbolized Iran's servility as well as the arrogance of the United States in considering itself above the laws of other countries.[41]

Ahmadinejad's longstanding animosity toward the United States is primarily political, focused on its "imperialist expansionist policies."[42] He sees the country as an empire that wants to expand in the Middle East and in the third world, as evidenced by its support for Israel and the invasion and occupation of Iraq. Ahmadinejad believes the United States wants to do the same in other parts of the world by assisting corrupt and weak regimes so that they depend on American support for their stability. Sometimes referred to as "the Great Satan" by Ahmadinejad, the United States is willing to achieve its expansionist goals through the use of brute force, but if force is not in its interest, it will do so through the spread of its "neoliberalist" ideas such as democracy and capitalism.

Ahmadinejad's experience under the shah also reinforced his distrust of capitalism and its values. At that time, Iran's economy was primarily capitalist and the rich, including the shah's family, abused it to their own advantage.

Poorer families, such as Ahmadinejad's, suffered. Furthermore, many cheap U.S. products entered Iran at the expense of Iranian products and jobs, adding to the misery and anger of the working poor.[43]

Ahmadinejad's only obvious religious dissatisfaction with America is that he expects it, as a predominantly Christian country, to follow the teachings of Jesus Christ and turn the other cheek if attacked. So he was disappointed to see the United States attack Iraq and Afghanistan, and kill their civilians.[44]

In fact, Ahmadinejad is sincerely interested in developing dialogue with the United States, as his unexpected but enthusiastic letter to President Bush in the summer of 2006 demonstrated. When the eighteen-page missive was dismissed without a reply, he felt let down and angry, warning the president that declining an invitation to do good will end badly.[45] Three months later, still bitter over his inability to galvanize President Bush with his letter, Ahmadinejad declared that the U.S. president was inspired by Satan, while he himself had a direct connection with God.[46] Despite his humiliation over the letter, however, he tried again on November 29, 2006. But this time he addressed Americans directly. By calling them "God-fearing, truth-loving, and justice-seeking," he hoped to show that he is not against the American people, only against the Bush administration.[47] The letter, which was suffused with attacks against the U.S. government and Israel, failed to reach the American public.

A surprising repercussion of Ahmadinejad's ideology is his contempt for England. Until his election, cries of "Death to England" were not standard at demonstrations. Now they are in fashion. Ahmadinejad holds England responsible for the creation of Israel, through the Balfour Declaration issued in 1917 by the British government, which recognized the legitimacy of a Jewish homeland in Palestine. Tony Blair's support for the war in Iraq and the United Kingdom's seemingly tough stance against Iran's nuclear program have intensified Ahmadinejad's animosity toward what he and his IRGC colleagues call the Anglo-Saxon empire.[48] However, interestingly, Ahmadinejad avoids using the word "Britain" in his harangues because it would imply he is speaking of the Scots, Welsh, and Northern Irish as well. Iran considers these peoples victims of "English occupation" and as potential allies against the "Anglo-Saxon" colonialists.

Ahmadinejad has extensively used Imam Hussein's teachings and the concept of martyrdom to prepare the Iranian population to confront the West, especially in the current struggle over the nuclear program.[49] But of all his convictions, he believes in the arrival of the Mahdi most fervently. Imam Hussein may be martyred and in paradise forever, but the Mahdi is going to return one day and Ahmadinejad will do what he can to make sure that happens, even if it means creating a crisis. Soon after becoming president, Ahmadinejad met with the foreign minister of an Islamic nation, who suggested that Iran seemed to be heading toward a crisis. Ahmadinejad replied that the crisis would prepare the arrival of the Mahdi, which would take place in a few years.[50] He later made the timetable more specific, saying the Mahdi would reappear in 2007.[51]

To Ahmadinejad's pleasure, some of the Iranian public have started to echo his beliefs. "The story of the life and death of Imam Hussein tells us that when you rights are being challenged, you shouldn't surrender," said a merchant in Tehran's Bazaar (market). "You should be prepared to die, if that is what is necessary. Today we have to practice the same concept and teachings to achieve our right to enrich uranium."[52]

Ahmadinejad's belief that the Mahdi will reappear sometime in 2007 is a source of concern to many inside and outside Iran. With Iran now able to enrich uranium, it could become nuclear in 2007. If that happens, Iran's nuclear arsenal might give the regime the confidence it needs to start a war, which could then become the "platform" that Ahmadinejad has said he wants to create for the reappearance of the Mahdi.

Even if Iran is not a nuclear power, Ahmadinejad might be willing to engage the West in a war because a conflict against America could precipitate the Mahdi's reappearance. A deadlock in the nuclear negotiations may lead to an attack against Iran's nuclear facilities by Western powers, probably the United States, or Israel. If the former attacks Iran, Tehran will undoubtedly unleash its Shiite allies against U.S. forces in Iraq, since messianic extremists in Iran see the U.S. occupation in Iraq as an attempt to prevent the Mahdi from reappearing there.[53] As far as Ahmadinejad and his fellow ideologues are concerned, fighting and expelling U.S. forces from Iraq will set stage for the Mahdi's return in the land of his birth.

CHAPTER FOUR

Paying Any Price

ON WEDNESDAY, NOVEMBER 23, 2005, Mahmoud Ahmadinejad was sitting in the front row of the Majlis. He could not believe what he was seeing. His third candidate for the powerful oil ministry in four months had just been rejected by the Iranian parliament. To have one minister rejected is acceptable; it has happened before. A second rejected nomination raises suspicion. To have a third nominee for the same position rejected is downright embarrassing, especially for a newly elected head of government who considered himself the popular choice of the people. Such a thing had not happened in Iran since the 1979 revolution.

One of Ahmadinejad's most famous election campaign promises was to put "oil money on the table of every Iranian family."[1] The fact that he couldn't even get his own nominee through the door of the oil ministry was a huge blow. Ahmadinejad was so furious that he walked up to the podium and reprimanded the Majlis members for attacking his government.[2]

Events behind the scenes were compounding Ahmadinejad's nervousness. He knew that Ayatollah Rafsanjani was responsible for the humiliating setbacks he was suffering in parliament. And Rafsanjani was still stinging from Ahmadinejad's Khamenei-engineered victory. In the ensuing five months,

Ahmadinejad had repeatedly behaved as if he deserved the victory, almost as if he were God's choice.

Though defeated and hurt, Rafsanjani wasn't going to surrender. Nicknamed "the Shark" for his mastery at ambushing his enemies, he put his talent to use. His method usually entails circling his enemy behind the scenes, then launching a sudden attack when the prey is at its weakest. For months Rafsanjani had lobbied Majlis corridors, encouraging members to reject Ahmadinejad's candidates for the oil ministry. It worked each time.

On November 23, 2005, Ahmadinejad bore all the signs of a man subjected to multiple shark attacks. When it came to the oil ministry, Rafsanjani was far stronger and more influential than he. Years of wheeling and dealing have made him the kingpin of Iran's oil industry, the country's lifeline. This time Ahmadinejad couldn't beseech Ayatollah Khamenei for help. Khamenei needed Rafsanjani to counterbalance Ahmadinejad's possible increase in power. Playing different factions against one another is a central part of Khamenei's strategy of maintaining control. To use a popular Iranian analogy, to Khamenei the Iranian regime is like a bird that needs two wings to fly; no matter how much he may favor the ideology and behavior of one wing, he will never completely clip the other. Despite the animosity between the two men, Khamenei will never eliminate Rafsanjani's influence completely.

Realizing that Rafsanjani was here to stay, Ahmadinejad made sure that his fourth nominee would be acceptable to Rafsanjani and his allies. On Sunday, December 11, Ahmadinejad's fourth candidate, Kazem Vaziri-Hamaneh, was confirmed by the Majlis. Beaten but enthusiastic, at last, Ahmadinejad thought that at last he had taken over the oil ministry.[3] It seems unlikely. Vaziri-Hamaneh was a candidate of compromise. His loyalties will be divided between the Rafsanjani the Shark and the president.

Oil is Iran's biggest and most lucrative commodity, providing no less than 80 percent of the total income from all Iranian exports and at least 50 percent of Iran's budgetary expenditures. Oil prices reached record highs during Ahmadinejad's first year in office. According to many estimates, they are likely to stay high for the foreseeable future because of growing demand from

Western countries as well as India and China.[4] Ahmadinejad can therefore count on substantial oil income until at least the end of his term in 2009, and if he is reelected, until 2013. (Iranian presidents are limited constitutionally to two consecutive four-year terms.) In fact, with its 132 billion barrels of proven oil reserves, if Iran continues to produce oil at the current level of 4 million barrels a day, it will have enough oil for the next ninety years.[5] On top of its abundant oil resources, Iran also owns the world's second-largest gas reserves, with 970 trillion cubic feet (TCF). If Iran continues to produce gas at the current annual rate of 3.5 TCF per year, its supplies will last for 320 years.[6] The price of gas, like that of oil, has also been rising.

Ahmadinejad is determined to control Iran's oil and gas resources. He is even prepared to resort to brute force in order to protect the treasure. He showed his aggressiveness in August 22, 2006, when Iranian gunboats were sent to take over by force a Romanian oil rig working in the Persian Gulf. It was a rare case of the military's being used to settle a civilian contractual dispute. Although the matter was quickly resolved (Ahmadinejad personally called the Romanian authorities), it nevertheless showed that income from oil is so central to Ahmadinejad's policies that he would do whatever is necessary to maintain control, including the use of violence.[7]

Oil is not only Iran's economic oxygen but also, in Ahmadinejad's eyes, a shield against international sanctions or a military attack on Iran's nuclear sites. In fact, the president's allies and advisors have threatened on a number of occasions that in such an event, Iran would punish the world economies by stemming the flow of oil.[8]

Just the mention of such actions pushes the price of oil upward. If Western threats of military action, or full economic sanctions against Iran were to become reality, Iran would almost certainly cut the sale of its oil, at least for a limited period, to ram prices to unbearable levels for Western economies. So far, it seems that this deterrent is working. The "awakening" market of China is already scared because Iran provides more than 15 percent of its oil supplies. Iran, together with Saudi Arabia and Angola, is among the top three suppliers of oil to China.[9] Because of that, China, a permanent member of the UN Security Council, with veto power, is very reluctant that the UN imposes tough sanctions against Iran. This is a significant achievement for Iran.

Russia, another Security Council member with veto power, has decided to join the "Chinese wall" and block U.S. efforts to impose broad economic sanctions on Iran. Although Russia does not need Iranian oil, Iran is a key market for Russian military, nuclear, and civilian goods, worth $3 billion annually. Russia is also building a nuclear power plant in Bushehr, located in southern Iran. The project is very important to the Russians, and they worry that if full sanctions were imposed, Tehran would no longer be able to sell oil to finance its Russian shopping spree.

Despite Russia's and China's defense of Iran against sanctions, past experience has taught Iran that both countries can be fair-weather friends. They have sided with Iran's enemies before and could do so again. Ahmadinejad follows Khamenei's precept that to maintain balance, more than one wing is needed to fly. Iran is not willing to rely solely on its Eastern wing. Consequently, the Iranian regime is ready to sleep with the enemy, so to speak, even if that contradicts its declared principles. Since the revolution Western oil companies have been traditionally presented in Iran including by Ahmadinejad as exploitative, manipulative tools of colonialism representing Western capitalism. Yet to defend itself, Iran's leadership has agreed to cooperate with the world's major oil companies, with the ultimate aim that they will unintentionally turn into supporters of Iran's nuclear program.[10] The logic is simple: if Iran is attacked, they will also have something to lose. This strategy may have started before Ahmadinejad's presidency, but he has done little to halt it. Iran's nuclear program takes precedence, and Ahmadinejad is ready to protect it even at the cost of working with international oil companies. It is conceivable that had the U.S. government not forbade it, Ahmadinejad might be dealing with U.S. oil companies today as well.

A further consequence of Ahmadinejad's focus on the nuclear program is that the country's fiscal problems are being neglected. The Iranian people want economic problems to be the government's top priority and the nuclear program second or even third, and they say so openly, without fear.[11] Some Iranians complain that Ahmadinejad is acting as if he could feed Iran's children with nuclear energy and that he shouldn't forget he was elected to fight poverty and unemployment. They point to Pakistan, whose citizens live in abject poverty despite the country's nuclear capabilities. The government needs to come up with sound economic policies first, they say, and then worry about nuclear technology.[12]

Ahmadinejad seems to think he can do both at once. While enhancing his nuclear program, he is trying to tackle poverty. Wages for civil servants, especially nurses, have been raised 30 percent.[13] He has also started providing financial assistance to some of Iran's elderly pensioners, many of whom suffer in acute poverty.[14] To help the underprivileged with housing problems, Ahmadinejad allocated $1 billion in his first budget (March 2006–March 2007) for the construction of low-cost housing, as he did when he was mayor of Tehran.[15] To improve his image among Iranian expats, he included in the budget flight discounts (as high as 50 percent) for Iranian students abroad as long as they flew Iran Air. However, some of his schemes, such as his Iran Air discount scheme have hit turbulent waters. Another example is his highly publicized Imam Reza Love Fund, named after the eighth Shiite imam, aims to provide financial support to young Iranian couples who cannot afford a wedding. It also provides them with affordable housing loans. To the delight of many struggling young couples, $1.3 billion was allocated to this project. To date, though, the majlis has failed to approve the plan, officially because of bureaucratic problems. Unofficially, some believe that the bureaucratic hurdles have been created once again by Rafsanjani's allies in an effort to undermine Ahmadinejad.[16]

Such failures, and the inherent contradiction between his insistence on having a substantial nuclear program (probably to produce nuclear weapons) and his promise to help the poor, do not hold Ahmadinejad back. Since most of his genuine supporters came from among the poor, Ahmadinejad's administration has been creating lavish plans to provide financial assistance to help them and ultimately, himself. These plans, however, are so extensive that his administration has started raiding Iran's oil stabilization fund, whose use is reserved exclusively for times of low oil income. Many Iranian economists contend that contributions to this fund should be increased when oil prices are up, but Ahmadinejad is instead removing money from it.

The economists have responded with anger, opening another front for the president to deal with. Ahmadinejad, for his part, appears unfazed.[17] He justifies draining the stabilization fund by arguing that the government needs to invest directly in antipoverty and employment projects sooner rather than later. His first budget set aside $18 billion (8 percent of the total) for a single project to fight unemployment. The program calls on banks and quick-loan agencies to distribute the money in the form of low-interest unsecured loans to Iranian businesses employing fewer than fifty people. Ahmadinejad hopes that this cash infusion will enable Iranian companies to boost their manpower and in the process significantly reduce unemployment. The government estimates this initiative will result in 844,000 new jobs, assuming the entire amount is spent on job creation.[18]

This ambitious target is also unrealistic. It will be a major achievement if this project fulfills even half of its goal. With no mechanisms in place to track the money after it has been disbursed, businesses will doubtless manipulate the system.[19] They might use the funds to finance other debts or to purchase raw materials immediately rather than wait for the spiraling inflation to make them more costly. They might simply save the money for the day sanctions are imposed.

Despite the project's likely shortcomings, Ahmadinejad envisions expanding it. This is one of the characteristics of Ahmadinejadenomics. The president of Iran believes that increased expenditures on economic plans, even those with dubious long-term results, are justified as long as they also improve his standing. Even a short-term boost to his popularity is sufficient, which is why Ahmadinejad has promised that the cheap-loan budget will increase from $18 billion to $30 billion in the March 2008–March 2009 fiscal year. Those who did not obtain a loan this year should have a better chance next year, and those who did will probably be able to get their hands on another one next year.

Another special characteristic of Ahmadinejadenomics is that a single populist economic plan never suffices. If one fails to produce the economic results or does not reach the intended segment of the population, then the others can cover it. Not surprisingly, Ahmadinejad has backed a number of other plans, notably a highly publicized one called the Justice Shares program. This plan was created during Khatami's presidency, but its implementation has only just begun. Ayatollah Khamenei wanted a dedicated soldier to follow his orders about this program, and Khatami, with his reformist agenda and corrupt backers, did not fit the profile. Ahmadinejad does, and follows orders without question. According to the constitution, Khamenei calls the shots and all government agencies are subject to his final verdict.

Under this scheme, parts of Iran's numerous state-owned companies will be privatized. While this is taking place, the government will denominate the country's poor, each of whom will be offered shares in the companies once the shares are ready to be listed on Tehran's stock exchange. To persuade the poor—who don't have money—to buy shares, the program allows the buyer up to ten years to pay for them. Until the poor are fully able to pay for the shares, Ahmadinejad's administration plans to finance the privatization process with Iran's oil money. Ahmadinejad sees the program as a unique scheme for social justice based on Islamic values. In truth, this concept owes a great deal to Margaret Thatcher's privatization policy, which denationalized the majority of Britain's state sector in 1980s and 1990s.

The plan's overt aim is to give Iran's poor a stake in the economy so they will be able to enjoy its profits directly. However, below the surface the Justice Shares program has two other important goals. First and foremost, it aims to correct the mistakes of the past. Khomeini's mantra of the 1979 revolution was "social justice and redistribution of national wealth," but the revolution has generally failed on both counts. Khomeini's regime focused on purging its enemies and fighting the Iraqis, and subsequent presidents allowed a new class of privileged officials to profit from their positions at the poor's expense. In fact, many Iranians see the postrevolution officials as more incompetent and corruptible than the shah's notoriously crooked officials had been. A large number of state-owned companies became staffed with corrupt managers who do not think twice about lining their own pockets and those of their families and friends. This enraged the poor, which helped Ahmadinejad come to power. Khamenei and Ahmadinejad hope to use the Justice Shares privatization program to review the management and accounts of state-owned companies. The review will be used to identify and replace corrupt officials with new managers who will be more efficient and ethical, it is hoped. Those who voted for Ahmadinejad because of his anticorruption stand, it is also hoped, will be mollified.

The second goal of this plan is to reduce Rafsanjani's influence. Many of the supposedly corrupt managers were installed during his tenure or are his allies. The Justice Shares program will allow Ahmadinejad to weed out Rafsanjani's allies and strengthen his own position both economically and politically.

Ahmadinejad has been involved in other anticorruption efforts as well. Ghaem Maghame Farahani Street (formerly Bucharest Avenue) is a fashionable neighborhood in the northern part of Tehran, home to high-profile lawyers and doctors and a number of foreign embassies. Real estate there is expensive. During Khatami's tenure Iran's ministry of cultural heritage was looking for a property where it could host its guests and carry out some of its administrative duties. This ministry is neither the biggest nor the most important and could have housed its offices in any middle-class neighborhood with reasonable prices. Instead, it chose to purchase a twenty-two-story building on Bucharest Avenue, costing taxpayers $50 million, the equivalent of the total monthly salary of 200,000 Iranian civil servants. Not only was the price exorbitant but the money was taken—illegally—from the country's job-creation program. Considering it wasteful and fraudulent, Ahmadinejad ordered the cancellation of this project, which had been approved during Khatami's tenure.[20]

Ahmadinejad also ordered a review of other contracts concluded during Khatami's presidency and found more cases of excessive expenses. Ahmadinejad canceled the contracts, renegotiated them, and returned the saved amount to the country's coffers.[21] To prove that he practices what he preaches, the president even went after his own bodyguards. Told that they had ordered Ray-Bans on his office's budget, Ahmadinejad was furious and forced them to pay for the sunglasses.[22]

Despite Ahmadinejad's persistent promises to fight corruption, he cannot completely solve this problem. Even with the support of Khamenei's Article 44 decree, which seemingly gives him the legal basis to fight corruption, Ahmadinejad will not be able to get rid of one-fifth of the corruption problem. He simply lacks the will. Corruption is so widespread in the upper echelons of power that to eradicate it means taking on the leadership, which would mean risking his power and probably his life, too. For many politicians in Iran, a fight against economic corruption equals a fight against their own political power, and they are ready to kill to defend that power. Ahmadinejad well knows that Khamenei is widely reputed to be corrupt. Many Iranians believe that the Supreme Leader is one of the richest people in Iran because he has amassed his wealth by taking a cut of both major government contracts and the income of many state-owned charitable organizations, such as the multibillion-dollar bonyads. If Ahmadinejad looked hard enough, he could prove it. But to do so would be very dangerous.

Although it may seem far-fetched that internal forces would assassinate the president of the Islamic Republic of Iran, many Iranians believe that however slight, the possibility exists. The example of Seyyed Ahmad Khomeini, the son of the founder of the Iranian revolution, is frequently cited. He died in 1995 at the age of forty-eight under what many consider mysterious circumstances. At the time he was attempting to moderate the regime's abuse of power and its fiscal corruption. Many believe he was killed by senior members of the regime even though he was the son of Imam Khomeini. This theory gained more credibility when Hussein Khomeini— Seyyed Ahmad's nephew and Ayatollah Khomeini's grandson—fled the country in 2003. Taking refuge in Iraq, he called for the Americans to invade Iran and topple the regime, which he described as the world's worst dictatorship.[23] Many attributed his escape and hostility to the fact that he held the regime responsible for the death of his uncle Ahmad. If the regime isn't afraid to remove the son of Khomeini, the thinking goes, then eliminating the president is certainly not out of the question. Ahmadinejad knows this and though the likelihood may be small, he is not willing to risk his own life.

Not to mention that his own reputation was stained. He claimed that he worked for free as mayor of Teheran with no wages from the city hall. This looked admirable, especially because his predecessors were renowned to be corrupt. But in June 2006 the reformist daily newspaper *Rooz* raised suspicions about Ahmadinejad's honesty and source of income. Quoting Nader Shariatmadari, a member of the Tehran city government, the paper alleged that the city audits had discovered that $350 million of its funds had been disbursed without a trace. The receipts had been lost. Some $300 million of the money was spent during Ahmadinejad's term as mayor. Nevertheless, no concrete action has been taken by Iran's judiciary to find the culprits, and since the publication of his findings Shariatmadari has complained of a threatening atmosphere in the city government.[24]

This could explain why Ahmadinejad refused to accept the mayor's salary: he had a bigger and better income from elsewhere.

Moreover, were Ahmadinejad to pursue corruption seriously, he would have to hold accountable some of his very friends, allies, and family members. In his native Aradan, Ahmadinejad's cousins boast about the fact that Mahmoud has never offered them privileged status because to him that would be cronyism.[25] However, when Mahmoud was mayor of Tehran, Ahmadinejad's brother Davood was awarded a lucrative contract, and later the city reportedly accused him of embezzling $2 million.[26] Ironically, Mahmoud has now appointed Davood to investigate government fraud. Similarly, his sister Parvin received positions in the government, despite her lack of qualifications. She later used her brother's name to run for Tehran City Council elections in December 2006, where she managed to win a seat. This was in sharp contrast to his other candidates who miserably lost in Teheran and elsewhere. While Ahmadinejad has lectured his staff about the advantages of meritocracy and the evils of nepotism, he himself is an unequivocal practitioner of it.[27]

Ahmadinejad's allies have also been guilty of installing family members in government positions, though they were more discreet than he: Instead of giving posts to family members who had the same surname, they gave jobs only to in-laws who had different surnames. These practices were eventually exposed and became known in the press as *bajenagh bazee* (the in-laws trick). Ahmadinejad's colleagues were forced to reveal the details of how they distributed jobs to their own relatives, against the government's and Ahmadinejad's instructions.[28] The in-laws in question were subsequently dismissed from their posts.

However, it appears that the government's anticorruption measures do not apply to the Islamic Republic Guards Corps and Ahmadinejad's Basiji allies. Since his rise to power, companies these groups control have won many contracts for which they were clearly not the most suitable choice. Many of the Basij and the IRGC corporations have established their own business empires via corruption, particularly in construction. The IRGC has set up its own construction empire in Iran, building neighborhoods for its members without regard for the laws and planning permissions. Neighborhoods composed exclusively of IRGC members exist in Tehran. A famous one is Shahid Mahalati, where Davood Ahmadinejad lives and Ahmad Ahmadinejad died.

The IRGC is heavily involved in business dealings with Hezbollah in Lebanon, which imports and sells a wide range of products, including household goods, that it buys from the IRGC. Many IRGC companies do business and own companies in Persian Gulf countries, especially the United Arab Emirates. IRGC companies frequently do not pay import taxes. Furthermore, using an IRGC company involves cash, less hassle, and less waiting time. And IRGC companies are also becoming involved in foreign-exchange scams in Iran. As state companies, they are entitled to purchase dollars at a lower rate, which they then sell on the black market at a hefty profit. This long-established scheme has been practiced mainly by companies associated with Rafsanjani.[29]

Ahmadinejad's penchant for spending money to increase his popularity has exacerbated other problems as well. Shopping for food is a depressing experience for many residents of southern Tehran and the rural areas. Inflation keeps pushing prices up, putting the Iranian consumer in a stranglehold. Some Iranian families can no longer afford to buy meat more than two or three times a month, if at all. It's bad enough that many are unemployed, but with inflation so high even those with a job find their cash isn't worth much.[30]

Although inflation existed before Ahmadinejad was elected, he does not appear to be taking any concrete action to curb it. In fact, in 2006, when every government agency clearly stated that the rate of inflation in Iran was 15 percent, Ahmadinejad insisted publicly that this figure was incorrect and that inflation was "only" 10 percent.[31] He seems to have become disconnected from the country's inflation-related woes.

Ahmadinejad's solution to this problem is more imprecise than his opinion about its size. When inflation is high, governments usually cut spending and raise interest rates to control the flow of money, but Ahmadinejad is doing the exact opposite. His budget for the year 2006–7 is 26 percent higher than the previous year's, resulting in higher expenditures and more money being pumped into the economy. And instead of raising interest rates, Ahmadinejad has lowered them to reduce the power of private banks. Newly established quick-loan agencies are also offering cheaper loans, which has brought more money into the economy, further increasing inflation.

For some Iranians, banking their money no longer makes sense—in some cases the level of inflation is greater than the interest rates themselves, so their money loses real value. It's more profitable to take out loans from the banks and invest the cash in business projects, which offer better returns. The rich are eager to invest, which drives inflation even higher, because there is more money chasing after fewer goods. And since the loan rates are low, borrowers are willing to spend, especially on construction, seen as the safest sector of the economy. The situation is a bit like the West's Internet-bubble days in the late 1990s. Well-heeled Iranians are buying at a ferocious pace, sending the price of property soaring. This is disastrous news for the poor because the lack of affordable housing, more acute than ever is coupled with inflation and high unemployment. Ahmadinejad may not realize it, but his administration's approach is having the same effect as Rafsanjani's: making the rich richer while the poor remain in the same miserable position.[32]

Although he has shown remarkable stubbornness in implementing unsuccessful economic policies, Ahmadinejad realized that one program may push the Iranian public over the edge—the fuel rationalization plan. Originally it was not Ahmadinejad's idea, but since he became president he was identified with the program. There are several reasons, all of them very convincing, for the plan. Because of poor maintenance, Iran is losing roughly 10 percent of its oil production capacity every year. A recent study predicted that by 2015, Iran would stop being an oil exporter.[33]

By reducing the amount of subsidized fuel available to Iranians, Ahmadinejad intended to cut the government's huge subsidy bill for fuel, $6 billion, and reduce the budget deficit. He also hoped to reduce the level of both traffic (especially in Tehran) and pollution, which is choking many of Iran's citizens. The fuel rationalization plan also has a strategic goal: to lessen Iran's dependency on gasoline imports. Despite being a major oil producer, Iran imports 40 percent of its refined oil because it lacks refining capacity. Rationalizing gasoline consumption would have reduced Iran's dependency on foreign countries for this critical commodity and helped prepare the nation for the possibility of international sanctions.

On the downside, the rationalization plan would have led to an increase in fuel prices, pushing up inflation even more. Making oil more expensive would also have affected the majority of Iranians, among them a substantial number of poor people, who own old cars and rely on the cheap subsidized gasoline. This would have made Ahmadinejad extremely unpopular and would run counter to the main goal of Ahmadinejadenomics. Unsurprisingly, in 2006 Ahmadinejad suspended the fuel rationalization plan. However confrontational he may be toward the West, Ahmadinejad is not politically suicidal. To cut the gasoline subsidies practically means punishing the public. Like any politician, he wants to be elected and reelected. And yet, difficult to explain the rationale behind it, at the beginning of 2007, he found himself having to implement the plan, which he tried to delay. This happened because Khamenei believed, with oil prices falling, that Iran's economy can afford less and less to subsidize gasoline prices for domestic consumption. One could argue that the nuclear program is gobbling up Iran's oil wealth and isolating the country globally, but Ahmadinejad remains unmoved. He knows very well that his country's nuclear dreams are supported by the majority of his countrymen and are an extension of Iran's historic aspirations.

CHAPTER FIVE

The Grandfather of Iran's Bomb

"I HAVE NO doubt—the answer is yes with a capital Y. He wanted the bomb and he would have gotten it had he stayed in power," says Dr. Akbar Etemad.[1] He is referring to His Imperial Majesty Muhammad Reza Pahlavi, the King of Kings, the shah. As head of the shah's nuclear energy agency, Etemad was responsible for making the shah's wish come true by the mid-1980s. He could have been the father of Iran's nuclear bomb, but his work was interrupted by Khomeini's 1979 revolution. Etemad, like many other loyal monarchists and servants of the Peacock Crown, had to flee his homeland. Had he stayed under the new regime, he certainly would have been killed, as were tens of thousands of military personal, SAVAK officers, cabinet ministers, government officials, court cronies, and scientists.

Etemad found safe haven in a posh suburb of Paris, his home for the last quarter century. "I remember numerous occasions," he said, "when I was sitting in his office and His Majesty was talking about the bright future that nuclear power would bring to Iran. On one occasion, at least, he talked to me about the need in the future to consider having the bomb. For him *nuclear* meant glory, pride, power regional hegemony."[2] These words are key in understanding Pahlavi's dreams, aspirations, and actions.

The Pahlavi dynasty was founded in 1925 by Reza Khan Pahlavi, an officer in the elite Russian-trained Cossack Brigade of the Persian army. In 1921, together with Seyyed Zia'eddin Tabatabaee, a young politician from the southern city of Shiraz, he staged a coup d'état against Ahmad Shah of the Qajar dynasty. After the coup Reza Khan took charge of the military and its affairs until 1923, when he became prime minister. But like Napoleon, he would be an emperor. He mobilized support among the members of the Persian parliament, even then called the Majlis, persuading them to crown him Shah of Persia on December 12, 1925. In 1935 he changed the country's name to Iran, a word derived from *Aryan* and mentioned in the Avesta, the ancient book of the Zoroastrians, an ancient religion from the fifth century B.C. which still has followers in today's Iran. This was to underscore that Persians considered themselves not Arabs but descendents of the Aryan race.

The shah ruled the country with an iron fist, infamous for his cruelty and merciless attitude toward his enemies. He tried hard to instill the same traits in his son, Muhammad Reza. There is a legend in Iran that before handing the reins of power to Muhammad Reza, the shah told him, "Listen, my son. I give you one piece of advice: *Az hichi natars*—don't be scared of anything." At the outbreak of the Second World War, Iran formally declared neutrality, but it was a biased neutrality. Reza Khan didn't hide his Nazi sympathies, which infuriated the British and the Russians, who had traditionally been involved in Persian politics. However, they did nothing until June 1941, when Germany invaded the Soviet Union. Fearing that the shah would eventually ally Iran with the Nazis, the British and the Red Army forced Reza Shah to abdicate. His son, twenty-two-year-old Muhammad Reza, replaced him.

One characteristic that father and son shared was an antipathy to religion's playing a role in Iranian politics. In their drive to modernize Iran economically and culturally, they could see no place for a 1,400-year-old ideology. As far as they were concerned, an ayatollah's job was to run the mosque and serve the local community. To weaken the hand of Islamists, they first discouraged and then banned Muslim women from wearing the *hijab,* the head scarf. They also allowed the consumption of alcohol in public places. During Reza Khan's reign many religious leaders were killed or imprisoned, though his son preferred "only" to imprison or deport them. Mohammed Reza was less disposed to murder, and had a greater fear of the power of the religious leaders, than his father. Some of his famous prisoners included the ayatollahs Rafsanjani, Khamenei, and Mesbah Yazdi. His best-known deportee was an ayatollah from Qom, Ruhollah Khomeini, who later deposed him and became the founding father of Iran's Islamic revolution.

Another feature common to the two rulers was their nationalism. Father and son possessed the same ambition of making Iran into a regional and eventually an international power. They wanted Iran to regain its historic place among the world's powerful, as when the Persian empire ruled from India to Ethiopia.

To justify his family's claim of having God's authority to usurp the throne, Muhammad Reza Shah spent lavishly on pomp and ceremony. He built palaces for himself and his family, mingled with the international jet set, and squandered the country's wealth on luxuries. "I was disgusted," recalled Israeli ambassador Uri Lobrani, "when one day I was invited by the shah to the isle of Kish. Luxurious palaces, posh hotels, and state-of-the-art casinos were built there to accommodate not only wealthy Iranians but also Arab sheikhs from the nearby Persian Gulf Emirates. This was just weeks before the revolution. People were demonstrating in the streets, soldiers were killing them, and the shah was telling me how the island would attract the world's richest people. He was completely out of touch with reality. He was living in his own world of dreams."[3]

Muhammad Reza Pahlavi assumed such titles as Shahanshah Aryamehr, meaning "King of Kings and Light of the Aryans." Politicians had to clap every time his name was mentioned in the Majlis. Iranians who met him were advised to bow down or kiss his hand as a gesture of gratitude. Others kissed his feet as a sign of respect. Hundreds of millions of dollars were spent on the shah's palaces. One of the most lavish signs of Pahlavi reign was the Peacock Throne, which the shah kept in his Golestan Palace in Tehran and used for official ceremonies. The throne was originally designed in the early nine-teenth century for Fathali Shah. It was named after his wife, Tavous, whose name means "peacock" in Farsi.

But pomposity alone does not build one's power. For this the shah needed weapons, and he spared no expense on the latest devices. In some cases Iran purchased weapons that were too expensive even for more developed coun-tries, such as Canada and Japan. A prime example is the purchase from the United States of F-14 Tomcat fighter jets by the Imperial Iranian Air Force in the late 1970s. One of the most sophisticated and expensive jets of its type built at the time, the F-14 was simply too costly to operate. Even the Israelis, who were receiving direct financial assistance from America, did not acquire any. The shah's appetite for modern military might was so insatiable, though, that he would pay any price to make Iran the power he wanted it to be.

Subsequent American administrations encouraged the shah to spend more. Not only was the exchange extremely profitable for American arms manufac-turers but it also led the United States to believe it had a strong ally in the region. Washington encouraged the shah to act as America's "police officer" in the Middle East, protecting the flow of oil through the Strait of Hormuz to feed American and other Western economies. The shah's appetite only grew, and he set his sights on nuclear weapons. His aspirations were reflected in the carefully drafted words of one of his closest confidants, Asadollah Alam, his minister of court. Alam kept a secret diary in which he detailed major developments in the daily life of the shah, his family, the court, and the country. On Saturday, November 29, 1975, he wrote: "Passed on reports prepared by Dr. Etemad, head of the Nuclear Energy Agency, detailing his recent agreements with France and Germany. HIM [His Imperial Majesty] has a great vision for the future of this country which, though he denies it, probably includes our manufacturing a nuclear deterrent."[4]

The shah, supported by his generals, wished to be involved and informed about the developments of the nuclear program. He easily lost his temper over the subject. During a meeting in April 1976, the ambassador of the African country Gabon asked the shah for financial assistance. "Why on earth should we support you?" he retorted. "You promised to sell us uranium, but it now appears that you don't have full control over your supplies." After the meeting the minister of court tried to calm the shah, wrote Alam in his diary: "I remarked that according to the poor old ambassador, they indeed arranged to supply 120 tons of unrefined uranium below the market price. HIM denied any knowledge of this, instructing me to contact Dr. Etemad, head of our Nuclear Energy Agency. If what the ambassador said was true, then we shall respond favorably to all his requests."

Iran got a late start in the nuclear race. Israel showed great enthusiasm about nuclear technology from its founding in 1948. Egypt began doing nuclear research in 1957. Iran showed faint interest, preoccupied as it was with the Mossadegh affair. In 1951 newly elected Prime Minister Dr. Mohamad Mossadegh took advantage of the weakness of the young shah by nationalizing the country's oil industry. Mossadegh became the most popular figure in the country, while British and American oil corporations, which controlled Iran's "black gold," utilized their influence in Whitehall and Washington, D.C. In 1953 British and American agents, led by CIA senior officer Kermit Roosevelt, orchestrated street demonstrations and organized corrupt elements within the police and the army to depose Mossadegh in a coup. The shah, now little more than a Western proconsul, was left as the dominant figure in politics, and the Iranian oil industry remained under the control of Western companies.

Iran's nuclear program began under the U.S. Atoms for Peace program, proposed in the early 1950s (see chapter 7). One of the first steps in the shah's nuclear voyage was to send a few young students abroad to master the art of nuclear power. Among them was Akbar Etemad, who studied nuclear physics in France and Switzerland. Upon his return to Iran he taught at some local universities and eventually became the chancellor of Tehran's New University. In 1974 he was summoned to the shah's palace and instructed to build the Atomic Energy Organization of Iran (AEOI). By this time Iran's civilian nuclear program was already at a relatively advanced stage, but the shah and his top military and political echelon were ready to move secretly from civilian to military applications. For this they needed an organization to unify and direct all the elements involved in the nuclear research and development. Dr. Etemad was the right choice in the right place. A talented scientist with strong ties to leading nuclear research centers and institutes in the West, he was, above all, a loyal servant of the shah. He believed strongly in Iran's right to have nuclear technology and would not hesitate to develop nuclear weapons if asked to do so.

The shah may have asked Israel for assistance in his nuclear project. Despite the general antagonism toward Israel among Iran's populace, the two states had previously cooperated on classified military projects. The alliance had grown out of strategic and ethnic factors in the Middle East. The shah respected Israel's struggle against the larger Arab countries and admired its formidable military. The Israelis saw Iran as a potential ally against their more rabid Arab neighbors.

Even before its 1948 independence, Israel sought alliances to combat Arab hostility. Israeli leaders divided the region into two circles. In the inner circle was Egypt, Jordan, Syria, and Lebanon, all of which shared a border with Israel. In the outer circle were Libya, Iraq, Sudan, and several northern African states also hostile to Israel. But there were several non-Arab states on the periphery: Turkey and Iran in the north and Ethiopia in the south. Moreover, within the Arab states themselves there were religious and ethnic minorities that might identify with and support Israel—the Christian Maronites in Lebanon, the Druze in Syria, and the Kurds in Iraq.

Israel hoped to form covert alliances with the countries on the periphery and the minorities who were suffering from the rise of Arab nationalism and radicalism (which was spearheaded in the mid-1950s by Egyptian president Gamal Abdul Nasser). The Israeli concept of maintaining contacts with these nations, known collectively as the peripheral alliance, can be summarized in the dictum "The enemies of my enemy are my friends." Any force that opposed or fought Arab nationalism was considered a potential ally of Israel's and Iran's. The people of Iran, although a great majority of them are Muslim, they always proudly affirmed that they were Persians, not Arabs.

Israel perceived radical and militant Iraq as a threat to its existence even before Saddam Hussein's rise to power in the early 1970s, as did Iran, which was involved in territorial and border disputes with its neighbor.

Thus out of the common interest, a secret alliance was formed between the shah's regime and Israel. Turkey was the first Muslim country to recognize de facto, though not de jure, the right of Israel to exist as a sovereign state, in March 1949. A year later Iran followed. Then in 1951 the shah authorized direct but secret flights from Tehran to Tel Aviv to take Iraqi Jews to their new homeland. He also agreed to sell oil to the Jewish state. By the end of 1958 the Israel's Mossad, Turkey's National Security Service, and Iran's SAVAK formally joined in a covert alliance for comprehensive cooperation called Trident.[5] In the seventeen years from 1961 to 1978, every Israeli prime minister from David Ben-Gurion to Menachem Begin visited Iran and engaged in lengthy meetings with the shah. Israeli defense ministers never turned down an invitation to come to Tehran.

Israel also saw the Iraqi Kurds, who were fighting for autonomy against the central government in Baghdad, as an ally. Iran saw the Kurds as a force that would destabilize the Iraqi government. Mossad sent weapons, medical aid, and military instructors via Iran to help the Kurdish rebellion in the 1960s and the early 1970s. In return, the Kurds provided Mossad agents with information about Iraq's military capabilities. The SAVAK (the National Organization for Intelligence and Security) was an enthusiastic partner. Instructors from Mossad and Shabak (Israel's domestic security service) trained SAVAK interrogators and case officers. Some SAVAK units, especially those in charge of technological espionage (which primarily entailed eavesdropping on the shah's political opponents), were established and run by Mossad and Shabak experts.

"To a certain degree, we were the masters of SAVAK," says Eliezer Tsafrir. As a young officer Tsafrir served as a Mossad liaison to the Kurdish headquarters in the mountainous northern region of Iraq. He arrived there by infiltrating Iraq from Iran with the help of SAVAK. A decade later he was the last chief of the Mossad station in Tehran, in the shah's last days. "Whatever we asked in terms of assistance to our needs, SAVAK responded favorably," concludes Tsafrir.[6] It enabled Mossad case officers to run agents and networks of spies inside Iraq. One of them was Shabtai Shavit, who in the early 1990s would become the head of Mossad. Shavit's career as an intelligence officer began in Iran and Kurdistan. It was for him a strange and twisted closure of a circle when, as head of Mossad in the early 1990s, he was entrusted with the mission to find out whether Iran under the ayatollahs was seeking to acquire nuclear weapons.

The relations between the two countries became even closer after the astonishingly quick victory of the Israel Defense Forces over the Egyptian, Syrian, and Jordanian armies in the June 1967 Six-Day War. Israel's stock soared in Tehran. The shah believed that a strong and technologically advanced army such as Israel's would elevate Iran's strategic posture as a major regional power. Hatred of Israel among the general population remained widespread, as evidenced in 1968 when its national soccer team was loudly booed when it came to Tehran to participate in the Asian Championship. Spectators burned the Israeli flag and chanted anti-Israeli, anti-Zionist, and anti-Semitic slogans. The shah was astounded at the degree of animosity that his subjects displayed toward Israel, but he continued his clandestine cooperation with the country. "His Majesty the Shah approved to the General Staff and the SAVAK to institutionalize relations with our Israeli counterparts. For us Israel was an important ally," said General Fereidoun Jam, the chief of the General Staff of the Iranian Imperial Army.[7]

Israel embraced the idea wholeheartedly. Not only was the strategic alliance bearing diplomatic fruit, but it was also producing economic and defense gains. Israel's major defense contractors saw Iran, with its oil wealth, as a lucrative market. The shah wanted to challenge his rivals in the Arab world—Iraq, Egypt, and Saudi Arabia. "He was a true megalomaniac," said General Yitzhak Segev, who served as Israel's last military attaché in Tehran before the fall of the shah.[8] "He was buying everything. Every new weapons system initiated or thought about in America or Israel was immediately offered to the army. Iran purchased from the U.S. twelve Boeing 747 carriers for midair fueling, and 650 helicopters. Most of them couldn't take off due to a shortage of pilots. He ordered 200 F-14 fighters and another 200 F-16s. He spent tens of billions to purchase more than his small and poorly trained army could swallow. For us in Israel, Iran was a gift from heaven."[9]

Geopolitics aided the shah in his efforts. In retaliation for their support of Israel in the October 1973 war, the Arab world stopped selling oil to Western Europe and the United States. Oil prices soared, making Iran, which didn't join the boycott, a major beneficiary. Its oil revenues tripled, with daily revenues reaching $180 million. Israel's defense minister, Shimon Peres, went to Tehran and persuaded his counterparts to sign a memorandum of understanding for strategic cooperation.

On the Iranian side, the architect of the newly elevated alliance was deputy defense minister General Hassan Toufanian.[10] In May 1977 Peres instructed Segev to enhance the agreement. "I didn't want to do it because I already had my doubts about the future of the regime," said the military attaché. "There had been warning signs, but Peres was completely blind. He told me, Iran is the most stable country in the region. Mind you, that was less then two years before the downfall of the shah."

Peres and his successor, General Ezer Weitzman, eventually instructed Segev to pursue six defense contracts worth an estimated $1.2 billion, under which Iran paid roughly $300 million in cash up front and another $250 million in oil. Iran would finance several research and development projects carried out by leading Israeli defense corporations. The armies of both countries would purchase the systems once they became operational.

For this purpose, Israel and Iran established a web of companies, which were registered in Panama and Switzerland. The central legal entity was called Trans-Asiatic Oil, jointly owned by the government of Israel and the National Iranian Oil Company. Israel Aircraft Industries (IAI) was designated to develop a modern advanced fighter code-named Lavi ("cub" in Hebrew). Another company, Rafael—the Hebrew acronym for the Armament Development Authority—would develop a new generation of sea-to-sea Gabriel missiles, based on the U.S. Harpoon missiles.

The jewel in the crown, according to CIA documents captured by Iranian students at the American embassy, was a new ground-to-ground, Israeli-made missile. (This missile was originally manufactured in France, which sold it to Israel in the late 1950s.) Israel's IAI and Rafael, which produced an Israeli version of the missile, later called it Jericho. The plan was that the prototype missile would be build in Israel but tested on Iranian soil. The Iranian-Israeli Jericho was designed to hit targets up to 500 miles distant, with a warhead capacity of 1,650 pounds of explosives. It was also intended to carry nuclear weapons. This was for Israel a clear indication about Iran's plans in the nuclear field. "Why would they need a sophisticated long [-range] ground-to-ground missile? There could be only one answer. The shah and his generals were thinking about the future, how one day they would become a strategic power like India, Pakistan, and their archenemy Iraq, which was already developing a nuclear program in the 1970s."[11]

Had the Jericho missile been completed, Iran's current leadership could have used it to hit targets in Israel. Fortunately for today's Israel, the ambitious projects never got off the ground. After Khomeini came to power, he instructed his government to cut off all relations with the Small Satan, as he dubbed Israel. Nearly thirty years later, batteries of Israeli, Iranian, and European lawyers with hefty salaries are still trying to untie the corporate knot of Trans-Asiatic Oil in various international tribunals and arbitrations in Geneva and elsewhere in Europe, but in vain.

There may have been additional reasons for Israel to cooperate with Iran on nuclear projects. By 1967 Israel had a nuclear reactor, a plutonium separation facility, and, according to CIA estimates, a nuclear device.[12] Israel, for its own interests, needed foreign suppliers and a large uninhabited territory where it could test its nuclear devices without notice. For this, according to the international media, Israel turned to South Africa's apartheid regime in the late 1960s and early 1970s. According to the reports, senior officials of the Israel Atomic Energy Commission (IAEC) secretly visited South Africa, among them Professor David Ernest Bergman, the father of the Israeli bomb. South Africa provided Israel with natural uranium (yellowcake) and other precious metals and in return received technological expertise and assistance in building nuclear warheads and delivery capability.

"We knew of course about the shah's nuclear ambitions," said Uri Lobrani, the former Israeli ambassador. "I personally met with senior cabinet ministers and other officials who were in charge of the nuclear program. They told me about Iran's program. I said nothing about Israel. But it was a general and cautious conversation without getting into details."[13] The nuclear issue was also raised at a more senior level during visits to Iran by Israeli premiers and cabinet ministers. "They heard from the Iranians that nuclear technology held tremendous interest for the shah," recalled Lobrani. "The Iranians even went one step further by saying that they knew that this topic was also of interest for us. But that was that. They didn't ask us for any help in the nuclear field and we never offered it."[14] According to IAEC officials, there had been no visits by Israeli nuclear experts to Iran.

When asked about a possible exchange of nuclear knowledge between Iran and Israel, Dr. Etemad replied, "Why should we? I knew the Israelis. I met some of their students during my studies in France and Switzerland. I toured Israel for three weeks in 1965 during a private visit. But we didn't need them. They had their own program and we had ours. We had our experts." There were better candidates with more advanced technologies. Many Western countries would have been only too willing to help Iran with its nuclear program. The Americans, the French, the Germans, and the South Africans were simply waiting for a nod from the shah. It is ironic that the United States, now leading the rearguard battle to stop the nuclearization of Iran, was the first to lend a nuclear hand to the shah.

A prominent reminder of America's shortsighted attitude stands at the heart of Tehran—a domed building housing the Tehran Nuclear Research Center (TNRC), part of Tehran University. It has an operating five-megawatt research reactor, a radioisotope production facility, radiochemistry laboratories, and a waste-handling facility. Most of its components, facilities, and equipment were sold to the shah by U.S. companies with the approval of the administrations of presidents John F. Kennedy and Lyndon B. Johnson.

U.S. involvement started in 1957, when that nation and Iran signed a civil nuclear cooperation agreement as part of the Atoms for Peace program. Two years later the shah ordered a nuclear reactor built at Tehran University and arranged for the purchase of the research reactor. It took eight years, but in 1967 TNRC, the first significant nuclear facility ever established in Iran, was inaugurated and went critical. Since then it has served as a launching pad for nuclear progress. The United States provided 5.58 kilograms of highly enriched uranium (HEU), or weapons-grade uranium, to be used in the facility. From its spent fuel, the reactor could produce each year up to 600 grams of plutonium.[15] The supply continued annually until it was halted in 1979 after the Islamic revolution.

In July 1968 Iran signed the Non-Proliferation Treaty (NPT) in an effort to speed up its negotiations for nuclear deals with the United States, and two years later it ratified the treaty. Article 4 of the NPT recognizes Iran's "inalienable right to develop, research, produce, and use of nuclear energy for peaceful purposes without discrimination, and acquire equipment, materials, and scientific and technological information."

After the traumatic repercussions of the oil shortages caused by the Arab embargo after the 1973 war, nuclear power was advanced as an alternative to petrochemical fuels. A 1974 study by the influential Stanford Research Institute concluded that Iran would need about 20,000 megawatts of energy by the end of the twentieth century, an amount that would require at least twenty nuclear reactors.[16] The shah adopted the recommendations and, according to State Department officials and documents, agreed to purchase eight nuclear reactors from the United States.[17]

American corporations were exuberant. After the 1973 war they had tried hard, usually unsuccessfully, to persuade the American public that there was a need to build more nuclear reactors to reduce dependency on oil. The shah became their salesman, prominently figuring in a huge advertising campaign in the American media, featuring him in regal military dress. The advertisement read:

Guess who is building nuclear power plants? The Shah of Iran is sitting
on top of one of the largest reservoirs of oil in the world. Yet he is
building two nuclear plants and planning two more to provide electricity for his country. He knows the oil is running out—and time with
it. But he wouldn't build the plant if he doubted their safety. He'd wait.
As many Americans wanted to do. The Shah knows that nuclear energy
is not only economical, it has enjoyed a remarkable 30-year safety
record. A record that was good enough for the citizens of Plymouth,
Massachusetts, too. They've approved their second nuclear plant by a
vote of almost 4–1. Which shows you don't have to go as far as Iran for
an endorsement of nuclear power.

The shah's program was an ambitious one to diversify its energy sources to
accommodate Iran's future energy needs. Dr. Etemad explained that Iran was
already worried on one hand about the depletion of its oil reserves and on the
other about the rapid growth of its population and energy demands.[18]

The site selected to house the first two reactors was Bushehr, where the
ayatollah's Iran is building its first nuclear power station. A warm, humid,
southern Iranian port, Bushehr is noted for its friendly people and energetic
folk music. It was selected because seismic and geological surveys determined
that the area is one of the few places in the country not on an earthquake fault
line. The contract to build the first two reactors, worth nearly $3 billion, was
awarded to Kraftwerk Union, a subsidiary of Siemens, the giant West German
engineering corporation.[19] Four years after the project broke ground in 1974,
90 percent of the first reactor had been built and almost 60 percent of the
machinery and equipment had been installed. Fifty percent of the second
reactor was completed by the time of the revolution. Khomeini's first premier, Mahdi Bazargan, canceled the contract.

In 1975 the Massachusetts Institute of Technology signed a contract with
the government of Iran to provide training for the first cadre of Iranian
nuclear engineers. To further enhance Iran's nuclear program, Dr. Etemad
traveled there, met with Indian premier Indira Gandhi, and signed a nuclear

cooperation treaty. Then the French were awarded a contract to build a nuclear technology center in the town of Esfahan; its main goal was to provide training for the staff working in the Bushehr reactors.

The French envied the Americans' lucrative deals in Iran and were ready to offer the coin of the Iranian realm—kickbacks. "You couldn't do any business in Iran without bribing top officials, and I know from my observations that the French were masters of the art," said a senior Israeli diplomat who was stationed in Iran during the 1970s.[20] Framatome, a French nuclear company (called Areva NP today), won a major contract to build two 950-megawatt nuclear reactors at a site outside the city of Ahvaz, near the Karun River. Framatome experts surveyed the area and began preparations, but construction had not yet started when the revolution took place. Immediately afterward Premier Bazargan canceled this contract, too. Iran was busy consolidating the revolution and had no interests then in pursuing the Sha's nuclear aspirations. The area is close to the Iraqi border and was severely damaged during the Iraqi invasion.

The shah and his advisors, especially Etemad, were eagerly looking for sources to provide them with uranium. Etemad first turned to Gabon, in 1975. The same year, at the instruction of the shah, the newly created AEOI established a joint Iranian-French venture, Solidif, which purchased a 10 percent stake in Eurodif. Eurodif, an acronym for European Gaseous Uranium Enrichment, is a French, Belgium, Spanish, and Swedish consortium that specialized in uranium enrichment. Iran also purchased a stake in the RTZ, a uranium mine in Rossing, South-West Africa (now Namibia). Two other important sources were South Africa and Argentina. The same year the AEOI signed a $700 million contract to purchase natural uranium from South Africa. Meanwhile, Argentina signed an agreement with Iran to provide expertise and enriched uranium, small quantities of which were sent to the TNRC. Etemad even sent experts to conduct geological surveys in Iran in search of uranium mines. Some were found in Saghand desert, near the city of Yazd in central Iran, and since 2003 the Islamic Republic has been mining its natural uranium deposits there.

Etemad revealed that under his directorship, the TNRC carried out an experiment to separate plutonium from spent reactor fuel and a series of research tests in laser technology. There are two major ways to enrich uranium—to separate uranium isotopes and isolate U-235, which can be enriched—in order to produce fissile materials. The most common way is an enrichment process using gas centrifuges. The other method employs laser irradiation technology. The plutonium extraction and laser tests were clear signs that the shah was not interested in merely diversifying energy sources and building nuclear plants for electricity. He was making sure that his nation would be acquainted with all available technological methods to gain nuclear weapons.

The Americans became suspicious, fearing the shah would repeat the Israeli precedent of building a nuclear weapon under the pretense of civilian purposes. Etemad said that he became worried about the American concerns. "We wanted to know what was being discussed in the government and in the congress about Iran's nuclear program." For this purpose Iran hired a lawyer to find out what the administration was up to and to try and mollify the Americans. Although the shah and his people were evasive about their real intentions, they eventually managed to calm U.S. jitters.[21]

The shah was America's friend and ally. The Americans trusted him. Above all, America—along with France, India, Argentina, South Africa, and Germany—was interested in the shah's money. The shah envisioned a nuclear-armed Iran, but unwittingly he left the remains of his dream in the hands of his and his father's sworn enemies: the ayatollahs, and in 2005, a messianic president.

CHAPTER SIX

Ayatollahs and Atoms

WHEN AYATOLLAH RUHOLLAH Khomeini came to power in February 1979, nuclear power and national glory were among the least of his concerns. In the first months after the revolution, Khomeini was busy building alliances, purging real or imagined enemies, and consolidating the theocracy. But in addition to these urgent topics, Khomeini also had serious reservations about nuclear weapons, which he identified with imperialism and the "decadent" culture of the West.

"Khomeini, as a Shiite Muslim theologian, felt that nuclear power was evil and certainly nuclear bombs were evil," Professor Juan Cole of the University of Michigan pointed out. "It's forbidden in Islam to murder innocents, and it's certainly forbidden in Islam to kill large numbers of civilians in the course of warfare. In medieval Muslim ethical thought about the 'just war,' you have to be chivalrous, you have to tell the enemy you're coming three days before you arrive, you have to give them an opportunity to back down, or if they're not Muslims, to convert to Islam. When you fight them, you may not kill women and children who are noncombatants. So, from a Muslim point of view, from the point of view of Muslim jurisprudence, dropping bombs on Nagasaki and Hiroshima was clearly evil, and Khomeini said so."[1]

It was natural, then, for Khomeini to restrict the nuclear energy program. Other revolutionary leaders, however, believed that Iran's geostrategic priorities hadn't changed significantly and that the country would need its nuclear program. Among them was Ayatollah Muhammad Beheshti.

Born on October 24, 1928, in the city of Esfahan, Seyyed Muhammad Hosseini Beheshti came from a religious family whose ancestors claimed to be direct descendents of Prophet Muhammad. At a young age Beheshti dedicated his life to learning about and teaching Islam. In the 1960s he worked closely with Ayatollah Boroujerdi, Iran's most senior cleric in Qom, and it was there that he met Khomeini, with whom he later planned and fomented the revolution. Idealistic and fervently antiroyalist, Beheshti was known for his dedication to the spread of Islam and his insistence on the religion's use as the basis for governance in Iran. He taught at the Islamic center in Hamburg, Germany, in the 1960s and traveled to the United States, France, Syria, and Lebanon in his efforts to form a united Islamic revolutionary front. Not long before the revolution, he set up the Daftare Tahkim Va Vahdat (the Office for Strengthening and Unity, or OSU), which aimed to solidify the relationship between university students and religious seminaries in Qom. There he met Mahmoud Ahmadinejad. The young student's dedication so impressed Beheshti that after the revolution, he granted him an audience with Ayatollah Khomeini, a favor for which many revolutionaries yearned. Beheshti was second only to Khomeini as an idol for and mentor to Ahmadinejad.

Following the revolution Beheshti held several influential and prestigious posts in Iranian politics and public life, including minister of justice. He established the ruling party, Hezbe Jomhouriye Eslami (the Islamic Republic Party), and took part in the election of the Experts Assembly. As a vice president of the Majlis, he oversaw the writing of the constitution. Yet despite his political achievements, Beheshti died in 1981, a bitter and disappointed man because he had failed to become president of the Islamic Republic of Iran. He felt he was far better qualified than other ayatollahs as he had lived and traveled abroad more. He had proven himself a skillful administrator prior to and immediately after the revolution. But Khomeini decided he did not want a cleric as president, deeply frustrating both Beheshti and his archrival, Ayatollah Rafsanjani. Nonetheless, the two continued to jostle for position behind the scenes, waiting for the day Khomeini would change his mind.

On June 28, 1981, during a political gathering in Tehran, Justice Minister Beheshti and approximately seventy others—cabinet ministers, parliamentarians, and various senior officials—were killed by a powerful bomb the opposition Mujahedeen Khalq movement had planted. Ultimately, the number of the dead was fixed at exactly seventy-two, to echo the number of people killed with Imam Hussein in the famous battle of Karbala in A.D. 680. Beheshti's supporters spread rumors that Ayatollah Rafsanjani had mysteriously left the hall minutes before the explosion, hinting that he was actually involved in his rival's murder or at least had prior knowledge of the plot.

Some Iranian observers believe that had Beheshti lived, he would have remained a prominent leader and advanced the nuclear program. In a meeting with his associates three months after the revolution, Beheshti said that Iran needed nuclear weapons regardless of the financial burden.

Challenging the prevailing ideology set by Khomeini would have been almost unthinkable, however. Even apart from the theological precepts, nuclear issues were not on the agenda of the newly established Islamic republic, for very practical reasons. The general atmosphere of fear, uncertainty, and instability discouraged the pursuit of science and learning. Many scientists left the country, among them Akbar Etemad, who believed that the Islamic Republic of Iran was no place for Western-educated people. The insufficient electrical infrastructure, the dwindling oil revenues, the withdrawal of foreign corporations, and the abandonment of nuclear power agreements exacerbated the energy gap.[2] In 1979 alone, the following events took place:

- The United States stopped supplying highly enriched uranium to the Tehran Nuclear Research Center.

- The Iranian government canceled its agreement with Eurodif, demanding full repayment of the $1 billion loan it had given the consortium.
- The West German government refused to grant further export licenses for the construction of the Bushehr reactors, although some of the equipment and systems was shipped and reached its destination.
- Framatome of France, which had not been paid its bills since October 1978, pulled out of Iran.
- Kraftwerk Union halted construction there and recalled its staff, though by mid-1979 half the work on the two reactors was already completed.[3]
- Fereydun Sahabi, Iran's deputy minister of energy and supervisor of the shah's Atomic Energy Commission, said his organization was cutting its program significantly.[4]

In November 1979 the nuclear debate and the developments surrounding it were suddenly overshadowed by a more urgent crisis. In a burst of revolutionary fervor, Khomeini's young disciples from the Islamic student movement—with Mahmoud Ahmadinejad reportedly among the leaders—took over the "den of spies," the U.S. embassy in Tehran.[5] Khomeini gave his blessing to the operation but didn't envision that it would grow into a 444-day confrontation with the "Great Satan."

Ruhollah Mousavi Khomeini was born on September 24, 1902, in Khomein, 100 miles southwest of Qom, not far from Arak, where Iran is building its heavy-water nuclear reactor. Khomein is on the trade route to Tehran and has been known for its vineyards, some of the finest in the region. (Jewish families in the nearby village of Lilian produced a very fine arak, an anise-based spirit.) Khomeini came from an extremely devout family. As a Mousavi Seyyed, it is claimed that he was the descendent of the Prophet Muhammad and Imam Mousa Kazem, the seventh Shiite imam. After a pilgrimage to the holy city of Najaf in Iraq, Khomeini's grandfather moved to

Khomein. Khomeini's father, Mustapha, died when the future ayatollah was just six months old. A religious man, he was killed by two local landlords on his way to complain to the governor about the oppression of the local inhabitants at the hands of the landlords.[6]

Ruhollah Khomeini's formal education began at the age of seven at a *maktab*, a school that combines secular and religious studies. Pupils were required to memorize the Koran, an experience that could literally be torture: if a pupil failed to repeat verses correctly, his feet would be caned until they bled. To the terrorized maktab students, finishing school for the day was like being freed from prison. After school Khomeini played games such as Dozd o Vizier, involving a thief and a judge, which may have piqued his appetite for power. Khomeini liked to take the role of the vizier, who determined the thief's fate.[7]

Khomeini's mother died of cholera when he was sixteen, whereupon his elder brother Seyyed Morteza became his guardian and helped him complete his basic education.[8] Khomeini immersed himself in religious studies. In 1930 he married the daughter of a rich Tehran ayatollah who saw a bright future for his "village mullah."[9] From then on, Khomeini devoted his life to teaching. Among his best students were Ayatollah Motahari, Ayatollah Montazeri, and Rafsanjani, all of whom would play prominent roles in his Islamic revolution.[10]

The period from the 1930s to the late 1950s were Khomeini's "quiet" years. He lived in the shadow of more influential and authoritative clerics, especially the conservative ayatollah Boroujerdi, the most prestigious religious leader, whom no one dared to challenge. During these two decades Khomeini stayed out of politics, though he had no inhibitions about criticizing the shah, publishing his first attack on the Pahlavi regime in 1944.[11]

In 1961, however, the death of Boroujerdi left a religious vacuum and Khomeini took advantage of the lack of spiritual authority, defining a turning point in both his own life and the history of Iran. He opened a school, where he developed a devoted coterie. He started to openly politicize his theological concepts, or rather, theologize his politics. One of his most controversial statements was delivered on June 3, 1963. Enraged by the shah's "White Revolution" (an ambitious plan to modernize Iran and reduce the clergy's power) and his close relations with the United States, he likened the shah to the hated Yazid, the man who beheaded Imam Hussein. Khomeini warned, prophetically, that one day the shah would suffer Yazid's fate: the people of Iran would turn against the modern-day traitor. The shah ordered SAVAK, the feared state security service, to arrest Khomeini, which provoked massive unrest and street demonstrations in Qom on June 5, a day now celebrated annually in the Islamic Republic.

Khomeini was jailed for a year but resumed his attacks on the shah as soon as he was released. Their conflict came to a head when he attacked the shah's agreement to grant immunity from Iranian law to U.S. servicemen in Iran. This time the shah had no mercy on the sixty-two-year-old cleric. He deported Khomeini to Izmir, Turkey, where, he knew, Khomeini would chafe under the rigid secular laws. In less than a year Khomeini went to Najaf, home to a number of famous Shi'a schools. He stayed there for thirteen years, during which he continued to attack the shah's regime. Despite his hatred of Western culture, Khomeini utilized Western technology, recording his tirades on audiotape, which were then smuggled into Iran by his disciples. There they were played in mosques, schools, and bazaars, and were used by opposition groups, not all of them religious, in the struggle against the shah.

Khomeini's favorite themes were that Islam was in danger of corruption from perverse doctrines and that materialism, Christianity, and Zionism were being encouraged in Iran by the imperialist powers. Khomeini urged the clergy to purify Islam from within; Iran must become a true Muslim republic.[12] In 1977, under pressure from shah, Saddam Hussein deported Khomeini to France. In spite of the increased distance, Khomeini was the spirit and inspiration for the street demonstrations against the shah that ultimately led to the monarchy's downfall. Khomeini paid a heavy personal price for his political battles. In 1977 his eldest son, Mustafa, died in mysterious circumstances in Iraq. Many believe that SAVAK was behind the killing.

Khomeini's unadulterated hatred toward the United States stemmed from his firm belief that America intended to replace Islam and Islamic values with its own "decadent" materialistic and imperialist beliefs. His rage against the country intensified as he saw his own homeland become infused with Western values. Under the shah, Iranians were told that Islam was holding their country back. Women were encouraged to dress in revealing Western fashions; their traditional hijab were ripped off their heads. Materialist and secular values were spread by the government-dominated press and government officials. Iran was openly dealing with Israel despite its occupation of Palestinian lands, selling oil to the Jewish state, and purchasing weapons from it. Khomeini perceived Israel and Zionism as a creation of U.S. imperialism.

America was the Great Satan and Israel the Small Satan, characterizations with origins in Khomeini's theological interpretation. "*Aozo Billahe Mina Shaytane Rajim*," reads the introduction to the reading of the Koran—"I ask for refuge in the Almighty from the cursed Satan." In his vision, the Islamic Republic would serve as a holy refuge from the Satan, which is why he initiated the "Islamization" of Iranian life—press, politics, and economy—as soon as he came to power. However, creating an Iran free of America's "satanic" influences was not sufficient. Khomeini also wanted to eradicate the influence of the United States from the entire Islamic world. He saw that as his holy mission.

The first great test of the Islamic Republic began on September 22, 1980, when Iraq invaded Iran. Saddam Hussein's move was precipitated by the hostage crisis but was based on many other factors as well. Hussein believed that the endless purges of Iranian army officers and air force pilots (Khomeini had thousands of them killed because he suspected them of being loyal to the shah) and the lack of spare parts for the country's military hardware because of the American embargo had inflicted irreversible damage to Iran's armed forces. He was convinced the war would be a stroll in the countryside, as did the CIA and Israeli intelligence. "We thought that the Iranian army would surrender after six days and this would finish off the Khomeini regime,"[13] explained Uri Lobrani, a former Israeli ambassador to Iran.

The invasion had several objectives: to topple the newly established Islamic regime in Iran, which threatened to spread its brand of revolitionary Shia radicalism to Iraq; to aquire the Shatt-al Arab waterway, Iraq's only connection to the Persian Gulf; to annex Khuzestan, Iran's rich oil province; and to control of the flow of oil via the Strait of Hormuz.

However, within weeks, the Iraqi military encountered unexpectedly fierce resistance. Khomeini and his ayatollahs knew how to inspire the masses with a combination of religious fervor and Iranian patriotism. Rather than turning against the ayatollahs' government, as Saddam Hussein thought would happen, the people of Iran rallied around the regime.

Iran compensated for its inferior military equipment with a callous disrespect for human life. Hundreds of thousands of volunteers were rushed to the front in November 1980 and stopped the Iraqi offensive with their bodies. Moreover, Saddam Hussein and his generals found the Iranian military not nearly as depleted as they had assumed. By June 1982 a successful Iranian counteroffensive recovered the areas previously lost to Iraq, including the Khuzestan province and the city of Khoramshahr.

After that, most of the fighting occurred on Iraqi territory, in a six-year trench war not unlike that on the western front in World War I. Now it was the turn of the Iraqi regime to appeal to its people's national pride. While the Iranians continued to employ unsophisticated human-wave tactics, the Iraqi soldiers managed to stop their advance.

As the war sank deeper into stalemate, several of Khomeini's advisors and allies revived the topic of nuclear weapons behind closed doors. These "atomic ayatollahs" conspired to resurrect the nuclear program, though without infringing on Khomeini's religious strictures or challenging his authority.[14] They raised the topic delicately, occasionally telling the Supreme Leader that Iran would need a nuclear program for peaceful purposes, to improve its scientific and technological infrastructure to meet the Iraqi challenge.[15]

"The Almighty will provide the ground for the defeat of America with his own invisible hand," Khomeini had promised the Iranian people, meaning that the Almighty would provide his guidance to defeat the U.S. ally, Iraq, and drive U.S.-dominated forces and U.S. influence out of his country. Evidently, in the Almighty's view, the time was not ripe. Khomeini accepted a cease-fire in 1988, making the Iran-Iraq war the longest conventional war of the twentieth century, responsible for 1 million casualties.[16]

The war was a traumatic experience for Khomeini. His theological views about nuclear and other weapons of mass destruction were deeply shaken and reshaped by the horrors of war—particularly the use of chemical weapons against not only Iranian soldiers but also civilians. The latter happened in July 1988, in Zardeh, tucked away in the mountains of Kurdistan region. A resident of the small village described the attack: "It was six in the morning. A man had passed away. We had gathered for his funeral. We saw two planes come over us and then turn back. They dropped six bombs here and four bombs in the streams. The ones in the stream were cyanide. The bombs dropped here were nerve gas. It killed a lot of people. There was a cloud of smoke and the birds started to drop out of the sky. People asked me, 'What is this?' I said, 'It's chemicals. Run away.' "[17]

There were in fact twelve chemical bombs dropped, which killed 275 people. In a matter of minutes, one-fifth of the population was wiped out. Eighteen years after that fateful day, there remains a 30 percent miscarriage rate among Zardeh's women. Almost all the survivors are still sick and getting progressively worse. Afshin Ramezani, an IRGC soldier who fought at the front and lost friends in the chemical attacks, put it this way: "They [the West] talk against genocide and the use of weapons of mass destruction. Well, during the Iraqi invasion, chemical weapons were used against Iranians with the West's full knowledge. But just because the victims were from Iran, a country that was not a friend of the West, they were considered expendable. No Western country took any active measure to stop the Iraqis." He added, "It shows that the West sees Iranians as subhuman, because if animals were gassed at that scale, I am sure Western animal rights organizations would have done something about it."[18]

After Khomeini's death in 1989 and especially in recent years, there have been many rumors, incorrect assumptions, and deliberate disinformation claiming that he even issued a fatwa, a religious decree, against nuclear weapons. But there is no written record of what the Supreme Leader really thought about nuclear weapons. The only existing document that attempts to explain the religious thinking of the Iranian leadership is from a later time. Issued in September 2005 to the IAEA in Vienna on behalf of Aya-tollah Ali Khamenei, Khomeini's successor, it read: "The Leader of the Islamic Republic of Iran, Ayatollah Khamenei, has issued the Fatwa that the production, stockpiling, and use of nuclear weapons are forbidden under Islam and that the Islamic Republic of Iran shall never acquire these weapons."[19] But this document should be viewed very skeptically. It was released three months after Ahmadinejad's election, when Iran was under tremendous pressure from the IAEA and the international community to halt its uranium enrichment program. The document was intended to appease the world. The fatwa, which was neither attached to the statement nor shown to anyone, could be a sham. There is a concept in Shiism called *taghiye,* which says that a lie is justified when it protects oneself from danger. There may already be a fatwa allowing the development of nuclear weapons or a document explaining that Khamenei's fatwa was reluctantly and tem-porarily issued because of special circumstances that threatened the Islamic Republic's interests.

There is growing evidence that after the war Khomeini realized Iran would need to develop its own version of weapons of mass destruction to defend itself or to deter enemies from future chemical weapons attacks. His change of heart became public knowledge when a confidential letter written in 1988, the last year of the war, was leaked to the Iranian press in 2006. The publication of the letter created a major scandal in Iran. Its origins date back to the late 1980s, when Hashemi Rafsanjani, then in charge of the war efforts, asked General Mohsen Rezai, then commander of the IRGC, to provide him with an estimate of the military hardware needed to win the war.[20] Rezai's reply, written in the aftermath of the traumatic chemical attacks, stated that Iran needed 300 new fighter-bombers, 2,500 tanks, 300 attack helicopters, and a substantial number of laser-guided missiles capable of carrying nuclear warheads. Without these, Rezai said, Iran would be unable to achieve its national goals, which included defeating Saddam Hussein's army, installing an Islamic regime in Baghdad, proceeding to "liberate" Jerusalem from Israeli occupation, and wiping the Jewish state off the map.

Unbeknownst to Rezai, Rafsanjani gave the information to Khomeini. Because the military requirements were beyond Iran's reach, Khomeini reluctantly decided that the war was not winnable and ordered the government to agree to a UN-endorsed cease-fire, despite his disdain for Saddam Hussein. Khomeini compared the cease-fire to "drinking the poison chalice." In his later published letter to the senior commanders of the army and the IRGC and the ministers, Khomeini addressed Rezai's list and made direct reference to nuclear warheads. The sensational revelations of the letters in 2006 were part of a power struggle between Rafsanjani and Ahmadinejad, but above all they contradicted both Ahmadinejad's claims that Iran was not interested in developing nuclear weapons and Khamenei's supposed fatwa.

After the war, Iran had to start its nuclear program over almost from scratch. Before 1979 AEOI employed more than 4,500 scientists. After the revolution barely 800 remained.[21] The two nuclear reactors in Bushehr were bombed six times between March 1984 and November 1987, and their cores destroyed. The Iranian leaders initially attributed the attack to the Israeli air force. They wished to believe that Iraqi pilots were incapable of reaching the sites and dropping bombs on them and that only the experienced Israeli pilots could have repeated their successful raid on the Iraqi Osirak (Tamuz) reactor near Baghdad. But eventually Iran acknowledged that Iraq was the culprit.

Slowly, in the second half of the 1980s, Iran began to release itself from its Khomeini-imposed nonnuclear policy. The most active among the atomic ayatollahs was Rafsanjani, especially after 1989, when he replaced Ali Khamenei as president. To understand how deeply Rafsanjani was involved in reawakening his country's nuclear program, it is sufficient to read a November 1985 advertisement in the foreign edition of the Iranian daily newspaper *Kayhan*. The ad, jointly sponsored by Rafsanjani's Majlis office and the AEOI, invited expatriate Iranian nuclear scientists to participate in a March 1986 technical conference, all expenses paid. Very few scientists responded, but among them was Fereydun Fesharaki, head of the shah's secret nuclear weapons program, who returned in 1987 after seven years in exile.[22]

In October 1988 Rafsanjani openly appealed to Iranian scientists to return home permanently. At the same time the government dispatched thousands of students abroad for nuclear-related training. The preferred destinations were still American and western European universities, but students also went to Chinese and Pakistani research centers and universities. China had begun training fifteen Iranian engineers from the AEOI in nuclear reactor design and research in 1987, and from 1988 to 1991 many more AEOI engineers traveled to China to learn about nuclear technologies, which were then applied at the Esfahan Nuclear Technology Center.[23] In Iran new research centers and nuclear-related departments were created at universities. For example, Sharif University of Technology in Tehran was established at that time for the indigenous education of physical scientists and engineers. The head of AEOI, Reza Amrollahi, announced that deposits of natural uranium (which were surveyed under the shah) had been discovered near Saghand.

Initially the atomic ayatollahs, led by Rafsanjani, tried to renew nuclear relations with the West. Even the United States was considered a suitable candidate despite the inflamed rhetoric and bad blood between the two countries. But the Reagan administration's anti-Iranian, pro-Iraqi strategy excluded Iranian emissaries and middlemen. Iran turned to West German's Kraftwerk Union and asked it to complete the Bushehr project. Iran had already paid for the work and most of the equipment, which was stored in West German warehouses. Kraftwerk Union considered the Iranian request but refused it after strong American pressure was applied.[24] An attempt to recruit a consortium of Argentine, Spanish, and West German companies to build the reactors at Bushehr met the same fate when the United States interrupted the deal at the last moment; the Argentine equipment for enriching uranium had already been packed and was ready for shipping.

The Rafsanjani government was forced to look elsewhere for help. Since the late 1980s China, Pakistan, and Russia have been the three supporting pillars of Iran's nuclear edifice. Rafsanjani was particularly enthusiastic about links with China. In 1984 China helped expand the Esfahan Nuclear Technology Center (ENTC), in part by supplying a small nuclear research reactor. Sometime in the mid-1980s the nuclear organizations of the two Asian powers signed secret agreements with Iran's AEOI to train personnel and provide nuclear technology and hardware. According to the agreement China would train Iranian scientists, technicians, and engineers and provide the knowledge to design and build nuclear facilities, especially in the area of uranium conversion. In 1985 Iran brought on line a fuel fabrication laboratory, also in Esfahan.

All involved tried to conceal the existence of this agreement. In October 1985 Rhode Island state senator Alan Cranston accused China of helping Iran with a nuclear weapons program, but China asserted there was "no relationship of cooperation between China and Iran."[25]

The major breakthrough in the relations between the two countries occurred in 1991, when China agreed to supply engineering designs and to construct a complete uranium conversation facility (UCF), again in Esfahan. Uranium conversion facilities usually consist of several conversion lines. The principal among them converts uranium-ore concentrate (UOC), known as yellowcake, into uranium hexaflouride (UF6).

The project was intended to produce UF6 on an industrial scale, but strong, almost unprecedented, pressure by the Clinton administration persuaded the Chinese to cancel the contract in 1997. This was after the engineering drawings had been delivered, however, and by the end of the 1990s Iran was able to build the facility with its own materials and human resources.[26] In 1991 several shipments of nuclear materials arrived in Iran from China, including at least one ton of natural uranium and nearly 1,000 pounds of processed uranium tetraflouride and uranium hexaflouride. In a clear violation of Iran's Safeguards Agreement with the International Atomic Energy Commission, these deliveries were not reported. The materials were used clandestinely in laboratory experiments and bench tests at the ENTC and at the Radiochemistry Laboratories of TNRC. In the experiments Iranians conducted tests to convert UOC to UF4 and UF6 in order to understand and later master the art of uranium conversion—the first important step on the road to nuclear weapons.[27]

China also clandestinely supplied Iran with the fuel fabrication laboratory and minireactors mentioned above, as well as a zirconium production plant. A metal used to prevent the spread of corrosion in nuclear facilities, zirconium is a vital cladding material for nuclear reactors. The plant is due to be operational in 2007 or 2008. Another important Chinese contribution was the sale in 1990 of a calutron, a device for separating nuclear isotopes, to the Center for Agriculture Research and Nuclear Medicine at Karaj.[28] Generally used for peaceful purposes, the calutron can also be used in the production of weapons-grade uranium. One was used in the development of the atomic bomb in the United States during World War II.

In 1992 Rafsanjani paid a state visit to China—accompanied by the then-head of AEOI, Reza Amrollahi—where he signed an agreement to purchase four nuclear power stations and another nuclear reactor in addition to the one supplied to ENTC. This was to replace the reactors that France's Framatome corporation agreed to build for the shah at the same site nearly two decades before. But American strong-arm tactics put an end to this project as well. China explained to Iran that because of a "technical reason," it could not honor the contract and supply the reactor.[29] Still, the Chinese contribution to Iran's renewed nuclear program was essential. It came just when Iran's scientific and technological infrastructure was at its lowest point—after the war, a time when no other nation with a nuclear know-how was ready to assist Iran.

Shrouded in deeper secrecy were the ties with Pakistan. Unlike China, which is a signatory to the Non-Proliferation Treaty (NPT) and the IAEA charter and allowed to produce nuclear weapons, Pakistan was—and still is—not a signatory party to the NPT. It would be highly embarrassing for Iran, a member of both the NPT and IAEA, to be exposed as having deals, not to mention secret ones, with Pakistan.

A 1987 deal called for at least six Iranians to be trained at Pakistan's Institute of Nuclear Science and Technology in Islamabad. In another arrangement, a number of Iranian students were trained in uranium centrifuge technology at what was then called the Engineering Research Laboratories (now the Khan Research Laboratories), founded by Dr. Abdul Qadeer Khan, the father of Pakistan's atom bomb. In February 1986 he secretly traveled to Iran, where he held meetings with his Iranian counterparts and was taken to visit Bushehr. According to intelligence sources, Khan also had a meeting with Rafsanjani. The meeting was aimed to massage Khan's ego and show him how important he was to his Iranian hosts. A year later Khan paid a return visit.[30] These initial interactions between Khan and Iranian nuclear scientists led directly to the doctor's assistance in procuring designs and equipment for Iran's uranium enrichment program (see chapter 7).

Iran, it turns out, was simultaneously dealing behind the scenes with the Soviet Union. The two countries had signed a memorandum of understanding about nuclear cooperation in 1987, but the collapse of the Soviet Union had slowed progress. In 1993 Russian president Boris Yeltsin gave the green light for his country's nuclear industry to enhance the cooperation. Victor Mikhailov, Russia's minister of atomic energy and the AEOI's Reza Amrollahi signed an $800 million deal to build a 1,000-megawatt nuclear reactor in Bushehr to replace the destroyed German-built nuclear reactor. A more detailed follow-up agreement was signed in 1995. Slated for completion in 2007, it paves the way to overcome one of the most disturbing obstacles in Iran's nuclear road: to complete the construction of the damaged and bombed German-built nuclear reactor. With 1,000 Russians at work on it, this reactor is intended for peaceful purposes: generating electricity. Of course it also may serve to help Iran master the various nuclear crafts.

What Iran couldn't get from Russia—highly enriched uranium—it tried to obtain illegally from the former Soviet republics. Iran initiated several purchasing networks to capitalize on the instability in Central Asia. They tried to purchase the uranium from the Ublinsky Metallurgical works in Kazakhstan, and if they could not buy it, they planned to steal it. The plot was exposed by

U.S. intelligence, which arranged to buy the material and transport it to safety at nuclear laboratories in Oak Ridge, Tennessee.[31]

But other purchasing networks, usually run by Iranian businessmen living abroad who still have strong family ties in Iran, went undetected by intelligence agencies and the IAEA. Iranian intelligence agents disguised as businessmen or government salesmen approach an Iranian expat they trust and ask him or his company to purchase some innocent items from European, Asian, or Russian suppliers. The authorities appeal to their sense of patriotism, also offering handsome financial rewards (money is not a problem for the Iranian government). Once a relationship is established, the businessman would be asked to purchase "dual-use" materials—technology or equipment that can be used for both legitimate civilian uses (such as agriculture, medicine, and industry) and less innocent purposes.

This technique, called industrial or technological theft or espionage, is widely practiced around the world. Israel has been engaging in it since the 1950s to meet its military and nuclear needs, even occasionally stealing from its allies, America included. The Soviet Union and its Communist satellites stole many technological innovations and scientific products from the West via the same methods. Beginning in the late 1980s and throughout the 1990s, Iran's underground purchasing networks managed to acquire high-strength aluminum balancing machines and a special kind of steel essential for producing rotors for centrifuges, electronic beam welders, and high-powered computers from Austria, Germany, Spain, Great Britain, and Switzerland.[32]

Recognizing the need to improve Iran's technical infrastructure, in 1993 Rafsanjani established a special task force charged with attracting scientists and easing the political climate. Scientists who had been arrested as political enemies of the Islamic regime were released from prison. They were offered luxury homes, cars, and large salaries, and the regime appealed to their national pride as well.

Eight years after Rafsanjani's first newspaper advertisement, the efforts to realize his nuclear vision were paying off. Tens of thousands of expatriate engineers, chemists, mathematicians, and physicists had returned home to work on the secret nuclear program. Research centers and laboratories were expanding. Contracts had been signed for the purchase of engineering designs, materials, equipment, and even whole plants. Basic but very important nuclear experiments were being conducted.

Between 1988 and 1993, experiments on plutonium separation were carried out at TNRC, producing a few grams—not a great deal, but a start. In a place called Lashkar Abad, northwest of Tehran, another plant was built where Iranian experts conducted tests to enrich uranium with laser technology. The Laser Separation Laboratory and Comprehensive Separation Laboratory at TNRC was carrying out similar experiments. These facilities had been supplied by the United States during the shah's reign.

But perhaps Iran's most significant achievement was concealing its true intentions from the world. While the country was reactivating its nuclear program, the international community was fast asleep.

CHAPTER SEVEN

Evading the Nuclear Police

I HAVE SEEN this before, thought Hollie Juha Heinonen. The fifty-six-year-old Finnish scientist and deputy director general at the department of safeguards of the International Atomic Energy Agency was standing at one of the production halls of Natanz, Iran's pilot fuel enrichment plant. Meanwhile, he and the director general of the IAEA, Dr. Muhammad El-Baradei, were listening to a blatant lie, while trying to maintain neutral expressions. It was February 2003 and it had taken them months to reach this point. Their host was Gholam Reza Aghazadeh, vice president of the Islamic Republic of Iran and the president of the Atomic Energy Organization of Iran (AEOI): the man in charge of the country's officially transparent nuclear program.

Heinonen, El-Baradei, and a half dozen Iranian AEOI officials, security guards, and intelligence officers were talking about fifteen or so centrifuges, which had been constructed in the big hall for the purpose of enriching uranium. Aghazadeh proudly, if dishonestly, described Iran's achievement. "See how good Iranian scientists are," he boasted. "We did it. It's our own work. It's our own invention."[1] But Heinonen knew better: The machinery installed at Natanz was exactly the same kind of centrifuge that had been designed and manufactured more than thirty years ago at the Uranium

Enrichment Corporation of Western Europe (URENCO). Heinonen and El-Baradei exchanged a knowing glance—the Iranians had purchased the centrifuges from abroad. But the IAEA brass chose not to press their Iranian hosts for information at the moment.

They decided to return to Tehran, hoping that the drive would be better than the hair-raising, high-speed trip from Tehran through the mountains to Natanz, roughly 250 miles away. Rocky mountains looms over the town, and local residents point to it while telling how the troops of Alexander the Great fought in the area.

The IAEA officials would discuss their Natanz experience with the people at the Iranian embassy to the IAEA in Vienna, officially known as the permanent mission. Ironically, the Iranian permanent mission was located on Leonard Bernstein Strasse. Leonard Bernstein represented everything that Mahmoud Ahmadinejad hates. He was an American Jew. He supported Israel and conducted its philharmonic orchestra. A talented composer and conductor whose music became one of the pillars of Western culture, Bernstein was a homosexual and a Western liberal to boot. To compound the irony, when the embassy later decided to move it wound up on Heine Strasse. Heinrich Heine was Jewish, too, and one of the nineteenth century's most renowned poets and journalists. From its offices there, Iran conducts its rearguard battle aimed to keep the international community from denying it membership in the nuclear club.

Officially, the embassy staff consists of members of the ministry of foreign affairs and experts from the AEOI who are diplomatically accredited with the IAEA. They have diplomatic status and enjoy diplomatic immunity. They participate in the long, usually boring, deliberations of the various committees of the IAEA, write memos and reports, and comply with all the rituals that come with the territory. But among the embassy staff are also intelligence officers, the eyes and ears of Iran's secret nuclear program, who have a multifaceted agenda. Their primary goal is to convince the world that Iran is a country that honors its international obligations and that its goal is innocent: to master nuclear technology for peaceful purposes, such as medical research and the well-being of the Iranian people. Their second goal, no less important, is to know what is thought of them a few streets away from Heine Strasse.

Vienna is one of four United Nations headquarters, along with New York City, Geneva, and Nairobi. The IAEA was the first and most prominent international guest in Vienna, arriving there in 1957, when the country was still recovering from World War II. It was first housed in the Grand Hotel, next to Vienna's famous opera house in the heart of Vienna's historic Ring center.

In 1979 the IAEA moved to its current home, the Vienna International Center, which the Viennese call Uno City—United Nations city—a monstrous complex of three connected buildings on the left bank of the Danube that houses several UN organizations in addition to the IAEA.

Upon its completion Uno City was a source of local pride for Austria and Vienna. However, because it was constructed with asbestos it has become a health hazard for the 4,000 employees from more than one hundred countries who work there. After a long struggle the employees forced the management to clean up the problem in 2007. No one has dealt with the other problem, the labyrinthine nature of the complex: convoluted corridors, connecting bridges, a complicated system of doors and elevators that usually take you to the wrong building. The employees joke that if they lost their way, no one would notice and their skeletons might never be found.

The spacious office of the IAEA's Director General is located at the top of the complex, on the twenty-eighth floor, commanding a splendid view of the town and river (which, unlike the Danube of Johann Strauss's era, is not blue at all).[2] The DG, as he is known, has a controversial, thankless, and near impossible task: to safeguard world peace by preventing the proliferation of nuclear technology for the production of WMD. At the same time he is supposed to foster the spread of atomic energy for peaceful uses. He needs acrobatic skills to maneuver between conflicting interests. On one side, there are the five permanent members of the UN Security Council, who have veto power and nuclear weapons. On the other is the rest of the world.

The DG also has to manage conflicts between the poor Southern Hemisphere and the rich Northern one, between the club of nations who possess nuclear weapons and technology and those who do not, and between the industrialized world and the developing countries. As if that is not enough, the DG also has to maneuver between President Bush's America, President Putin's Russia, Communist China, and the European Union.

Moreover, he must do so without real support or backing. What Stalin said condescendingly about the pope—"How many troops does he have?"—can also be said about the DG. He doesn't have any soldiers at his disposal; his only power comes through his ability to persuade and the authority given to him by the UN. In a fragmented world rife with greedy thieves and specious politicians, the DG is like the little Dutch boy trying to stop the dike from flooding by plugging the hole with his finger.

The IAEA was conceived in December 1953, when U.S. president Dwight D. Eisenhower addressed the 470-member plenary meeting of the United Nations General Assembly and warned that events forced him to speak in a new language, "the language of atomic warfare." He added, speaking of proposed diplomatic talks: "The United States would seek more than the mere reduction or elimination of atomic materials for military purposes. It is not enough to take this weapon out of the hands of the soldiers. It must be put into the hands of those who will know how to strip its military casing and adapt it to the arts of peace."

Eisenhower suggested that "the governments principally involved, to the extent permitted by elementary prudence, should begin now and continue to make joint contributions from their stockpiles of normal uranium and fissionable materials to an international atomic energy agency. We would expect that such an agency would be set up under the aegis of the United Nations."[3]

The thirty-fourth U.S. president's ideas helped shape the IAEA statute, which eighty-one nations unanimously approved in October 1956. By the end of 2006 the membership had grown to 143 states. Article 2 of the statute says "The Agency shall seek to accelerate and enlarge the contribution of atomic energy to peace, health, and prosperity throughout the world. It shall ensure, so far as it is able, that assistance provided by it or at its request or under its supervision or control is not used in such a way as to further any military purpose"[4]

The two most important aspects of the agency's work are nuclear security and safety and the transfer of technology from scientifically advanced nations to those that are less advanced. They are the core of Eisenhower's Atoms for Peace idea: nuclear research and technology for the welfare of the human race, to provide electricity, to develop better medicine and food, to improve agriculture, and to eliminate poverty. However, these nonglamorous ideas-barely get any play in the media.

However, the agency's third task, nuclear inspection, is what grabs most of the headlines. In the years preceding the U.S. invasion of Iraq in 2003, the IAEA sent its inspectors to Saddam Hussein's nuclear sites on numerous occasions. They found nothing. No smoking gun. No evidence that the regime was involved in any illegal activity to produce nuclear bombs. President George W. Bush and his administration remained adamantly unconvinced. If the IAEA, led by the DG and his teams of professional inspectors, could not find proof of Saddam's nuclear weapons, the Bush administration, with the help of U.S. intelligence and the Pentagon, would find—or invent, if necessary—their own evidence to justify the decision to invade and change the regime there.

The IAEA was formally created in 1957. As more countries mastered nuclear technology, concern grew that they would sooner or later acquire nuclear weapons, particularly after two additional countries—France in 1960 and China in 1964—joined the club by developing and testing nuclear devices.[5]

The growing desire for internationally binding commitments to prevent the spread of nuclear weapons found its expression in July 1968, with the adoption of the Treaty on the Non-Proliferation of Nuclear Weapons, which took effect in March 1970. Known as the NPT, the treaty essentially freezes the number of nuclear weapons states at the five permanent members of the

UN Security Council—the United States, the Soviet Union (now Russia), the United Kingdom, France, and China. Other states are required to forfeit the option of developing nuclear weapons and to conclude comprehensive safety and safeguards agreements with the IAEA for their peaceful nuclear technology. The signatory members of the NPT are required to cooperate fully with the agency, to be transparent (to report about their nuclear materials and storage sites), and to open the sites to scrutiny and verification by IAEA inspectors. In order to fulfill its mission, the IAEA promotes safe nuclear power by running technical-aid programs with most of its member states.

The West, and to a lesser degree the Soviet Union, transferred knowledge, nuclear materials, and equipment to other countries. Though the aid is meant exclusively for civilian use, certain countries used what they gained to begin a secret parallel program to produce fissile materials and nuclear weapons for military purposes. Israel was the first country to do this, beginning with the big research reactor it received from France between 1958 and 1960 and a smaller reactor from the United States.[6] India followed a few years later by taking advantage of Canada, the United States, and the Soviet Union.[7]

France and Holland became casualties of Pakistan's secret plans in the 1970s, when a young Pakistani scientist named Dr. Abdul Kadir Khan interned in Dutch laboratories at the Uranium Enrichment Corporation. URENCO was established in 1970 as a British, German, and Dutch consortium to provide a supply of enriched uranium to fuel their reactors. There, Khan learned how to enrich uranium-using centrifuges. He also stole blueprints and drawings from the facility, smuggled them back to his country, and helped Pakistan become a nuclear power.[8] Thus he became the most successful nuclear spy since German Klaus Fuchs stole secrets from America and Britain in the 1940s for his Soviet masters. Khan, admired in his country as the Father of Pakistan's Atom Bomb, would later sell his knowledge to North Korea, Iran, and Libya and would offer to do so to Egypt, Syria, Algeria, and Saudi Arabia but was turned down.

There have been countries that possessed nuclear weapons, or planned to do so, but chose to dismantle their program, as South Africa did in 1993, after the collapse of apartheid. Ukraine, Belarus, and Kazakhstan did the same after the dissolution of the Soviet Union. Libya announced that it had decided to give up its intention to acquire nuclear weapons in late 2003. Other countries—Japan, South Korea, Brazil, Argentina, Italy, and Germany, to name a few—possess advanced technology that would enable them to produce nuclear weapons at any time, but so far they have declined to do so.

Paradoxically, a state that has not signed the NPT but has nuclear weapons can still be a member of the IAEA. India and Pakistan, which have publicly declared that they possess nuclear weapons and have tested them, and Israel, which has not and maintains a policy of "ambiguity," do not permit IAEA inspections of their nuclear sites yet remain active members of the agency. India and Pakistan even have representatives on the IAEA's primary decision-making body, the Board of Governors. On the other hand, Iran, which signed both the NPT and a Safeguards Agreement with the IAEA, finds itself under intensive scrutiny. These are the rules of the game—dictated by the international community, headed by the five major powers.

Additionally, in order to fulfill its mandate the IAEA has been promoting safe nuclear power by running technical aid programs with most member states. Some of that knowledge could be useful in a weapons program, though the aid is intended exclusively for civilian use. The agency still helps Pakistan, which exploded a nuclear bomb in 1998. It also helped North Korea until a decade ago. Even today it is assisting Iran, which many experts fear is close to mastering the basics of bomb-making. It has fourteen programs under way with Iran, including a study on upgrading a nuclear research laboratory, as well as helping it start up its Bushehr reactor.[9]

The DG was designed to be a job exactly tailored for the gray and staid diplomats of typical UN bureaucracies. It is true that El-Baradei is a cautious man, sometimes speaking in the politically correct diplomatic jargon of the

United Nations and signing reports written in technical terminology. However, he shook up a sleepy organization, gave substance to its mission, and became a focal figure in the international arena, a household name. He received the Nobel Peace Prize in 2005. He achieved success because he rose to the occasion and turned his office into one of the most important jobs of the twenty-first century. He became a champion of the prevention of the spread of nuclear weapons. North Korea and Iran receive his closest scrutiny.

Dr. Muhammad El-Baradei was born in Egypt in 1942. He studied law at Cairo University and then specialized in international law at New York University. He began his career in the legal department of the Egyptian foreign ministry. He came to the IAEA in 1984 as the agency's legal advisor and has been the DG since 1997. In 2006 he was reelected for his third term, despite U.S. reservations.[10] The United States and Israel are especially suspicious of the bold, tall, smiling Egyptian who always dresses impeccably in tailored suits. His nationality and ethnicity lead Israeli decision makers, especially the Israeli Atomic Energy Commission, to fear that he is anti-Israeli. His tireless work to promote a nuclear-free world, and especially his extensive efforts to establish a Nuclear Weapons Free Zone (NWFZ) in the Middle East, didn't win him friends in Israel. The Jewish state, in theory, is ready to accept a NWFZ in the Middle East, but only after all its Arab and Muslim enemies recognize Israel's right to exist and confirm that with peace treaties and security arrangements. Until then, Israel won't even discuss the idea.[11]

Both the Bush administration and Israel believe that El-Baradei is too soft on Iran. To undermine El-Baradei's credibility, the United States, Israel, and some Western European countries spread a rumor that he was married to an Iranian woman, suggesting that he cannot be an honest broker in Iran's case. He is, in fact, married to an Algerian, but the fabrication served the Bush administration's campaign against him.

American officials also suggest that the DG should have shown more determination once Iran admitted it had breached its obligations to the IAEA, even by minor technical infringements. Instead he showed patience and tolerance toward Iran. In 2003 the United States demanded that Iran be declared a noncompliant state according to the IAEA statute. El-Baradei refused, arguing that the matter was political. The United States claimed that noncompliance is a professional and legal status, not a political one.

El-Baradei and his assistants have been accused of removing some sensitive facts and important paragraphs from IAEA reports on Iran because they didn't want to poison the atmosphere and increase tension with the country. The whole drafting process was masterly crafted to avoid embarrassment and offending the Iranians and their supporters. The IAEA reports dealing with Iran resemble a dinosaur. They have a fat body with a lot of meat, but a small head and skinny legs. The introduction and the conclusions of these reports are short and evasive, while the body of the reports contains a lot of findings, which unfortunately are not compatible. One of the major handicaps of the report is that they were not written by the inspectors who had visited the sites. The inspector's reports were viewed, reviewed, and rewritten by El-Baradei, his top assistants from the IAEA Secretariat led by the Canadian Tariq Rauf, head of the Verification and Security Policy Coordination Department, and herds of lawyers. They made sure that everyone would not be terribly offended. By trying to please all parties, they pleased no one. Occasionally there had been arguments between El-Baradei's Secretariat and Heinonen's inspectors. In such incidents, the Belgian Pierre Goldschmit played an important role. Goldschmit preceded Heinonen as head of the Safeguards Department. Heinonen was the head of the B division, responsible for Iran. The division of labor between them became clear. Heinonen was the bad cop, while Goldschmit was the good cop, protecting Heinonen from El-Baradei's rage and making peace.

For example, IAEA officials initially refused to admit that Iran was conducting a certain kind of laser enrichment test that usually has only one purpose—producing nuclear weapons. The information was subsequently inserted in a seasonal IAEA report on Iran, which stated that "Iran has a substantial R&D program on lasers."[12] The work was done in two secret locations that Iran should have revealed but did not, as it has become its common practice to hide some of its facilities. One of the locations was Ramandeh, which belongs to the AEOI and is part of the Karaj Agricultural and Medicine Center near Tehran. The other site was the laser laboratory at Lashkar Ab'ad, also part of the AEOI.[13] Such actions lead Israeli and American officials to accuse El-Baradei's agency of ambiguity, if not outright deception.

Israeli and American officials claimed that the DG's accounts have deliberately delayed by at least two years the referral of Iran to the UN Security Council.[14] The first evidence that Iran was violating its safeguards agreement with IAEA was revealed in 2003, but it was not until February 2006 that the Board of Governors declared Iran a noncompliant state and referred the case to the Security Council. On the other hand, the nonaligned countries, especially Iran, see El-Baradei as a puppet controlled by the United States. El-Baradei rejects both accusations. He states he is doing an honest and professional job as required by his mandate and the international community's rules of the game. He is proud that all sides are dissatisfied; for him that is a sign of a fair, unbiased, and fearless attitude. "I can know only what we are told and what we find. The IAEA doesn't have its own intelligence," he says, and adds for emphasis, "We are not an intelligence organization."[15] One of the top officials of the IAEA elaborated. "We don't have human sources. We don't cultivate agents. We don't have satellites," he said. "We buy satellite imagery from commercial companies. If a state wishes to deceive us, it will be difficult for us to find out." While correct, these statements don't tell the whole truth.

IAEA established its satellite department in 2003 after the North Korean crisis. U.S. intelligence satellites discovered that North Korea was building nuclear weapons. The United States offered the images to IAEA. At first the agency refused to accept the photos. It was something that had never been done before. IAEA always relied only on its own experts and rejected outside information. But after long and arduous deliberations, their operating procedures were modified. Since then IAEA is willing to receive information from any source and to examine it. IAEA nowadays has its own special imagery unit. The unit commissions commercial satellites and its own in-house experts to decipher the images. They don't wish to rely and maybe be manipulated by outside experts, who may have hidden agenda.

Considering that the IAEA is not an intelligence agency, it is nonetheless one of the most intelligence-ridden international organizations in the world. During IAEA gatherings and especially when the board of governors discusses Iran, Vienna turns into a hotbed of intelligence activity. It's reminiscent of Vienna after the Second World War, when Austria was divided into four zones run by the four victorious powers. The magnificent Orson Welles film *The Third Man* accurately describes Vienna then as crowded with spies, case officers, agents, and informers.

Today many intelligence organizations, especially those who have keen and an immediate interest in Iran's program are increasing their presence in Vienna, hoping to establish contact with and eventually recruit someone important in the Iranian delegation. They follow delegation members and consider breaking into their rooms. They send communication technicians to install bugging devices and code-breaking experts to listen to messages between the Iranian missions, IAEA headquarters, and Tehran.

Naturally, during significant discussions, the volume of communication and messages increases dramatically. Experts talk over the phone and send e-mails and faxes. This can help the code breakers. "We know that we are bugged, that we are listened to, and that the place is full of spies," a top IAEA official says with a smile of acceptance. "We take it into account, and there is nothing we can do about it. This is the nature of a high-profile international organization that deals with such a sensitive issue."[16] To be on the safe side, the IAEA security department has the organization's computers and sealed rooms inspected, but they know that a determined person could eventuality break into the IAEA's computer network.

Iran, too, knows that it is on the radar screen of Western intelligence communities, especially during deliberations. Its mission is beefed up, with security guards and intelligence experts. It instructs its delegates in Vienna not to be in contact with non-Iranians, not even strangers at restaurants, hotel lobbies, and bars. The delegates are asked to report any suspicious activity. For their part, Iranian intelligence officials try to intercept communications coming out of Uno City headquarters. In recent years there have been several cases in which Iranian intelligence officers tried to recruit employees working for the IAEA. As of 2007 there were at least twenty Iranians employed by the various IAEA departments. They were hired in accordance to IAEA contractual regulations. The Iranian are not allowed to work in Division B of the Department of Safeguards tasked with monitoring and inspecting Iran's nuclear sites. Nevertheless, the interested intelligence agencies suspect that some of the Iranians were installed there to be the eyes and ears of Iran's government. Iran's intelligence wants to be kept informed about IAEA plans regarding inspections of Iranian nuclear sites and about future IAEA reports on Iran. Austrian counterespionage and security officials discovered several attempts by Iranian intelligence to tap telephone lines of top IAEA personnel.[17] However, Iran's technological capabilities in the area of signals and communication intelligence, interception, and code breaking are still inferior to Israel's and the West's.

IAEA delegations to Iran's nuclear sites are also subjected to intensive monitoring by Iranian security officials. The Iranians suspect that the international inspectors are not only working for the IAEA but also collecting information for foreign security services, especially the CIA, MI6, and Mossad. Iranian intelligence tries to break into inspectors' hotel rooms, scan their documents, and listen to their phone conversations. It tries to spot weaknesses that can be exploited, such as drug habits or sexual preferences. On several occasions the Iranian liaison officials attempted to bribe the inspectors. Hollie Heinonen was sometimes sent gifts by his Iranian hosts but returned the boxes unopened.[18]

The truth is that Iran has grounds for its suspicions about the IAEA. Since 2003 the IAEA maintains strong ties with the intelligence communities, including the CIA and Israeli intelligence. El-Baradei himself admitted he didn't see any problem in cooperating with anyone who could provide the agency with information that would enable him to fulfill his mission— preventing the proliferation of nuclear weapons.[19] The CIA, Mossad, MI6, and other intelligence organizations have provided very useful data about

Iran's nuclear program and its efforts to acquire equipment and technology. IAEA officials, however, complain that Western intelligence agencies, especially the CIA and Mossad, don't share what they have or give it only after considerable delay. These agencies in fact suspect that the IAEA leaks like a sieve. Every piece of information that is provided might reach Iranian eyes and ears and, worse, could endanger sources and agents. The have also given the IAEA information that proves false. "We could have been much more effective," senior IAEA officials emphasize, "had we received more solid information." The reality is that all involved parties—the Iranians, Israelis, Americans, Russians, British, and French—have been working hard to influence and even manipulate the IAEA reports on Iran. Unlike the Israeli and U.S. intelligence communities, the British MI6 had more faith in IAEA and has closely cooperated with it.

One piece of information that landed in IAEA headquarters in August 2002 was not false, though. It was very accurate and shocking in part because of its origin: the National Council of Resistance of Iran (NCRI). The NCRI is the political stepchild of the MEK, considered the largest, most vociferous, and most militant opposition group to the ayatollahs' regime. The NCRI is essentially a cover organization for the MEK, which is still on the State Department list of terrorist groups.

However, Israel and the West couldn't dismiss the NCRI report out of hand. Despite its past record as Marxist and anti-Americans a well as despising Israel, the NCRI had knowledge of Iranian politics and the ability to recruit agents and infiltrate the IRGC and AEOI. The CIA and Israeli intelligence had formed secret channels of communication with the group even before the Natanz revelation.

The Iranian government claimed that the NCRI was used by the CIA or Israeli intelligence, or both in a joint operation, to launder their own information in order to protect their sources and modes of operation. Nevertheless, it was NCRI that got the headlines and the glory. The organization published a report on its Web site, then called a press conference and eventually informed the IAEA that Iran was building two nuclear sites. One was a uranium enrichment plant in Natanz, the other a heavy-water production facility and a nuclear reactor in Arak that would allow Iran to produce plutonium.

This revelation was a watershed in the attitude of the IAEA and its relations with Iran. A signatory of the NPT that has a safeguard agreement with the IAEA is supposed to report to the IAEA about all its nuclear sites and materials. Iran was one of the first states to join the IAEA in 1958, a year after the agency's founding, and it ratified the NPT in 1974. Since then the country usually enjoyed smooth relations with the IAEA. Until the summer of 2002 Iran had never been mentioned in IAEA documents.[20]

The IAEA was not alone in ignoring Iran. In the 1990s some intelligence agencies dealt with Iran's nuclear capabilities (see chapter 9), but basically Iran was a prime target of neither these communities nor the IAEA. Since the gulf war of 1991, the United States and the rest of the world had focused on Iraq. The NCRI exposé of Natanz and Arak made the intelligence communities frantic. They became more motivated to get their hands on valuable and accurate information.

The NCRI's ties to the MEK were the cause of some of the frenzy. The MEK was established in the late 1960s by Marxist Iranian students who opposed the shah and his pro-Western policies. Their left-wing ideologies did not prevent them from embracing Shiite-Islamist beliefs, nor did those beliefs stop them from using violence. They targeted the shah's generals and officials and also assassinated foreigners, especially Americans. The State Department includes the MEK on its list of terrorist organizations because "during the '70s it conducted several attacks against American military and civilian targets, and participated in the capture of the U.S. embassy in the revolution."[21] The report also notes, "The MEK has not attacked or targeted U.S. interests since the 1979 Islamic Revolution in Iran."

The members of the movement, which was banned, were persecuted by the feared SAVAK security service. In the mid-1970s they joined forces with the Islamic revolutionaries of Ayatollah Khomeini, proving the dictum that politics makes strange bedfellows. At the time it was said in Iran that the young, urban bright students joined the MEK, whereas the slower, more parochial students joined Islamic groups. Mahmoud Ahmadinejad's excellence at his studies was in a way an exception.

But Khomeini had plans other than sharing his power and his vision about an Islamic republic with Marxists. Within two years of consolidating his power he banned the MEK, arrested thousands of members, and executed many. The remainder went into exile in Paris. The group's leaders include Massoud Rajavi, one of the founding fathers of the movement, who was nominally replaced by his wife, Maryam Rajavi, as part of the group's attempt to improve its image. To date, most male members of the MEK can be recognized by the mustaches they wear in imitation of their founder, which contrast starkly with the full beard the Iranian government supporters sport.

In the mid-1980s, President Francois Mitterrand's Socialist government struck a deal with the Khomeini government. In return for the release of French hostages captured by the pro-Iranian Hezbollah movement in Lebanon, the French government would expel the MEK and its headquarters. With the Iran-Iraq war still raging, the group then found shelter in Iraq, forming a partnership with Saddam Hussein. With this alliance, the MEK stained itself forever, becoming shameless traitors in the eyes of even staunch opponents of Khomeini's. Hussein's regime equipped them with weapons, such as tanks, and they reciprocated by attacking Iranian soldiers at the front and stabbing the regime in the back by targeting senior government officials and military personnel. Among their victims was President Muhammad Ali Rajai, who was assassinated in 1981 in a bombing that also killed Justice Minister Muhammad Beheshti, Prime Minister Bahonar, and many other officials. Another notable hit was the murder of the director of Iran's prison system, Asadollah Lajevardi, labeled the Butcher of Evin, after the notorious prison in northern Tehran. Despite the MEK's ailing reputation, many Iranians appreciated Lajevardi's death. The 1999 assassination of the deputy chief of Iran's armed forces, Ali Seyyed Shirazi, was also another important attack carried out by the MEK.

The MEK's record of killing Americans and their alliance with Saddam Hussein have been hard to digest for consecutive U.S. administrations, the present one included. But the information about Natanz and Arak couldn't be ignored, and Israeli and American intelligence communities trained their satellite cameras on the newly revealed installations. The NCRI proved to be right. U.S. intelligence explained that the National Reconnaissance Office (NRO) had detected the digging and construction at Natanz a year earlier but couldn't determine its true purpose, whereas Arak "was not flagged as being nuclear-related," wrote Jeffrey T. Richelson, "because from above it looked like a common factory."[22] Israeli intelligence offered a similar excuse, claiming that "we knew a year before the NCRI exposé but, because of safety concerns for the sources that provided the information, couldn't reveal it in public."[23]

On August 16, 2002, IAEA Deputy Director General Heinonen wrote a letter to Ali Akbar Salehi, the Iranian ambassador (or to be more precise, "Head of Mission") to the IAEA, demanding to know what was going on at Natanz and Arak. Ironically, the well-groomed Salehi is a professor of mechanical engineering who used to teach and do research at the Sharif Technical University in Tehran, one of the facilities suspected of developing Iran's secret nuclear plans. The robust Finn with an impeccable memory recalled that the professor turned ambassador's signature appeared on several purchasing documents from 1989 to 1991, supposedly for the university laboratories. Sources indicate that Salehi took advantage of his academic credentials to cover his involvement in, and evidence of, his country's nuclear program by serving as a conduit for the purchase of materials and equipment from Austria and other countries that would not otherwise have sold to the Iranian government. Heinonen demanded in his letter to know what was happening a Natanz and Arak. The answer from Leonard Bernstein Strasse came quickly.

Salehi quickly responded that the NCRI report was baseless propaganda spread by Iran's enemies. Regardless of the truth about the report's origins, even the Iranians knew that the MEK indeed has had good networks of sources in Iran. The IRGC, which is in charge of the nuclear program, and VAVAK (Vezarate Ettelaat va Aminiyate Keshvar) Iran's ministry of information and security, conducted several investigations to find out who leaked the information. They questioned scientists from the AEOI and subcontractors who were involved in the work there. Security, already strict, was further tightened.

At the September 2002 annual IAEA General Conference, El-Baradei met with Gholam Reza Aghazadeh. Aghazadeh stated that Iran was embarking on a long-term plan to construct six nuclear power plants with a total capacity of 6,000 megawatts. This ambitious plan would complement the Bushehr nuclear reactor already under construction, which would have a capacity of 1,000 megawatts. The head of AEOI also stated that such a sizeable project entitled Iran to have access to all aspects of nuclear technology, including uranium enrichment.

The DG demanded that his Iranian guest confirm or deny whether Iran was building a large underground nuclear facility at Natanz and the plant at Arak. Aghazadeh was evasive, yet during the meeting he agreed that an IAEA team could visit Iran. After an exchange of letters in which Iran began what became a pattern of delaying tactics, the country was forced to allow the first visit by El-Baradei, Heinonen, and some of their aides. The original visit was scheduled for October 2002, but the Iranians found more reasons to postpone it until February 2003. In the meantime, Iran's nuclear program moved to the center of the IAEA's radar screen and remained there.

This was the inspection tour in which Heinonen recognized the URENCO-style centrifuges. On February 21 and 22, 2003, Aghazadeh provided for the first time details about Iran's uranium enrichment program and the two facilities. He conceded that Iran was building three new facilities at Natanz. One was a pilot fuel enrichment plant, which was nearing completion. The other, still under construction, was a larger, commercial-scale fuel enrichment plant. The third facility, which has not been constructed at all, should be for fuel fabrication. In an effort to mitigate his country's violations,

Aghazadeh also declared Iran's intention to extend the Safeguards Agreement with the IAEA by joining what is known as the regime of "Additional Protocol," a set of more rigid inspections enabling IAEA inspectors to conduct inspections with a shorter lead time.

Finding out about Natanz and Arak was only one goal on the agenda of the DG and his deputy. They also had information about another site, the Kalaye Electric Company. El-Baradei left Tehran for Vienna, but Heinonen demanded to be taken to the Kalaye factory. The Iranians were polite but not welcoming. "Why do you want to go there?" they asked him. "What are you going to do there? It's a private company that has nothing to do with nuclear work." Heinonen insisted he be shown the company's workshop, located in an industrial zone in a Tehran suburb.

Aghazadeh's people took the deputy director general to the company headquarters in downtown Tehran. Although he didn't like the cat-and-mouse game, Heinonen noticed that the people at the headquarters were indeed engaged in nuclear-related paperwork. He saw that the staff was drawing, planning, and dealing with documents for subcontractors hired for the Natanz facility. Caught red-handed, the Iranians didn't blink. They claimed there was a misunderstanding. Heinonen asked, "Where is the workshop?" "We have never heard of it," they replied. "There is no workshop for Natanz."

Heinonen flew back to Vienna and with his team of experts continued to uncover more about Natanz and the Kalaye workshop. A few weeks later, in late March 2003, he and a couple of inspectors returned to Iran, now equipped with very precise information (probably supplied by the Americans and Israelis). The Iranians had no choice but to take him to the address he gave them, which they explained was used by a subcontractor "to manufacture civilian components."

The Kalaye factory consisted of four buildings and some additional roofed structures. From the main office, the IAEA inspection team noticed a hall 60 feet wide and 200 feet long, and asked what it was. The Iranians said it was storage but refused to allow the inspectors to see it. "We don't have the key and anyway, there is nothing there." The inspectors looked through the windows and saw a run-down storage hall. Decrepit and dirty, it was blocked with boxes. Their request to take environmental samples was also rejected. They departed but continued to press the Iranians.

A couple of weeks later the Iranians relented. In April another IAEA mission went to Iran and this time, after exerting extreme pressure the inspectors were allowed to enter the hall. The "storage" building was empty. All the structures had clearly been renovated—the walls were newly painted and the floors retiled. Even the restroom was unusual for an Iranian warehouse: shining clean, it had lights that flicked on as soon as a person walked in. No switch, no buttons. The Iranians probably didn't want to give the inspectors an excuse to touch the walls, fearing they would leave microscopic devices to measure radioactivity. *What a miracle,* thought one of the inspectors. *Only three weeks ago this place was filthy. The walls were stained and black, and the paint was old and peeling.* Still, the inspectors managed to take some samples.

The Iranian liaison officials explained that the Kalaye workshop was manufacturing electrical wall clocks. To prove their point, they even showed Heinonen and his team an attic in which one hundred or so clocks were packed in boxes. At least one of them was purchased by a member of the IAEA team and today adorns the wall of his office. One hopes the IAEA's security department checked it to make sure there were no listening devices inside.[24]

All in all, three hundred samples from Kalaye, Natanz, and other facilities were examined at IAEA laboratories near Vienna, and found to contain particles of highly enriched uranium (HEU) mainly used to produce nuclear weapons. Now the Iranian officials had to come up with a new story. The HEU, they asserted, were contaminates from centrifuge assemblies that came from a foreign supplier, which they refused to name.[25] In other words, they were used centrifuges. They also admitted that their scientists had enriched uranium, but only to 1.2 percent. (The level of enrichment required to produce fissile material for a nuclear bomb is 90 percent.[26]) The IAEA analysis showed evidence of uranium U-235 enriched to a composition of about 70 percent. Other traces of contamination ranged between 36 percent and 54 percent. The Iranian experiments indicate that Iran was trying to test its machinery to master the process and perfect it.

The more findings were revealed by the IAEA, the more the AEOI panicked. To cover one exposed lie, they concocted new lies, and eventually Iran found itself surrounded by a thin web of lies, easy to tear apart. Iran promised time and again in the period from the end of 2002 to mid-2004 to fully cooperate with the IAEA. "A decision had been taken to provide the agency with a full disclosure of Iran's past and present nuclear activities," stated an official letter from Dr. Hassan Rohani, secretary of the Supreme National Security Council, one of Iran's highest bodies, where strategic topics are discussed. Rohani's promise proved an empty one.

Rohani, a senior official considered a moderate, also served as the chief nuclear negotiator on behalf of President Khatami with the IAEA and the European Union. After Ahmadinejad's election, he was replaced by the conservative Ali Larijani.

In June 2003 the DG submitted a report to the board of governors. The report is titled "Implementation of the NPT Safeguards Agreements in the Islamic Republic of Iran." In the "Finding and Initial Assessment" chapter, it is stated that "Iran has failed to meet its obligations under its Safeguards Agreement with respect to the reporting of nuclear material the subsequent processing and use of that material and declaration of facilities where the material had been stored and processed." In plainer language, Iran did not report, as it was internationally obligated to, the following facts.

- The country was building two plants to enrich uranium in Natanz.
- It was building a heavy-water facility and nuclear reactor in Arak to produce plutonium.
- It purchased the designs for the conversion plant from China in 1991.
- It bought both natural uranium and converted uranium (UF4 and UF6) from China.

- It was processing and producing uranium metal.
- It did not report the existence of the storage and waste facilities for all these materials.
- It did not provide design information about a radioisotope facility in Tehran.
- It did not report the existence of the drawings for the centrifuges.
- It did not report that it was testing the centrifuges at the Kalaye factory and assembling them at Natanz.

Throughout this period, Aghazadeh maintained that Kalaye had nothing to do with his organization. Though his explanations for the workshop changed—first he said it was a private company, then that it served civilian purposes—he never admitted that it was connected to Iran's nuclear program and the AEOI. Heinonen and his staff eventually found out that not only was Kalaye Electric Company an organ of the AEOI but also its chairman was none other than Aghazadeh himself.[27]

Finally in October 2003 Iranian officials admitted they had tested centrifuges at the Kalaye workshop using UF6 for nearly five years. The IAEA inspectors eventually reached the conclusion that the Kalaye workshop "has been a central part of [Iran's] centrifuge testing program."[28]

In December 2003 the Iranians were forced to admit to another deception when Libya's president, Colonel Muammar Qaddafi, surprised the world by agreeing to discontinue his plans to build nuclear weapons in return for the lifting of sanctions on Libya and the establishment of diplomatic and economic relations with the United States and Britain. As part of this deal he gave the Americans huge boxes of documents about his nuclear plans, and they told a fascinating story. Pakistan's Dr. Khan had sold Libya blueprints of the P1 and the more advanced P2 designs for building centrifuges, as well as technical drawings showing how to assemble a nuclear warhead.

The Pakistani drawings supplied to Libya matched the design of the P1 centrifuges discovered in Iran, so the wandering IAEA inspectors added more stops to their itinerary. In Pakistan, Switzerland, Germany, Great Britain,

Malaysia, and the United Arab Emirates, they quizzed the members of the smuggling ring and eventually reconstructed the trail of the "black-market bombs."[29] Their scenario only involves the movement of centrifuges to Libya, but the IAEA and Western intelligence officials assume that similar operations were done with Iran.

A key figure in the ring was Buhary Syed Abu Tahir, a Sri Lankan businessman living in Dubai, who was described by President Bush as "deputy and chief financial officer and money launderer" of Khan.[30] Tahir set up a front company named SMB Computers, which assisted the smuggling operations into Libya and probably Iran. Gulf Technical Industries (GTI), a British company in Dubai that Tahir owned with his partner Paul Griffin, placed an order for the centrifuge components with a Malaysian steel company called Scomi Precision Engineering. The cover story was that the parts were for the gas and oil industry. After the parts were delivered to Dubai, they were loaded onto a German ship named *BBC China,* bound for Libya in the late summer of 2003. The ship, however, was intercepted in a joint intelligence operation by CIA, German, and Italian agents.

The Pakistani government of President Pervez Musharraf, supposedly a staunch supporter of the West and the United States in the war against terrorism, refused to allow access to Khan. Musharraf was probably afraid that he would be criticized for allowing foreigners to accuse a Pakistani national hero of theft and smuggling. We also know now that Khan threatened to reveal how subsequent Pakistani governments, the Pakistani military, and its intelligence community either condoned or turned a blind eye to his illegal sales of lethal merchandise.[31] Under pressure from the United States, the United Kingdom, and the IAEA, Musharraf put Khan under house arrest and sent Pakistani experts to interview him. He allowed neither the CIA nor IAEA inspectors to talk directly to the scientist. But the interview process was sufficient to prompt the Iranians to preempt his revelations with their own version, which this time was closer to the truth, if not yet the whole truth.

Iran had initiated its efforts in the field of gas centrifuge enrichment in 1985 with a search of available technical literature and expertise, during which they found. Khan. He met with Iranian AEOI scientists and security officials, who reciprocated with visits to his home country, and eventually Khan sold them his blueprints. Based on them, Iran manufactured the centrifuges discovered at Kalaye and Natanz.

This, of course, contradicted Aghazadeh's original claim presented to El-Baradei and Heinonen, but the IAEA accepted the explanation. The IAEA revealed in one of its later reports that components for the centrifuges came not only from Pakistan but also from another country, which the report didn't name. According to Western intelligence sources, the country was Russia.[32]

Iran admitted that it had P1 and P2 drawings purchased from the Khan network. In January 2004 "Iran acknowledged, for the first time, that it had received P-2 centrifuge drawings in 1994," the IAEA reported.[33] The Iranians insisted, however, that they had never looked at the P2 drawings but simply stored them in boxes. This was only the first of numerous peculiarities in the explanations.

The AEOI had signed a contract with a small company led by a young Iranian scientist to do research and development on P2 centrifuges and claimed that until the scientist was commissioned—a period of seven years—they didn't touch the P2 drawings, a statement the IAEA experts found hard to believe.

Next, although the Iranians claimed that they did not use the drawings, they immediately tried to upgrade them. In 2004 IAEA inspectors met with the scientist in Tehran, and he said he was trying to build rotors made with fiber-carbon technology for the centrifuges. Fiber carbon is an advanced technology that avoids the use of the standard steel (called maraging steel) specified in Khan's drawings. IAEA experts say that it is almost impossible to build rotors with fiber carbon material without first testing the rotors in the centrifuges. When confronted with this information, the Iranians came up with yet another implausible story. Yes, they said, that's how scientists usually do it, but our scientist employed an unconventional technique.

And that wasn't the last fantastical explanation the Iranians had up their sleeve. IAEA inspectors understood from the scientist that he was negotiating to procure 4,000 magnets from a European supplier "with specifications suitable for use in P2 centrifuges and that he had also mentioned to the intermediary the possibility that larger orders would follow."[34] But why would he order these magnets if the AEOI had no intention of building P2 centrifuges? The Iranians answered that even though they had the P2 drawings and had discussed procuring the magnets, they had no plan to manufacture or assemble the centrifuges. Neither the IAEA nor Western intelligence communities believed them. There is a strong sense that somewhere in Iran are other secret installations with the more advanced P2 centrifuges, which can enable the country to enrich uranium better and faster.

There is another, more important, puzzle. The Libyan records also disclosed that Khan had sold them designs for building nuclear warheads. This is the most complicated and sensitive stage in the process of building nuclear weapons. Once you enrich uranium or separate plutonium to produce sufficient fissile material, you have to design and manufacture a device that will hold all the relevant components—a bomb. This is called weaponization.

The Iranians never admitted that Khan sold similar drawings to them, but the professional echelon of IAEA, already very suspicious, became even more distrustful. No one rules out the possibility that the Iranians are already deeply involved in weaponization, though there is as yet no evidence of "military use," as far as IAEA inspectors have discovered.

CHAPTER EIGHT

A Shadow Program

AFTER A LONG period of failure and frustration, early 2004 was looking like a good time for Uno City. Its inhabitants were reaping a record harvest in their efforts to expose Iran's nuclear program. The IAEA inspectors and analysts, led by Hollie Juha Heinonen, were focusing on the question of whether Iran had, as suspected, a secret military program parallel to the official civilian "transparent" one that wasn't transparent at all.

But hidden hands were making very sure that the world's nuclear watchdog received some interesting information. Batches of documents landed at the IAEA headquarters at the end of 2003 and early 2004, drawing attention to the heavily fortified, huge military complex of Lavisan-Shian, in northern Tehran. Although the precise nature of their information and even their source remains unclear, they talked in general terms about the strong possibility that Lavisan was a site where nuclear activity—probably related to uranium enrichment—was being conducted, without its having been declared to the IAEA. There is no question, however, that the documents stirred the IAEA to great activity.

During the 1970s Lavisan was a military garrison housing the shah's Imperial Guards. When the anti-shah demonstrations and strikes dominated

Iranian streets, Khomeini supporters killed several Imperial Guards officers at Lavisan and occupied the base. Since the late 1980s it had been a manufacturing center, mainly of household products such as TV sets, washing machines and dryers, vacuum cleaners, stainless-steel pots, dishes, and automotive parts. The largest corporation there, Sanam Industrial Group (SIG), was a subsidiary of Iran's Aerospace Industries Organization (AIO).

But Sanam's innocuous products were merely a decoy for advanced defense and military research and development. After the revolution the base was put under the control of the defense ministry and Armed Forces Logistics, which turned it into a major high-tech research center housing nearly 10,000 technicians, engineers, chemists, biologists, and physicists. Several of Iran's most secret and prestigious projects have been developed there, including its first generation of missiles (Sayyad 1, based on Chinese–North Korean technology), jet engines (Tolu-4), and liquid fuel for more advanced missiles.

Lavisan attracted the attention of the American, British, and Israeli intelligence communities in the early 1990s. They received information that the site had become one of the centers for the country's chemical and biological weapons program, and probably nuclear, too. In 1992 a U.S.-originated report claimed there was a "98 percent certainty that Iran already had all of the components required for two or three operational nuclear weapons made with parts purchased in the ex–Soviet Muslim republics."[1] Six years later another report stated that Iran had stored nuclear warheads in Lavisan.[2] But these claims proved false, likely part of a disinformation campaign initiated by a psychological warfare department in one of the branches of Israeli intelligence, the CIA, or the opposition Mujahedeen Khalq.

Whatever the true nature of its activities, Lavisan was a busy place. Alongside its research and manufacturing facilities, it also became a center for scientific studies, beginning with the Physics Research Center (PHRC) in 1989. Its name and the nature of its studies suggested it was involved in aspects of nuclear research and in training young nuclear experts for service of the ministry of defense and the military. A few years later the Sanam Group opened its own college on the premises. The purpose of the school was to train students and experts in the art of building boosters and other components of long-range ballistic missiles of the Shahab (Comet) family. Iran is assiduously trying to engineer the missiles to carry its nuclear warheads in the future. "Shahab" is a generic name for a line of ballistic missiles that the Aerospace Industries Organization has been frantically developing since the early 1990s, a result of the lesson learned in the war with Iraq. Shahab missiles were originally based on the Soviet Scud missile, which was then upgraded in China and in North Korea. NATO code-named the North Korean missile No Dong. The Pakistanis also based their Ghauri missile on the Scud design.

With a range of 800 miles and a payload capacity of 1,540 pounds of explosives, the newly developed and tested Shahab 3 missile can hit almost any target in the Middle East, including Tel Aviv in Israel, Riyadh in Saudi Arabia, Ankara in Turkey, and Alexandria in Egypt. When it was introduced in Tehran in a September 1999 military parade for the annual Martyrs' Week commemoration, which honors the fallen soldiers and volunteers of the war with Iraq, the missiles were draped with a banner stating ISRAEL SHOULD BE WIPED OFF THE MAP.[3] (The Iranian practice of calling for Israel's obliteration began soon after the Iranian revolution of 1979. However it continued unabated during the 1997–2005 presidency of the "moderate reformist" Muhammad Khatami.) Iran also has the Shahab 4 missile, with a range of 1,250 miles, and is working on a new missile with an operational radius of 1,875 miles. This would put almost every major European capital within striking range.

In the second half of the 1990s, dozens of Iranian students from Sanam College were sent to Russia in an exchange program with the Baltic States Technological University, in St. Petersburg, and the Ustinov Military Mechanics Baltic State Technical University from St. Petersburg. Only after the U.S. Congress voted to impose sanctions on Russia—over its international commitment to control the spread of missile technology—did President Boris Yeltsin's administration expel twenty-two Iranian students from various universities where they had studied (see chapter 9).

Another supposed educational institute in Lavisan is a center for biological studies. It is not clear when exactly the institute was founded but, according to an Iranian opposition group, it happened sometime during the Khatami administration. "In May 2003 the ministry of defense and armed forces logistics formed a new biological weapons center to expand a biological bomb," a spokesman for the MEK-spawned National Council of Resistance of Iran claimed in May 2003.[4] Iran quickly denied the allegations.

Regardless of its veracity, the information the IAEA received about Lavisan triggered international interest. The National Reconnaissance Office (NRO) of the U.S. intelligence community trained its satellites on Lavisan. The photos taken were extremely detailed and clear, but analysts couldn't determine what was really happening inside the buildings. For such information, agents and informers—human intelligence—are needed.

In early 2004 more information arrived at IAEA headquarters, which concerned the installation of one or two "whole body counter" machines at Lavisan. This is a cage- or cell-like device that can identify and measure radioactive material in the bodies of both humans and animals. It uses sensitive radiation detectors and electronic counting equipment, as well as heavy metal shielding, to screen out naturally existing background radiation. Its main application is medical—to measure exposure to X-ray radiation in people at radioactive facilities—and the presence of a machine is in itself an indication of nuclear-related work. Searching its IAEA files, Deputy Director General Heinonen and his assistants from the Department of Safeguards found records showing that Iran purchased two such machines, reportedly for medical research, in the mid-1990s. One was bought directly from an Australian company.[5] The other was purchased with an IAEA grant as part of the agency's technical nuclear cooperation. IAEA officials made requests to visit Lavisan during February and March 2004, to verify the information and confirm their suspicions.

The Atomic Energy Organization of Iran took a few weeks—a typical delay—to give an answer that was itself a delay. "We are still considering the request" was the reply. Then the organization argued that Lavisan was beyond the scope of IAEA inspections because it was a military installation. When reminded that they had agreed to full transparency and cooperation under the "Additional Protocol," which allows for intrusive spot checks, the Iranians gave the most astonishing answer. "We had to dismantle Lavisan Shian," they said without blushing.[6]

In fact, the response surprised neither the IAEA nor the various Western intelligence organizations. They had already seen Iran wipe the whole Lavisan-Shian military base off the face of earth. A new round of satellite imagery showed clearly that what used to be a huge and active complex—fifty-five acres with hundreds of buildings, workshops, laboratories, production halls, roads, and trees—had become an empty space. From the photos it was determined that the demolition of the place took place sometime in November 2003, but bulldozers, tractors, and heavy trucks continued to work there. The IAEA insisted on visiting the abandoned site. The Iranians continued their evasive tactics. It would take another three months of arm-twisting and threats by the IAEA and the European Union before Iran approved the request.

In the meantime, the head of AEOI, Reza Gholam Aghazadeh, explained to IAEA DG Muhammad el-Baradei that the military had been forced to remove the facility because it belonged to Tehran. City managers, led by Mayor Ahmadinejad, had demanded their property back so they could build a public park. No one at the IAEA believed this obvious ruse, designed to justify its unprecedented removal of the facility to another location. Further inquires revealed that the defense ministry denied city authorities access to the site during the demolition.[7] In June 2004, following a stormy meeting of the IAEA board of governors, Iran was asked to provide access to the site "in the interest of transparency."[8] Eventually Iran agreed.

When the IAEA inspectors arrived there at the end of June, they saw, of course, nothing. "Unfortunately we were tipped off [about Lavisan] too late," said a senior IAEA official.[9] Still they noticed one interesting sight. Not only was there not one single standing structure but the whole area had been plowed, its topsoil removed, and new topsoil spread. "It was clear that

someone dug very deep to take out the soil," recalled a senior IAEA official.[10] Later, by comparing satellite images that IAEA purchased from commercial companies with photos taken by reconnaissance flights of the NRO,
it was determined that between twenty and a hundred inches of soil were
removed. The inspectors took two sets of samples from the area. For the
first, called a swipe sample, a special piece of cloth is used. These samples are
then examined in a process known as destructive analysis, because the cloth
is separated from the traces collected on it and destroyed. The second kind
involved samples taken from the soil, sewer, vegetation, and air in the area.
The samples were sent to the agency's laboratories at Sibersdorf, 35 miles
southwest of Vienna.

Lab tests showed that no traces of nuclear material were found. "It should
be borne in mind, however," the IAEA official said, "that detection of
nuclear material in soil samples would be very difficult in light of the site's
razing." Because the soil had been replaced and trees cut down, the sampling
was useless.

If the Iranians thought, though, that by destroying the evidence they
would put an end to the IAEA's curiosity, they were wrong. Heinonen and
his inspectors asked where the whole body counters and their trailers had
been moved. The Iranians responded that they had put them in storage,
along with the other equipment from the Physics Research Center of Lavisan,
in "a technical university in Tehran." The IAEA insisted on checking and
taking samples from the counters, but after another set of delays and evasions
the Iranians explained that one trailer was lost. The IAEA inspectors and analysts were astonished, as were researchers at Israeli intelligence and the CIA.
"You are so organized," they pointed out. "Everything is in its place. How
could you lose the trailer?" It can happen to anyone, replied the Iranians,
even to us.[11]

Eventually, in January 2006, nearly two years after their original request,
the inspectors were given access to the equipment, including the two body
counters and the one remaining trailer, all of which had been stored at a
technical university whose identity the IAEA didn't reveal. According to

Western intelligence sources, it was the Sharif University of Technology. The inspectors were also allowed to question a senior professor who served as one of the heads of PHRC. His answers were evasive and uncooperative—essentially variations on "I don't know," "I don't remember," and "It was not my responsibility." Tests and analysis of the samplings showed no significant traces of nuclear materials in the trailer or on the body counters. Still, however, the investigation was left incomplete. The Iranians refused to allow the IAEA inspectors to question another scientist involved in the project who could have shed light on the mystery. They also denied, on several occasions, another IAEA inspection team's access to Natanz. That was in March and April 2006. The Iranians accused the Belgian Chris Charlier, who was the head of the B division in charge of Iran, of spying activities. The Iranian permanent mission to the IAEA filed an official complaint that Charlier was "acting outside the responsibility of an inspector." Though not completely explaining what was his wrongdoing, AEOI officials claimed that he had been talking to the media and had made unauthorized tape recordings. Two other inspectors were subjected to similar accusations and treatment. IAEA officials defending Charlier said that he was a committed inspector who was doing his duty, and that the Iranians didn't like his thorough inspections.[12]

But what the inspectors did find on other equipment from Lavisan at the technical university increased their suspicion. Most of the items searched were "dual-use" equipment (such as pumps, balancing machines, mass spectrometers, magnets, and fluorine-handling machines), devices that can be used either for a civilian nuclear program or a military one. "Analysis of the environmental samples taken from equipment at a technical university in January 2006," concluded an IAEA report, "showed a small number of particles of natural and highly enriched uranium. The equipment had been shown to the agency in connection with the investigation into efforts made by the Physics Research Center to acquire dual-use material and equipment."[13]

How could equipment and machinery in Lavisan possibly be contaminated with traces of nuclear materials, highly enriched uranium included, in a facility that Iran had not declared as nuclear, as it was obliged to do by its agreement with the IAEA? The AEOI'S official answer was that the Physics Research Center had been established for the purpose of "preparedness to combat and neutralization of casualties due to nuclear attacks and accidents (nuclear defense) and also to support and provide scientific advice and services to the defense ministry."[14] When asked for a list of the activities and equipment there, "Iran provided a list of eleven activities conducted at the PHRC but, referring to security concerns, declined to provide a list of the equipment used at the Center."[15]

To add additional mystery to the whole incident, in February 2006 Tehran mayor Muhammad Bagher Ghalibaf followed in the footsteps of his predecessor, Mayor Ahmadinejad, and ordered thousands of trees in the area cut down. This was a further indication that Iran had something very important to hide in Lavisan—but that no traces of it would ever be found.

What was there in Lavisan that caused the Iranians such panic? The country had built a physics research center on a secret ministry of defense military base focused on aerospace research, without declaring its existence. When the site was revealed, Iran first refused the IAEA access, then delayed its answer, and eventually demolished the site. Only then did Iran admit that there was a research center in Lavisan. A similar pattern of delay, evasion, and complications involved equipment that had been removed and stored, and then some of it was "lost." Iran refused to let the IAEA interview the staff, but it was able to speak with one uncooperative scientist. Not until the IAEA managed to find dual-use equipment and traces of enriched uranium did Iran confess that Lavisan was the site of nuclear activity, but this activity, they argued, was purely for defensive research.

Inevitably, such a sequence of events will arouse suspicion. Even the IAEA stated, in its usual indirect language, that as with other locations "Iran has not expressed any readiness to discuss these topics." The prevailing assumption shared by analysts and experts from the French, American, British, and Israeli intelligence communities was that Iran was engaged in a secret operation to manufacture highly enriched uranium. Because of the missile research conducted at Lavisan, Western intelligence experts also assume that Iran was working there on weaponization.

For the first time, however, the IAEA had established a connection between nuclear activities and the defense ministry, a key piece of evidence in determining violations of nuclear protocols. In all the major nuclear powers of the world, the involvement of a defense agency and the armed forces indicate that the program is not just civilian but military as well.

Parallel developments in other parts of Iran related even more strongly to weaponization. One of them was the Green Salt Project, a code name the IAEA applied to a program or research study the Iranians were allegedly running to produce materials that would assist them in the conversion of uranium dioxide into UF4 (often referred to as green salt).[16] Asked about this project in 2004, the AEOI completely denied the allegation, describing it as "based on false and fabricated documents so they were baseless."[17] It explained that since the plant in Esfahan was converting yellowcake to uranium gas UF6, they didn't need another program for uranium conversion. However, the IAEA found out that the company allegedly involved in the Green Salt Project was the same one the AEOI used to procure equipment and materials abroad for the Esfahan conversion plant.

For that reason, some senior officials in the IAEA and Western intelligence communities tend to believe that the secret Green Salt Project existed and that its aim was mastering what is known as the fuel cycle. The fuel cycle is the whole process that enables a country to produce fissile material for a bomb: mining natural uranium, milling it, converting yellowcake into either metallic uranium (UF4) or gaseous hexafluoride uranium (UF6), then enriching it to levels of concentration at or above 90 percent. To complete the process, Iran would also need to assemble the material into a warhead or an explosive device. To explore the various stages of weaponization, Iran created several secret programs. One focused on the production of polonium-210, a highly radioactive material which in conjunction with beryllium is essential for "military purposes." [18] Another program dealt with the design of a warhead. Yet another tested high explosives. All these activities are essential to the development of a nuclear device.

The IAEA, during its lucky streak of early 2004, received information from unidentified sources that Iran was exploring these controversial areas. It is not clear if the anonymous sources were Iranian defectors, or walk-ins, as they are known in intelligence jargon. A walk-in is an informer who offers his services voluntarily, without being recruited. On the other hand, the information may have reached Uno City because someone made sure that IAEA would get the valuable tips.

According to the information, between 1989 and 1993 Iran attempted to extract polonium-210 in a series of experiments at the Tehran Research Reactor (TRR)." The experiments included the irradiation of bismuth. Some of the experiments were conducted at Malek Ashtar University of Defense Technology in Esfahan (which has a branch in Tehran) and has been known to Western intelligence organizations and the IAEA as one of Iran's important nuclear centers.

Bismuth is a reddish-white, easily fusible metallic element that has applications for the pharmaceutical industry but also in a nuclear program. Polonium-210 is used as a neutron initiator in some designs of nuclear weapons.[19] Beryllium is used to trigger a chain reaction inside the explosive device that causes a nuclear explosion. At first Iran informed the IAEA that it had never acquired beryllium. "It was not on our shopping list," announced Asghar Soltaneih, a senior Iranian official and future ambassador to the IAEA.[20] When IAEA inspectors found out that Iran tried to purchase the material from a Western European company, the country admitted trying but said the effort had failed. IAEA and Western intelligence agencies tend to believe that Iran managed to buy beryllium from another supplier.

Eventually Iran came up with another dubious explanation: that the experiments were part of a feasibility study and said that it didn't have "a project either for the production of polonium-210 or for the production of neutron sources using polonium-210."[21] The Iranian explanations about polonium and beryllium didn't ring true, even to the ears of IAEA diplomats. One of the agency's reports about the polonium/beryllium program says that "the plausibility of the stated purpose" of the experiments "remains somewhat uncertain." In plain English, the IAEA doesn't really believe the Iranian explanations and wonders why they have been involved in continual experiments with such materials.

Another discovery shed light on the dark side of Iran's nuclear program—the Parchin complex, 30 miles southeast of Tehran, a huge military base controlled, like Lavisan, by the defense ministry and devoted to research into and the production of ammunition, rockets, and high explosives. It consisted of hundreds of buildings and several heavily fortified underground sites used to test high explosives. According to U.S. intelligence assessments, the bunkers could have served as a perfect location to develop nuclear weapons.[22] Western intelligence believes that Iran had already conducted preliminary experiments testing its capabilities to simulate a nuclear explosion. When the IAEA asked that its inspectors be allowed to visit Parchin, Iran—as before—initially ignored the IAEA's request and eventually denied it.

Even more worrisome was information that reached Uno City about warhead design. The IAEA had suspected, as early as late 2003, that Iran had received technical drawings for the design of the bomb, because of the revelations in the Libyan archives. IAEA inspectors supposed that if Libya had received bomb designs from Khan, why not Iran?

But in the spring of 2004 someone made sure that IAEA experts would be privy to plans for a nuclear warhead, which were stored on a laptop computer. The laptop, which belonged to an Iranian scientist associated with the AEOI, contained drawings and designs for a uranium enrichment facility and for producing a small nuclear warhead. The designs were made by a company called Kimeya Madon, which was by then defunct, increasing the suspicion that it was a front for the Iranian ministry of defense.[23] The laptop had been smuggled out of Iran to Germany, where it was given to BND, the German foreign intelligence service. After evaluation the Germans handed it over to the CIA, which eventually decided that the IAEA should have a look at it.

When the shocked IAEA officials demanded an explanation, the AEOI almost reflexively claimed that there was no such laptop. Then they claimed the information was a lie, fabricated by the American and Israeli intelligence communities to make it seem as if Iran were working on a warhead design. The pattern was familiar: denial followed by accusations against the West followed, under pressure, by contradictory stories.

The Iranians stated that they never would have stored such supersecret information on a laptop, as the laptop was not secure enough. Not only that, they argued, the drawings were annotated in Farsi, which they said was clear proof that it couldn't have come from Iran. Since most Iranian scientists and experts are highly educated and have a good command of English, the reasoning went, the drawings and calculations should have been done in English, even if they were stored in an Iranian computer. Finally, they came up with the argument that the basic data should have been in the original language—Chinese, Urdu, or Korean—that is, any language but Farsi.

Some senior officials at the IAEA believed the Iranian version that the whole story was fabricated by a Western intelligence organization—the CIA, MI6, or most probably Mossad. Because Israel feels more threatened than any other country by a nuclear Iran, it has the biggest motivation to show the world that Iran is developing a nuclear weapon.

This Iranian government logic is that whoever was behind the fabrication didn't do a good job. Whether it was the CIA or the Mossad, they failed in their mission. Is it possible? Yes, of course. These intelligence organizations are not perfect. They have erred in the past, even at colossal levels. In his book *State of War*, James Risen tells about a CIA operation aimed at establishing contact within Iran's nuclear program by using a Russian scientist who had defected to the United States. The scientist was given information to convince the Iranians that he had something they could benefit from. That was the bait that would hook the Iranians to recruit the scientist, who in reality would be a double agent seemingly working for the Iranians but actually loyal to the CIA. The plot went awry because the CIA gave the Russian information that was too good. In other words, the United States helped Iran.[24] Just as the CIA messed up with the Russian defector, whoever invented the laptop plot could have botched it.

On the other hand, to base the argument on a failed mission impugns the most basic talents of the CIA, the Mossad, or the MI6. The truth is that the laptop drawings were genuine. The laptop contained one thousand pages of computer simulations and calculations for experiments that could have been part of a program to design a nuclear warhead that would be compatible with Iran's Shahab family of missiles. Some documents specified a blast of about 600 feet above a target, an altitude considered ideal for a nuclear explosion.

The CIA sent the laptop for further evaluation at the Livermore and Sandia National Laboratories, which certified its authenticity. British intelligence experts, who were asked for a second opinion, reached the same conclusion. The laptop contained the design of a nuclear warhead of 270 pounds that could be delivered by a missile.

Eventually Iran was forced to admit that the laptop was not invented but genuine. However, they said, these were not drawings of a nuclear warhead but rather of a reentry vehicle for a missile. The Iranians explained that they were, as was known, at very advanced stages of developing missiles and therefore they were engaged in research about reentry vehicles.

The IAEA top echelon remains divided on this question. While there were people at the agency who accepted Iran's explanations at face value, there were other senior officials who thought that the laptop and its contents were genuine. Consequently the IAEA continues to ask Iran for more explanations about the real nature and purpose of its nuclear program.[25] "The agency remains unable to make further progress in its efforts to verify the correctness and completeness of Iran's declarations with a view to confirming the peaceful nature of Iran's nuclear program," said the August 2006 IAEA report.[26]

But since February 2006, after the board of governors referred Iran's nuclear dossier to the UN Security Council, Iran has tremendously reduced its cooperation. Aghazadeh has sealed his lips, at least about what the IAEA calls "outstanding issues," the most burning of which are the sudden demolition of Lavisan, the Green Salt Project, Parchin's bunkers, and the warhead drawings.

All these questions have contributed to the growing fear that Iran has embarked on two or more roads toward its nuclear destination. One, the "official" program, is run by Aghazadeh's AEOI. The Atomic Energy Organization of Iran provides an acceptable cover. It exchanges information maintains liaison with other international atomic energies and commissions around the world. It is officially involved in nuclear projects for truly peaceful projects in medicine, agriculture, and energy

However, this organization is neither forthcoming nor fully transparent in its dealings with the IAEA. Even requests for the simplest facts are met with suspicion and reluctance. For example, the AEOI has never provided a full description of its structure and the names of its departments. It is increasingly clear that this supposedly "peaceful" nuclear agency has a lot to hide. Though the agency formally reports to the president of the Islamic Republic, it is in fact controlled and directed by the Supreme National Security Council (SNSC), which is under the thumb of the Supreme Leader. Inside the SNSC there is a smaller body—a committee on nuclear matters—that holds its meetings in secret. Iran's parliament has no oversight of the AEOI or the nuclear committee of the SNSC, as was proven by the decision in 2000–2001 to construct the uranium enrichment plant at Natanz and the heavy-water nuclear reactor at Arak. The budget for Natanz and Arak came from a secret fund set up by the SNSC for this purpose. The cost of the two projects will reach more than $2 billion, yet the highly influential finance and budget committee of the Majlis was not even informed of their existence, much less allowed to vote on them.

It is clear that the AEOI only provides the cover for Iran's more sinister efforts to acquire nuclear weapons. Its mission is primarily to prepare the ground for construction of the nuclear technological infrastructure, especially in the field of uranium enrichment.

However, parallel to the AEOI, or in its shadow, are other units and organizations that are very active but much more concealed. These special units within the IRGC and the ministry of defense are responsible for the nuclear program's other aspects and have almost unlimited secret budgets hidden from parliamentary oversight. It is estimated that in 2006 alone, the secret fund provided $600 million for enhancing the nuclear program. They have front companies operating abroad, usually from Bahrain and the United Arab Emirates, which purchase materials and equipment for the program. They can recruit almost any scientist in the government and at universities and civilian research centers such as the Malek Ashtar University of Defense Technology, affiliated with the defense ministry and Armed Forces Logistics. This university and its rector, Lt. General Muhammad Mehdi Nejad Nouri from the IRGC, were put, along with other organizations and individuals, on the sanctions list adopted by United Nations Security Council under resolution 1737 in December 2006. (See the full list in appendix B.)

The IRGC has additional scientific and technological training facilities—for one, the Imam Hussein University in a northern suburb of Tehran, which has a very large and advanced department of nuclear physics. One of the most important units is the research group of the IRGC, which coordinates all the elements of the clandestine nuclear program. This body sets the program's annual goals, prioritizes them, and makes the crucial decisions. While the AEOI is working hard to complete its mission in uranium mining, milling, conversion, and enrichment, the IRGC and the defense ministry are in charge of a parallel program that runs another enrichment program (apart from Natanz) using centrifuges and is advancing through the various stages of weaponization: the high explosives test, assembling fissile materials, designing the warhead, and other processes.[27]

Since the IRGC is the most important organ of the regime and is run and controlled by the Supreme Leader, it also clear that Ali Khamenei is in charge of the nuclear program, not President Mahmoud Ahmadinejad.

Seyyed Ali Khamenei was born on July 17, 1939, in the city of Mashad, to a family of Azerbaijani decent. He was the second son of Ayatollah Seyyed Javad Hosseini Khamenei, an Islamic scholar. From the age of four, Khamenei was sent to maktab. The young Khamenei adored his father and tried to follow in his footsteps. Together with passion for Islam, Khamenei developed his anti-Western and antimonarchist political ideologies at a very early age. In 1952, during Mossadegh's regime, Khamenei went to a sermon delivered by an Islamic scholar who vehemently attacked the shah and the British. Khamenei still vividly recalls the day. He became convinced that Islam needed to play a bigger role in Iranian politics.

In 1957, at the age of eighteen, Khamenei continued his Islamic studies in Najaf, in Iraq, and in 1958, in Qom. There he studied under a number of renowned Islamic scholars, among them Ayatollah Boroujerdi. However, it was during his studies under Ayatollah Khomeini that both his Islamic beliefs and political ideology were shaped. In 1962 he joined the ranks of Khomeini's antimonarchist activists and served as his emissary to other clergymen. In 1964 he left Qom to care for his ill father, but he remained loyal to Khomeini and his revolutionary vision. This earned him a number of stints in prison, where he was tortured by SAVAK, yet his revolutionary zeal was undimmed. In 1975 the shah deported the thirty-six-year-old Khamenei to Iranshahr, one of the few Iranian cities with a majority Sunni population and therefore one of the last places a Shiite ayatollah would want to go. It was a humiliating experience for Khamenei, who was ridiculed and even physically assaulted.

Prior to Khomeini's return to Iran in 1979, Khamenei, with other well-known revolutionaries such as Beheshti, joined the prestigious Shoraye Enghelabe Eslami—the Islamic Revolutionary Council. From there he went on to be one of the founding fathers of Hezbe Jomhuriye Eslami, the Islamic Republic party. These were major promotions for a cleric who for three years had been confined to a desert city and could not participate in any revolutionary activity. What gained him this position was his tenacity and Khomeini's good memory. Remembering that Khamenei had shown himself to be a dependable, loyal soldier in the 1960s and early 1970s, Khomeini promoted the man he knew and trusted.

Soon after the start of the Iraqi invasion, Khamenei was posted to a number of important military positions, such as secretary of defense and supervisor of the IRGC. His organizational skills were needed there, but in addition Khomeini wanted him to purge the armed forces of any vestige of the shah's days. Khamenei proved to be an uncompromising zealot. Despite the Iranian army's lack of military skills and the problems at the front, he insisted on keeping the shah's officers in jail or killing them.

This attitude put him on a collision course with the Islamic Republic's first president, Abdul Hassan Bani Sadr. Bani Sadr believed that the officers' professional skills were badly needed to fight the better-armed Iraqis. Initially Bani Sadr's advice won out, and Iran was able to check Saddam's army and then drive it back from major cities. But Khamenei was bitter. He joined Muhammad Ali Rajai, another sworn enemy of Bani Sadr's, and together they were instrumental in turning Khomeini against the president. In 1981 Khamenei personally delivered Khomeini's speech in the Majlis that resulted in the dismissal of Bani Sadr. Soon after, Bani Sadr fled Iran dressed as a woman. Ali Rajai replaced Bani Sadr as president, though his tenure was cut short after just two weeks by the Mujahedeen Khalq bomb that killed him along with Beheshti and others.

In the same year the MEK settled scores with Khamenei as well. Their operatives booby-trapped a tape player and placed it near a stage where Khamenei was giving a speech. The bomb ripped off Khamenei's right hand, which has since been replaced with an prosthesis. This disability earned him the epithet "the living martyr" among his supporters, while some opposition figures in the United States nicknamed him the one-armed bandit.

Rajai's death placed Khomeini in a dilemma. He had heretofore insisted that the president be a noncleric, but now there was no one he considered suitable. He was forced to unofficially back Khamenei, who became the third president of the Islamic Republic of Iran with 95 percent of the vote.

During the eight years Khameini served as president, Khomeini, whose health was declining, started to search for a successor to be Supreme Leader. Candidates included Rafsanjani (the former speaker of the Majlis), Ayatollah Montazeri (a senior clergy and admired religious scholar), and Khamenei. Khomeini chose Khamenei because, unlike Rafsanjani, he had managed to stay relatively clean of any allegations of corruption. He also had a better relationship with the IRGC, the regime's most trusted organization. Montazeri was labeled as moderate and soft because of his increasingly vociferous criticism of the regime's abuse of power in the name of Islam.

According to Khomeini's son Seyyed Ahmad, Khomeini finally decided to appoint Khamenei his heir in the mid-1980s. "When Ayatollah Khamenei was visiting North Korea, the late imam (Khomeini) watched the TV reports including a large number of people who gathered to welcome him, as well as his marvelous speeches and debates. Then he said that Ayatollah Khamenei really deserves to be a leader," said Seyyed Ahmad.

Soon after Khomeini's death in 1989, Khamenei was appointed to be Vali Faghih—Supreme Leader. His appointment was not easy. He had many enemies and his religious authority and credentials were doubtful. Khamenei was a mere Hojjatol Eslam, one rank below ayatollah. He did not have the necessary religious accreditations required by the constitution to become a Supreme Leader, and other ayatollahs were better qualified. However, Khomeini had been so adamant that the constitution was changed and Khamenei was made an ayatollah overnight. Nonetheless, Khamenei remained insecure about his religious credentials and by 1997 felt so threatened by Ayatollah Montazeri's opposition that he placed him under house arrest.

Upon his appointment as the Supreme Leader, Khamenei worked closely with Rafsanjani, who had replaced him as president, to reconstruct the war-ravaged parts of Iran. Although he was concerned about allegations of Rafsanjani's corruption, he needed his business connections, especially with foreign companies. Moreover, notwithstanding his public denouncement of corruption, Khamenei had amassed a huge private fortune and so had his children.[28] In fact, rumors fly today in Iran that Khamenei is the richest man in the country, even wealthier than Rafsanjani.

It was during the Khamenei–Rafsanjani tenure that Iran's nuclear program grew. The war with Iraq and Iranian fears that the Islamic nature of the republic might be changed one day by foreign invasion have convinced many that Iran's only ultimate guarantee would be nuclear weapons. Khamenei is considered a great supporter of scientific progress in Iran, a main supporter of stem cell research and cloning. He is also a news addict. According to his own accounts, he reads more than ten Farsi-language newspapers every day.

In 2005 Khamenei decided to do what Ayatollah Khomeini had wanted

to do all along and supported a noncleric for president. However, his decision to back Ahmadinejad was not merely a desire to implement the legacy
of Khomeini. It was motivated by his fear and hatred of Rafsanjani and also
his desire for a hard-line ultraconservative who would also be weak. When it
comes to the nuclear program, Ahmadinejad is Khamenei's puppet, though
a very vocal one.

On December 16, 2005, less than five months into his presidency,
Ahmadinejad ordered Iran's ministry of culture and Islamic guidance to commission a symphony, a rare event in the annals of Iranian classical music. The
symphony is to celebrate Iran's nuclear achievements and to honor the
"national pride," a phrase Ahmadinejad uses as code for Iran's atomic ambitions.[29] The commission was awarded to Behzad Abdi, one of the country's
most promising composers. Ironically, Abdi had been living and working in
Ukraine, 120 miles from Chernobyl, the site of the world's worst nuclear
accident. This irony was not lost on Anna Galabovskaya, an antinuclear cam-
paigner, who called using art to promote nuclear energy "lying to people. It's
a kind of deception, unfairly influencing peoples' minds." Nothing came of
her objections.[30]

The first movement is aptly named "Shokouh," "magnificence" in Farsi.[31]
Ahmadinejad has often used this word to describe the talent of Iran's youth,
whom he considers the main force behind Iran's nuclear program. Tellingly,
the second movement of the symphony is called "Aftabi Dar Mian," or "the
sun" in the middle. In Iran the sun is seen as a source of energy and light,
so this title suggests that Iran wants to use its nuclear technology for the
production of energy. The next movement is named "Solh"—peace. The
composer's decision to use the names Magnificent, Sun, and Peace reflect
the party line, explaining and justifying the nuclear program despite the
international pressures.

Yet it is the name of the fourth and last movement that is troubling:
"Pirouzi"—victory. It overtly shows Iran's desire to overcome technical challenges and complete the full nuclear cycle. But victory in this case can also
be interpreted as defeating Western efforts to deny Iran nuclear technology,

or worse, Iran's future victory on the battlefield using nuclear bombs against its sworn enemies—Iraq, the United States, Israel, and Great Britain.

If this is the rationale for Ahmadinejad and the powers behind him then they might be compared in future history books to Nero, whom the Romans blamed for setting Rome on fire for his own amusement while playing his musical instrument.

CHAPTER NINE

Intelligence Failures

BECAUSE SHABTAI SHAVIT was less a man of words than of deeds, his outspoken regret was surprising, and all the more so because it concerned something he had not done. For the sixty-seven-year-old former head of Mossad, his most humiliating professional failure in thirty-five years of service is that Dr. Abdul Qadir Khan is still alive. "Had he not been around, the world would be safer and Israel would have been better off," Shavit said. "He is one of the rare examples of a single person determining the course of history. What Iran has now in the nuclear field and might have in the future is essentially because of him."[1]

Israeli intelligence had the Pakistani scientist on its radar screens in the early 1990s. "We knew that he was an unstoppable proliferator of nuclear technology. We identified him as a target for intelligence information gathering. But we were not sufficiently sharp to perceive him as a threat and subsequently to deal with him." In the Israeli intelligence dictionary the expression *to deal with him* is a code word for liquidating a target. The question of what to do about the hyperactive "father of the Pakistani nuclear bomb" was occasionally raised in evaluation sessions in the years Shavit headed Mossad, but in the late 1980s and early '90s the focus of Israeli intelligence was elsewhere.[2] Iran, then considered a relatively low risk, was not high on the intelligence "menu."

However, there were a few renegade voices in the Israeli intelligence community trying to elevate the Iranian ranking. One of them was Colonel Opher Ben Peretz, who served as an air attaché at the Israeli embassy in Washington. "It was brought to my attention that hundreds of Iranian students and scientists were studying in nuclear-related fields, such as chemistry, physics, and engineering, at America's best colleges," Peretz recalled. "Many of them attended Harvard and other schools around Boston. Their extensive efforts left me with no illusions. I quickly reached the reasonable conclusion that they were there to promote a very active nuclear program." The Israeli attaché tried to ring alarm bells in both Israel and Washington "From an early stage," he explained, "I was trying to draw my colleagues' attention to the Iranian activities and change the priorities, but no one really wanted to listen to me."[3]

Information was gathered and exchanged on the Iranian students and on Khan's travels in the Middle East, but since Syria and Egypt had declined his offers of nuclear information, Israeli intelligence remained relaxed. Mossad did try to draw the attention of the CIA and MI6 to Khan's activities since both organizations maintained close relations with the Pakistani Inter-Service Intelligence (ISI). But the CIA and especially MI6 were skeptical, feeling that Mossad is perceived by some of its counterparts as an "alarmist" agency that deliberately doctors information to serve Israeli interests.

Even if the information regarding Khan had been taken seriously, it would not have produced much. The CIA had a full plate. Shavit recalled how one day in the early 1990s he went to Washington for a courtesy visit, to meet his American counterparts. In a meeting with the one of the heads of the U.S. Army intelligence he asked casually, "What are you up to?" without expecting a real answer. The U.S. general, however, took it very seriously. He ordered his secretary to bring in a tray. It held dozens of documents. "My host picked them up one by one," recalled Shavit, "and said nonchalantly, 'This is from this country and this is from that country.' These were intelligence reports from all over the world. When he'd concluded his *tour d'horizon,* he said dryly, 'This is only last night's harvest.' Until then I thought that Mossad was an organization with global reach. Talking to my American host, I realized the big difference between the organization I was leading and an agency with a truly international agenda."[4]

The CIA stored away Mossad's information on Khan to deal with another day. From the Israeli viewpoint, the Americans did nothing further. From the American angle, however, it looked altogether different. According to Jeffrey T. Richelson, author of *Spying on the Bomb,* by the early 1990s the U.S. intelligence community was already monitoring nuclear developments in the Islamic Republic of Iran by "employing high-tech intelligence systems including satellite imagery and human intelligence."[5] Through these means the United States discovered the contracts with China discussed previously and presented the information to Congress. As early as 1991, a U.S. National Intelligence Estimate warned that Iranian leaders were "committed to developing nuclear weapons."[6] A year later Robert Gates, then head of the CIA (currently secretary of defense), told Congress that Iran "was seeking to acquire an atomic bomb."[7] Yet at the same time, with typical intelligence caution, the reports and estimates also concluded that the country's nuclear program was badly organized and remained at a very preliminary stage.

"Intelligence agencies write reports and estimates that are sometimes based on intuition and extrapolations but lack a firm factual basis. It is much more difficult to cultivate sources of information and even more so, reliable ones," explained General Uri Saguy, who was at the time head of Israel's military intelligence (known by its Hebrew acronym, AMAN).[8] To a certain degree, Shavit and Saguy represent opposites. Saguy is more intellectual, interested in methodological and philosophical questions about intelligence work; Shavit is a man of action and operations.

Shavit wanted to expand Mossad's technological horizons into signals intelligence (*sigint,* for short): intercepting, deciphering ,and analyzing messages. However, sigint was the turf of AMAN's Unit 8200, Israel's equivalent of the National Security Agency. Saguy thought that Mossad operations of this kind would overlap with Unit 8200's, wasting financial, technological, and human resources. He also believed that Shavit's proposal was motivated by frustration and a lack of success in human intelligence (*HUMINT*, in intelligence parlance)—identifying, recruiting, cultivating, and operating human sources, in which Mossad should have excelled. The two organizations and the two chiefs found themselves engaged in futile battles about resources and the division of labor. These interservice rivalries, together with a lack of precise intelligence and the global priorities of the American intelligence, diverted them from the real goal: investigating Iran's nuclear aims.

Shabtai Shavit joined Mossad in 1964, after completing his compulsory national service with a tour of duty in Israel's top Special Forces unit, Sayeret Matkal. He was trained as a case officer and two years later was assigned to the shah's Iran. There, while undercover and using a false identity, he polished his Farsi strolling around Tehran's Bazaar, situated near the Pamenar neighborhood, the Ahmadinejads' first home after leaving Aradan. Maybe one of the children whom Shavit saw playing football in the streets was Mahmoud Ahmadinejad. Later, for the two years he was based in the oil-port city of Abadan, Shavit recruited and ran networks of informers and agents, coordinating with the shah's SAVAK as part of the intelligence cooperation between the two countries.

Shavit's Iranian experience brought him back to the region seven years later, for a shorter period, to help the Iraqi Kurds in their rebellion against Baghdad's central government. He would not return again for nearly twenty years, when Dr. Khan's name popped up in Mossad's records. In the meantime, in 1980 Shavit became the head of Caesarea, the operational division of Mossad. In 1986 he became Mossad's deputy director and in 1989 Prime Minister Yitzhak Shamir selected him to lead the agency. During these years he was privy to, and often involved in, some of the most daring Israeli intelligence collection and assassination operations, among them the killing of several leaders of Palestinian groups. These operations taught Shavit about the historical significance of certain individuals as agents of change and how removing them can have an immense impact. Unfortunately, his knowledge was not applied to Khan.

Three developments compelled Shavit and Saguy to pay greater attention to Iran's nuclear aspirations. The first was the realization that the ayatollahs were involved in terrorism. In 1992 General Saguy orchestrated the assassination of Abbas Mussavi, the secretary-general of the pro-Iranian Shiite Lebanese Hezbollah organization. To avenge his death Iran's Supreme Leader, Ali Khamenei, and President Rafsanjani sanctioned the bombing of the Israeli embassy in Buenos Aires, Argentina. The attack was planned by Imad Mughniyah, Hezbollah's chief of operations and its liaison to the Iranians' IRGC (see chapter 12).

The second development was the capture of Ron Arad, an Israeli air force navigator. Lieutenant Arad was captured by Amal, a moderate Shiite Lebanese organization, after his plane was shot down in 1986 over Lebanon. After eighteen months in captivity, he was sold to the IRGC's intelligence officers stationed in Lebanon as part of Hezbollah's fight against Israel. Arad subsequently disappeared without a trace and his case remained shrouds in mystery. Mossad and AMAN spared no human or financial resource to obtain information about his fate. Although they did not accomplish that goal, during the search Mossad and AMAN developed contacts that became instrumental in the efforts to unmask Iran's nuclear program.

Lastly, "my personal trigger regarding Iran's nuclear program," explained Shavit, "was their determined effort to obtain ground-to-ground missiles and later to acquire the know-how and technology to produce them themselves. As far as I was concerned, the turning point was when Iran started to increase the range of its missiles."[9] The basic missile model was the old Soviet-Chinese-made Scud B, which was later upgraded by North Korea to the Scud C, which had a range of 600 miles.

Though China and Russia were the first to supply Iran with missiles, missile parts, and missile technology, the main source for Iran's extensive missile program since the late 1980s has been the reclusive regime in Pyongyang. Khan played a major role in this, too, as an intermediary and mediator of differences. It was a marriage of convenience for the two countries: North

Korea exports its missile technology to earn revenue to feed its people; Iran gains long-range missiles as a deterrent.[10]

Israeli intelligence could tolerate Iran's interest in missiles with a range of up to 500 to 600 miles, which can reach Iraqi territory but do not pose a threat to Israel. "But when they started to work on increasing the range, said Shavit, "I asked myself, Why do they need it? For what purpose?" He continued. "The Iraq threat and Iranian preparations for another round of war with Iraq didn't justify the enlargement of the missile range to more than 1,000 kilometers. The Iraqi excuse didn't make sense. So for me there was only one explanation—they wanted a strategic capability against us that could be used as a delivery tool for their weapons of mass destruction."[11] Shavit's experts and advisors told him that the bottleneck of every military nuclear program was the delivery system. The Iranians were trying to open the bottleneck by manufacturing missiles that could carry warheads themselves.

Shavit instructed both his research department, led by Uri Neman and Uzi Arad, and the operational units to pay more attention to Iran's missile program and the entire nuclear field. Though General Saguy was more skeptical, he followed suit. The main focus of the efforts by the Israeli government and intelligence was to try to prevent the sale to Iran of technology for missile and nuclear programs. In the intelligence dictionary *prevention* means doing everything possible to thwart an event from occurring. Diplomacy and persuasion—called "diplomatic prevention"—are preferable, but if they fail, "violent prevention" (intimidation and even terror, as a last resort) might be applied. The combined preventive efforts were coordinated with the Clinton administration and its intelligence community.

Israel began by trying to persuade the North Koreans to stop cooperating with Iran, promising to urge Jewish businessmen in the United States and Europe to invest in the North Korean economy as compensation for lost missile technology sales to Iran. In 1993 Shavit secretly dispatched his deputy (and future successor), Ephraim Halevi, to Pyongyang. (Coincidentally, Israel's foreign ministry sent its own delegation there, and the two groups were quite embarrassed to find themselves on the same flight from the North Korean capitol to Beijing.) The North Korean operation failed. The compensation deal offered was not sufficiently attractive.

After that fiasco, Israel's main efforts turned to Russia and China. Almost naturally, a division of labor between Israel and the United States was arranged, since the Clinton White House had more influence over Beijing and was already trying to stop Chinese sales of missile and nuclear technologies to Iran (as discussed in chapters 6–8). Israel became more active on the Russian front, which demanded some Israeli "chutzpah." The Soviet Union had long been off-limits to Israeli intelligence, out of fear that any Israeli secret operation that went sour would have serious ramifications on Soviet Jewry. Since the 1970s Israeli agencies together with Jewish organizations around the world had orchestrated a systematic public campaign against the Soviet Union to "let their people go."[12]

But after the collapse of the Soviet Union, Jews were allowed to emigrate, and the risks of operating on Russian soil dwindled to a much more acceptable level. Moreover, with the old order gone and a new one not fully emerged, President Boris Yeltsin's Russia and the former Soviet republics were in semi-chaos. Instability coupled with a lack of law and order ultimately creates an administrative vacuum. The deterioration of the economy only increased the temptation to operate there. Worst of all, former Soviet Union nuclear sites were being ravaged. Sensitive equipment and radioactive materials, including very precious metals, were being stolen and offered to the highest bidder. Networks of greedy entrepreneurs and criminals teamed up. Prestigious Russian research institutes and plants found themselves without the financial resources to support themselves.

"Almost everything was for sale," said a former senior KGB officer turned businessman who was personally involved in one of the deals to offer Iran a small quantity of highly enriched uranium.[13] "The central government was hopeless and people took advantage of the situation. They realized that they had to take care of their daily needs. So they took action in all walks of life, including conventional and nonconventional weapons." Sometimes the authorities turned a blind eye to this theft of state property, but others fully cooperated, even against government directives.

Iranian intelligence and the Iranian Atomic Energy Organization took advantage of the situation. In the first half of the 1990s, they operated extensive networks in search of nuclear items in Russia, Ukraine, Belarus, Kazakhstan, Azerbaijan, and Uzbekistan. On their shopping list was everything from off-the-shelf nuclear warheads to highly enriched uranium to triggers used in nuclear devices. They also offered jobs to Russian nuclear scientists. Russia was fertile ground for Iran's hunting trips. In the post-communist era, a Russian scientist or engineer whose salary was barely $50 a month could have a job in Iran at $5,000 a month plus expenses. Who could resist? "Information started to arrive," recalled Shavit, "to the effect that Russia and the former Soviet republics had become a focal point for Iranian efforts. I personally and my organization had to acquaint ourselves with a new terminology in a field which was not known."[14] Mossad established and later enlarged a special unit to analyze information from Russia and other sources about non conventional weapons. Its findings were presented to Yitzhak Rabin's government and, after his murder, in November 1995 to his successors, Shimon Peres and Benjamin Netanyahu.

Concerns about Russian-Iranian encounters grew in 1995 when the two countries signed an official agreement for nuclear cooperation. The centerpiece of the agreement was to build the Bushehr reactor, but even more worrisome was the secret appendix to the contract which committed Russia to providing Iran with key installations to master the full nuclear fuel cycle, a light-water research reactor, and most significantly, a uranium enrichment plant.[15]

Throughout the 1990s Israeli governments employed a threefold policy to prevent or at least reduce Iranian efforts to purchase technology and materials from Russia and the former Soviet republics.[16] The major tools used were intelligence and diplomacy. The first step in the Israeli policy was to engage the United States in the process. "We pointed out to our decision-making levels that the U.S. administration was not sufficiently pressing the Russian government to stop its cooperation with Iran," said General Amos Malka, who became head of military intelligence in 1998.[17] Former Mossad operative (currently Netanyahu's diplomatic advisor) Uzi Arad was appointed to lead the Israeli charge. "We had to work very hard," he said, "to convince our American friends about the urgency of the situation and the need to act."[18]

In 1994 Clinton appointed Vice President Al Gore the point man to deal with Russia's nuclear issues. Washington adopted a carrot-and-stick policy: trade incentives were offered to Russian companies that would desist dealing with Iran, and those who would not were punished by sanctions. The ailing Yeltsin partially succumbed to the American pressure, appointing his premier victor Chernomyrdin to be Gore's counterpart in a joint oversight committee. The committee managed to force some Russian institutes that had been working with Iran to stop. In a few instances Iranian students studying at Russian universities were asked to return home. Yeltsin also secretly promised Gore that his country would restrict the supply of technology to civilian and peaceful purposes (with no military application). U.S. pressure also resulted in Russia's refusal to supply installations to Iran where Tehran wanted to enrich uranium to high levels. Russia did, however, provide some equipment and materials and knowledge for the Natanz and Arak projects.

Mossad has played a pivotal role in this effort, too, utilizing its contacts with its foreign counterparts to influence their respective governments. For example, Shavit traveled in 1992 to a Far East country in an effort to convince the chief of its intelligence organization to persuade his government to divest its interests in Iran. At the time that country was considering offering a $2 billon loan to Iran for a construction project. "I told my hosts that Iran was a state sponsoring terrorism," Shavit said. The leaders of that country were persuaded and halted the project, thus causing additional problems for Iran's economy. "We hoped that by such acts, Iran would change its priorities and realize that investments in missiles and nuclear materials would deprive her of the means to improve social economy conditions."[19]

The second step was to approach the Yeltsin administration directly, to persuade officials not to allow any unauthorized transfer (or in intelligence jargon, *leakage*) of nuclear technology to Iran and to minimize contact between the two sides. Little progress was made until 1999, when General Malka was suddenly invited to visit Moscow as a guest of GRU, Russian military intelligence, the first head of Israel's military intelligence to do so. Malka felt that the Russians wanted to either please Israel or fend off Israeli aggressiveness—or only acted because of American pressure.

That does not meant the Russians were forthcoming. "In retrospect," Amos Malka concludes, "they tried to put us into sleep. To calm us down." The Russians refused to act against any companies, institutes, and individuals that Israel named. "They always demanded that we give them evidence," said Uzi Arad, "but we couldn't because we didn't want to compromise our sources. And besides, we didn't trust them."[20] One such organization was a state-owned secret: the "Research and Development of Power Engineering—Nikiet Institute," which had a clandestine channel to Iran. The Nikiet Institute had long been one of the leading nuclear research and development groups in the country, having designed nuclear power installations for the first Soviet nuclear submarine in 1954. Its director, Evgeny Adamov, was President Yeltsin's powerful minister of atomic energy. The ministry and the institute, together with the famous Mendeleyev University of Moscow, collaborated on Iran's heavy-water reactor project in Arak.[21] Once completed in 2014, it will be able to produce plutonium.

When diplomacy and persuasion failed, Israel deployed the third approach: acting independently to maintain the pressure. The instability and chaos in Yeltsin's Russia was practically a double-edged sword. Just as Iran did, a Western government could take advantage of the fragile economic and social environment to influence events. Some scientists were actively discouraged from working for Iran's missile and nuclear program. The CIA and British MI6 approached others. These and other Western intelligence agencies conducted a few successful operations to recruit agents and sources among the Russians who worked for Iran's nuclear program. The success, however, was limited. Though some Russian companies were deterred and some experts refused to go to Iran, the Yeltsin administration declined to cancel the Bushehr reactor project.[22] The financial compensation offered to Russia by the Clinton administration—around $30 million—was no match for the $800 million (and the cost is still rising and estimated at $1 billion in 2007 dollars) and jobs for thousands of skilled workers in the nuclear energy sector.

Israeli intelligence, and to a lesser degree the CIA, found itself chasing around the globe for information about Bushehr. Most of it, as Shavit admitted, proved to be wrong. He justified the search by saying "But we had to check everything. This was our obligation."[23] It is clear now that Israeli intelligence overplayed the threat of Bushehr. Indeed, the Bushehr project distracted Mossad and other Western intelligence communities from more threatening Iranian projects and especially from Khan. It was not, after all, China or Russia that provided Iran with blueprints for centrifuges to enrich uranium. Khan's cooperation with Iran benefited from the overloaded agenda of the CIA, the internecine rivalries between Mossad and AMAN, and the narrow scope, the priorities and the shortsightedness of the Israeli intelligence community. The precious time lost in the search enabled Iran to enhance its crucial nuclear project at secret facilities such as Kalaye Electric Company, Natanz, Esfahan, and Arak, almost without being noticed.

It took Western intelligence organizations a while to regroup and redirect their operations, but once they did they were relatively successful. Some of the information about the nuclear sites and their activities had been known to the Israel, British, German, French, and American intelligence communities. But they faced essential dilemmas. What to do with the information? How to share it with others? How to release the information in order to make the world aware of it? And maybe the most important question was how to use the intelligence obtained to prevent or delay Iran's nuclear activities. "It is one thing to have the data and the information," explained Shavit, "but it is completely another thing to translate it into a useful and successful tool to achieve the goal, which in this case is to stop Iran from reaching its final destination: to acquire nuclear weapons."[24]

By nature, intelligence bodies don't like to reveal or share information. They fear that releasing it will jeopardize their modes of operations and endanger their sources. Nevertheless, a growing realization that international cooperation is necessary tipped the balance. In separate meetings American, British, French, and German intelligence heads agreed to enhance the collection efforts inside Iran through spy satellites, eavesdropping, and the deployment of agents. But this time there was one agreement that would have been almost unthinkable just a few years ago: they agreed not only to share the collected data but also to team up and perform joint operations.

Recruiting agents in any country is not easy. However many human weaknesses—such as greed, revenge, jealousy, ego, and ideology—make spying possible, it is nevertheless an unpleasant business. The recruit is asked to betray his country, family, or friends. It is even more difficult to recruit quality agents, those who have good access to real secrets. For such agents a case officer (the person who recruits, directs, cultivates, and operates human sources) stands ready to pay almost any sum of money. The best candidates are senior officials, scientists, or managers with access to classified information and secret sites who are relatively free to travel. But these potential candidates are also well protected. They are escorted on trips abroad by "minders," whose assignment is to not only protect but also shadow them and to make sure that unauthorized strangers do not approach them. In actuality, their security guards are spying on them.

Iran is a tough target to penetrate. It has several field security apparatuses whose sole mission is to protect the country's military secrets in general and the nuclear ones in particular. Iranians, even top officials, who are privy to Iran's nuclear secrets are occasionally invited by the security organizations to attend briefing sessions, which may evolve into tough interrogations. The AEOI and the other bodies involved in Iran's nuclear program maintain a qualified system of compartmentalization. Those who work at the program are trained not to ask unnecessary questions and are conditioned to know only what they need to know to carry out their work.

These counterespionage methods are run by the skillful Iranian security officers at the top of their craft. They had very good teachers—those in the shah's SAVAK, which had been trained by the Israeli intelligence and had enjoyed great deal of cooperation with the CIA. General Uri Saguy admitted that Iran is a very hard place to penetrate adding, "It is a closely monitored society. Foreigners are suspected. It is a theocracy with highly religious and ideologically motivated people who believe in the cause. All these things make it harder for the intelligence to operate, but it is not something which wasn't done or couldn't be done."[25]

Operations aiming to recruit agents among Iran's nuclear community are the most sensitive issue. Talking about these or revealing some details can cause the agents to die. Iran's field security is on high alert. They see real or imaginary spies everywhere. In the last few years Iran's ministers of intelligence and information (VAVAK) announced that several networks of Iranians working for Mossad and the CIA were cracked. Yet a few interesting developments in this area can be observed:

- Western intelligence coverage of Iran has improved and thus the country's nuclear program is better understood.
- There has been an increase in the number of joint operations.
- French, German, and British agents have become very active in the effort to collect information about Iran, partly because their respective governments have been involved in the intensive (but failed) negotiations to persuade Iran to suspend its uranium enrichment activities.
- The important contribution of MI6 wins praise from Israeli and American officials. "They are true professionals and masters in the art of HUMINT," said senior Israeli intelligence officials admiringly.[26]
- Some Eastern European intelligence organizations are also involved in the collection efforts. Because their respective countries have some commercial and business presence in Iran, they can provide documentation and cover for joint operations conducted by Western intelligence operations.
- A way to "launder" information from Western intelligence to the

IAEA was found so that agencies and the sources could be protected. Information is "filtered" to the IAEA via Iranian opposition groups, especially the National Resistance Council of Iran.[27]

All these developments and achievements coincided with a change at the helm of Mossad. At the end of 2002 Premier Ariel Sharon appointed his old friend and political ally, General Meir Dagan, as the head of the agency, replacing Ephraim Halevy. Though Halevy was trained primarily in the secret diplomatic alleys of Mossad and was less involved in operations, he did direct some successful operations against Iran's nuclear capabilities, some of which focused on the clandestine encounters with Russia. Yet he was largely seen as a director who avoided risky operations. Dagan's appointment was precisely aimed to replace that image with a new one and to shake up the organization.

Although Dagan has never been an intelligence officer in the true sense of running agents and evaluating their performance, he has the reputation of a man well versed in special operations. As a young captain in the military he was involved in controversial operations against Palestinians in the Gaza Strip and later he took part in sensitive military missions against Hezbollah in south Lebanon as a colonel and brigadier general. In one of his first meetings with the top echelon of Mossad, he stated that Iran was at the top of his list of priorities.

That in itself is not entirely new. Iran had been high on the list since Shabtai Shavit's days, but the prioritization of Iran had not been well received, for a simple reason: Israeli intelligence estimates about Iran's nuclear capabilities have changed every few years.[28] In the early 1990s Mossad and AMAN concluded that by 1997, Iran would have nuclear weapons. Then the date was delayed to 2002. This uncertainty gave the Israeli intelligence the image of an alarmist organization abroad and at home, rendering their estimates suspect. In addition it placed the Israeli intelligence community at odds with American intelligence. CIA director George Tenet declared in a declassified report to the U.S. Congress, "The United States remains convinced that Tehran has been pursuing a clandestine nuclear weapons program," but added that Iran would not be capable of producing nuclear weapons until 2015.[29]

The wide gap between the two estimates derived from the standard of evaluation. Until 2005 the term Israel used to define Iran's gallop to reach its nuclear destination was *the point of no return,* the moment when Iran would have the ability to manufacture, assemble, and operate the centrifuges to produce the necessary fissile material for a nuclear device. The United States thinks that having the capability to enrich uranium doesn't necessarily make a country a nuclear weapons producer. The American intelligence estimates talk about the technological difficulties facing Iran in assembling warheads.

The American intelligence community has been criticized, however, for not taking into account all of Iran's nuclear activity. "The American intelligence community may be seriously underestimating Iran's progress towards a nuclear bomb," wrote Graham Allison. "The judgment is based on Iran's overt enrichment program at Esfahan and Natanz. The dog that hasn't barked is Iran's covert program for acquiring nuclear weapons."[30]

Dagan, after some hesitation, moved to bridge the gap between the two countries. First, he approved an increase in collaboration with the CIA and other foreign intelligence agencies involved. Then he, together with the head of AMAN General Aaron Ze'evi Farkash, changed the terminology. They realized that the "point of no return" standard left the impression that once Iran reached that point, nothing could be done to stop them. "This was of course very wrong," said a senior Israeli intelligence official. "There is always room to do something, even if we reach desperation point."[31] The term was changed to "technological threshold," and Israeli intelligence estimates that Iran will reach this point sometime in 2007. Once they perfect the uranium enrichment technology and have a full control of it, according to the Israeli understanding, it would take them another two to three years to produce their first nuclear device.

In the meantime, the American intelligence estimate brought forward their projected date to sometime between 2010 and 2015. John Negroponte, the former director of national intelligence (currently deputy secretary of state), explained the difference in attitudes between Israel and the United States. "I think that we basically operate from the same knowledge base. We also happen to consult with the Israelis quite closely. We have intelligence-sharing arrangements, procedures. I think that sometimes what the Israelis will do—and I think that perhaps because it's a more existential issue for them—they will give you the worst-case assessment. We would agree that perhaps an equally valid assessment would be the same one that we put forward."[32]

Premier Sharon also instructed Dagan to coordinate the efforts of the various Israeli agencies working on the "Iranian file" and "to head the efforts to prevent Iran's nuclear program." Dagan and the Mossad are the facade for an interagency taskforce that includes the Israeli Atomic Energy Commission (IAEC), and the Israeli Air Force (IAF). Established in 1952, the IAEC is one of the most secretive organizations in Israel. Until a few years ago when it launched its official Web site, even its name was barely mentioned or known to the public. Its responsibility is to manage Israel's nuclear program and its various sites. Its jewel in the crown is the nuclear reactor in the desert city of Dimona. This is the site where, according to foreign intelligence estimates, Israel has been producing plutonium for an arsenal of up to two hundred nuclear warheads. The IAEC represents Israel in international organizations and forums about nuclear issues and policy. The Israeli ambassador to the IAEA in Vienna has always been a senior member of IAEC.

In the task force, the Mossad has responsibility for liaison with its international counterparts, the coordination of joint operations and the application of preventative measures through diplomatic persuasion or, if necessary, violence. Military intelligence is responsible for the overall and national estimate and together with the IAF, prepares files on sites and targets. These files would include what the target is made of and the type of armaments that would be necessary in case of a military strike. The IAF is especially proficient in performance analysis. Military intelligence also has the best units to deal with technological questions. The IAEC's part is to provide a higher-level analysis of Iran's nuclear program, and to convey the views discussed and attitudes presented at IAEA meetings. It is not an intelligence-gathering organization, but because of its experience and expertise, its contribution is noteworthy.

Since Dagan was put in charge, there have been notable successes, especially regarding international cooperation and prevention. The exchange of information between Israel and its Western counterparts led to a suspension of material and equipment shipped to Iran purchased through its front companies from Eastern and Western Europe, the Far East, and South America. An extensive international effort exposed several companies in Europe and Africa that were selling Iran dual-use equipment. In August 2005, Bulgarian custom officials stopped a truck carrying 1,000 kilograms of zirconium silicate "supplied by a British firm" that had reached the Turkish border en route to Iran.[33]

Another expose of Iran's endless efforts was revealed in early 2006 and led to the resignation of Koen Dassen, the head of the Belgium's security service. Agents from a Western intelligence informed Dassem in 2004 that Epsi, a Belgium company, was selling Iran an isostatic press, which can be used for the production of nuclear weapons. Dassem ignored the information and didn't stop the transaction.[34]

In summer 2006, another expose of Iran's purchasing front companies emerged. This time it was in Tanzania. Local officials told IAEA that they intercepted a shipment of uranium 238 originated from a mine in nearby Congo. The uranium was found hidden in a consignment of coltan, a mineral used to produce chips for cellular phones. "When we opened the container, it was full of drums of coltan. When the first rows were removed, we found behind them drums of uranium," said a Tanzanian customs official. The shipment handlers produced an "end user" certificate stating that the final destination is Kazakhstan. However, what arose suspicion was the fact that the shipment was going to travel via the Iranian port of Bandar Abbas.[35]

The end of 2006 witnessed another scandal. Tipped off by an intelligence organization, the Austrian police in southern city of Graz arrested a local businessman employed by a company called Daniel Frosch Export. The company owner, Daniel Frosch, escaped to United Arab Emirates in August 2006, a few days after the investigation was launched. As noted, the UAE is a preferred location for many purchasing and smuggling operations run by the IRGC's front companies. Some of Dr. Khan's network's shipments went through, or even originated in, the UAE. The Austrian company was suspected of supplying capacitors and accelerators that can be used in civilian industry but also in nuclear weapons.[36]

According to the Israeli intelligence estimates, 2003 was a turning point in Iran's nuclear program and its dealings with the international community. Several developments occurred that year. When sixteen years of concealment and deceit were eventually exposed, Iran realized that it could no longer continue using the Atomic Energy Organization of Iran to cover its tracks. AEOI had provided the infrastructure, know-how, technology, and international contacts. In the shadow of AEOI, Iran almost reached its nuclear destination. But with that path blocked, Iran had to look elsewhere. It therefore embarked on the secret parallel program that is only partly known to the intelligence communities and was totally unknown to the IAEA. And 2003 was also the year that Iran's Shahab 3 missile became operational, giving the country a means of delivering a nuclear weapon.

Western intelligence worked hard to keep up with these events. They had to provide not only general estimates but also solid and accurate information about them, and they had to figure out how to release the information plausibly and without burning their sources. They need what may be called "the smoking gun," which was exactly what they found with the controversial laptop discussed in chapter 8.

"The truth is," said Dr. Ephraim Asculai, a former member of the Israeli Atomic Energy Commission, "that in the nuclear field, there is no real smoking gun. What we have seen in Iran is a series of indications, developments and processes. All of them together can have only one interpretation—that Iran is seeking to produce nuclear weapons. Each of these indicators in itself cannot be the "smoking gun." As the saying goes, the proof of the pudding is in the eating. In the nuclear world, the smoking gun can be found only when Iran will have the bomb or when it tests it. But then it might be too late to act.[37]

CHAPTER TEN

Oil Punishment

A PHALANX OF gunships in battle formation roared at top speed toward the sandy beaches of the Persian Gulf. Soldiers in full combat gear jumped off onto the strand. Other ships took positions to secure the landing zone. Special and naval forces of the Pasdaran—Iran's Revolutionary Guards Corps backed by the Pasdaran's artillery and rocket units—were conducting a military exercise.

The Strait of Hormuz, a channel between Iran and Saudi Arabia, separates the Persian Gulf from the Gulf of Oman and the Indian Ocean. While it is thirty-four miles from shore to shore, its topography forces ships into two lanes only a few miles across and easily blocked. It is the narrowest point in the Persian Gulf. Through that narrow navigation lane, 40 percent of the West's oil flows from the Persian Gulf states of Iran, Iraq, Kuwait, Saudi Arabia, the United Arab Emirates, Bahrain, and Qatar. Iran took over three small islands in the Gulf in 1971, during the reign of the shah, to have full control of the traffic through the strait. The United Nations has declared that the islands belong to the United Arab Emirates but neither the shah nor Khomeini's Islamic regime have relinquished these strategic territories. Despite the Islamic regime's assertions that it is against occupation everywhere, notably

Palestine, Tehran refuses to return the islands, which significantly improve its ability to blockade the strait, to their legal owners.

The October 2006 drill was a simulated takeover of the Strait of Hormuz, which actually lay a few miles down the shore. Its real point was to show that the Iran of the ayatollahs will not tolerate sanctions and will retaliate if provoked. They have the experience, the capability, and the intention. They tried to seize control of the strait during the war with Iraq, and if they fail again, they may try to repeat an old plan—mining the shipping lanes and attacking oil tankers in the strait.

Like most of Iran's military maneuvers over the last few years, the exercise was highly publicized in the local press.[1] Video footage was given to any international television station willing to take it. The simulated takeover and especially the publicity that accompanied it were a preemptive strike against sanctions or attack. Iranian cabinet ministers, parliamentarians, military officers, and others repeatedly threatened that they would retaliate. "We have the power to halt oil supply to the last drop from the shores of the Persian Gulf via the Straits of Hormuz," Muhammad Nabi Rudaki, deputy chairman of the Iranian parliament's National Security and Foreign Policy Commission, said early in 2006.[2] This was the most explicit threat ever used by an Iranian official. Still, because Muhammad Nabi Rudaki is neither a household name in the West nor a powerful figure in Iranian politics, his threat carried little weight.

But a similar threat from Iran's Supreme Leader, Seyyed Ali Khamenei, shows the gravity of Iran's intentions. In a 2006 speech to commemorate the seventeenth anniversary of the death of Ayatollah Khomeini, Khamenei announced, "If the Americans make a wrong move toward Iran, the shipment of energy will definitely face danger, and the Americans would not be able to protect energy supply in the region."[3]

What is the true meaning of the Iranian threat? If the strait were hermetically sealed, oil prices could rise as high as $100 per barrel.[4] This, Iran believes, would be lethal to the health of Western economies. Western leaders fear that their constituents still have vivid memories of the winter of

1973–74 when the Arab oil embargo caused havoc in the West. Oil prices went from $10 a barrel to over $30, causing cold living rooms and long queues at gasoline stations. For some leaders, especially in Europe and Japan, to impose sanctions that provoke an Iranian retaliation is simply to shoot oneself in the foot. To Mahmoud Ahmadinejad, controlling the strait means the ability to change political decisions in oil-producing Arab countries. It also means that Iranian threats are palpably felt in the United Nations Security Council.

In February 2006 the IAEA decided that Iran's defiance and lack of cooperation regarding its nuclear program forced the agency to refer the Iranian case to the Security Council. The United States, which was the major advocate of punishing Iran for its nuclear violations, hoped that the five permanent members of the Council would reach a unanimous decision to impose sanctions. The Bush administration, led by its vociferous and controversial ambassador to the UN, John Bolton (who stepped down in late 2006), proposed a full range of sanctions: banning international travel by Iranian officials and scientists involved in the nuclear program, banning the sale of any nuclear-related technology or equipment, halting cooperation between the IAEA and Iran, and imposing heavier economic sanctions—mainly freezing Iranian accounts in international banks. Actually the United States desired harsher sanctions, such as a full embargo on the sale of Iranian oil, the pillar of the regime's survival.[5] But the Bush administration also knew that it would be very difficult to rally the support of its own allies—the European Union and Japan—for such a far-reaching endeavor. Therefore they settled for less.

To its disappointment, however, Washington couldn't even deliver its reduced sanctions package. After long delays and endless deliberations, the five permanent members of the Security Council reached a decision in July 2006 calling for sanctions on Iran, but without specifying their nature or their starting date. Eventually some toothless sanctions, excluding the Bushehr project, were adopted by the Security Council in late December 2006. China and Russia had refused to join strong sanctions, wanting to give

Iran more time to come to terms with the rest of the world and to agree to suspend its uranium enrichment program.[6] Resolution 1737 about sanctions on Iran bans the travel of some top Iranian officials and military personnel who are involved in the nuclear program and forbids all states in the world to supply, transfer, and sell any equipment that could assist Iran in enriching uranium and building the heavy water reactor in Arak. The resolution lists eleven officials and a few companies and organizations as being major participants in the nuclear program, headed by Atomic Energy Organization Iran.

China and Russia believed that they could convince Ahmadinejad's government to cooperate. However their political and economic interests were powerful unspoken factors in their positions. China is hooked on Iranian oil (as discussed in chapter 4), and Russia is building the nuclear reactor in Bushehr and hopes to win more contracts in Iran. Both countries also challenge U.S. supremacy in the international arena and wish to execute their own foreign policy. The sanctions imposed on Iran are symbolic and largely harmless.

Sanctions are in any case a double-edged sword. Their purpose is punishment—to force the other side to change policies or accept negotiating terms. There have been many examples of sanctions imposed either by a group of countries, such as the Arab embargo against the West in 1973, or by the UN Security Council against a single country, such as UN sanctions against Saddam Hussein's Iraq in the 1990s. But constructing useful sanctions and administering them effectively is a delicate art. The trick is to not throw out the baby with the bath water—to make sanctions work against a regime without hurting its citizens. Sanctions did not work against Saddam Hussein. Instead they hurt the Iraqi people, who already had very little, but not the elites and other beneficiaries of the regime. Similarly, sanctions on North Korea hurt the people, not the government. On the other hand, sanctions against the South Africa in the 1980s were very effective and one of the factors that brought down the apartheid regime in Pretoria in the early 1990s.

Iran is well aware of these precedents. It radiates a sense of self-confidence about surviving the sanctions and bristles with threats of retaliation. Despite its rhetoric, however, the Iranian leadership doesn't really want the international community to impose sanctions of any sort. If sanctions are imposed, their goal will be to hurt Ahmadinejad's government and the ruling classes of the theocracy. They will also undoubtedly make the poor even more desperate, and if Iranians of this class blame Ahmadinejad's government for their misery, they might turn them against him and his regime.

But in the Iranian case, such expectations could produce opposite results. Broad economic sanctions might actually rally the masses around the government and increase the popularity of Ahmadinejad. For Iranians, sanctions would not only mean punishment, but also foreign intervention and the Iranians have a bitter memory of previous foreign intervention in their internal affairs. A siege mentality and distrust of other nations is engraved in Iranian history. They feel they have been under attack from richer and more powerful countries for centuries: the Russians under the tsar, followed by the Soviet empire, on their northern border; the British circling them from the south and the east; and the Arabs from the south and the west. Some Iranians describe their country as a peacock, beautiful with colorful wings. Others are jealous and want to pluck her feathers. In the Iranian case, the feathers are her natural resources—above all, oil. National pride, foreign intervention, and oil have played a major role in shaping modern Iranian history. Foreign powers interfered with and exploited Iran during both world wars, but the most memorable incident was the deposition of Prime Minister Mossadegh, engineered in 1951 by the CIA (which we mentioned in passing in chapter 5).

Mossadegh's fateful decision was that Iran should have control over its own destiny. In that era of crumbling colonialism, he saw that there was no reason for British oil companies to rule over Iran's oil, then as today the major source of income for Iran. Mossadegh wanted to control the oil money so that it could be distributed in a more just way for the benefit of Iranians' health, welfare, education, infrastructure, and economy. In fact, Ahmadinejad's slogan of "putting oil money on every Iranian table" derives from Mossadegh's populist economic policies, which also called for the development of rural areas with oil money.

The British very quickly portrayed Mossadegh as a Communist, which he was not. Although he did ally himself with the Communist Tudeh party, which had strong ties with the Soviet Union, that was simply a tactical necessity to gain support for his nationalization policy. Dr. Mossadegh was, rather, the product of two traditions, one being the Iranian culture, which has been conservative for centuries. For example, Dr. Mossadegh did not advocate voting rights for Iranian women. That was only granted in 1963, under the shah. At the same time, he was strongly influenced by his Western liberal education. He studied law in Switzerland and believed in such basic Western principles as democracy. During his election campaign, which at times seemed like a crusade, the majority of Iranians supported Mossadegh. But he did not win the shah to his side. Ten years into his reign on the Peacock Throne, Muhammad Reza Pahlavi was still fragile, weak, inexperienced, and mostly pro-Western. He was jealous of Mossadegh's popularity and very quickly began to dislike him.

Surprisingly enough, the United States was Mossadegh's source of inspiration. He saw that U.S. oil companies were giving better deals in their contracts with countries in the region, and wanted the British oil companies to follow suit.[7] Mossadegh also sensed the increasing postwar rivalry between the British and Americans, and tried to create a wedge between them. The Iranian prime minister approached the United States for loans that would have enabled him to carry out some of his projects for the country. His scheme worked temporarily, as President Harry S Truman's administration rejected the British offers to join forces against Mossadegh. However, after Republican Dwight D. Eisenhower was elected in 1952, American policy changed. Under the influence of the Dulles brothers—secretary of state John Foster and CIA director Allen—President Eisenhower joined forces with the British on a plan to remove the Iranian nationalist "troublemaker."

In the rabidly anti-Communist atmosphere of the McCarthy era, Washington became increasingly wary of Mossadegh's close cooperation with the Tudeh party. American and British cooperation increased when Mossadegh's government nationalized the oil industry. The British immediately placed an embargo on the sale of Iranian oil and blocked the Strait of Hormuz with gunboats. Not a single barrel of Iranian oil left the Persian Gulf. The British also froze Iranian government money deposited in foreign banks. Like the Americans' hope about sanctions on Ahmadinejad's government, the British hoped that the oil embargo and sanctions would worsen living conditions for the masses, who would turn against Mossadegh and demonstrate in the streets.

They did not. Although the sanctions did create economic hardships for many, most Iranians were ready to suffer and to support Mossadegh. It was a matter of national pride and blatant foreign intervention. There were massive public demonstrations, but they were not the ones the British had wanted. Under the influence of the British and the Americans, the shah fired Mossadegh and replaced him with Ghavam el Saltaneh, who was ready to negotiate with the British to end the sanctions. When the public heard this, thousands poured into the streets around the country in protest. Riots broke out and continued for three days, until the shah was forced to bring Mossadegh back.

Eventually it was the shah who left the country. The British and the Americans instructed him to leave, hoping that it would create an uproar that would add to their efforts to destabilize Mossadegh's government. That did not happen either. Mossadegh's popularity worried the British and the Americans so much that they decided that the only way to get rid of him was through a coup d'état.

Consequently the CIA and Britain's MI6 set up Operation Ajax, whose aim was to stir up domestic trouble and provoke internal Iranian factions to turn against Mossadegh and depose him. Kermit Roosevelt, a senior CIA operative and nephew of President Theodore Roosevelt, was placed in charge of the operation.

To depose Mossadegh, the British and the Americans applied the same divide-and-conquer strategy that he had originally tried to use against them. Realizing that the Tudeh party provided much of Mossadegh's parliamentary support, the CIA paid demonstrators to dress up as Tudeh supporters, hold up pro-Tudeh placards, and incite riots.

Mossadegh, worried about increasing instability in Iran, ordered the police to suppress the rioters, which in turn angered his Tudeh allies. They withdrew their support for him, costing Mossadegh his major ally. Although the religious establishment was opposed to the Pahlavis, the ayatollahs also condemned Mossadegh's close relations with the Tudeh and therefore they sat on the fence. Mossadegh was cornered. Street violence spread, the police did not obey his orders and he lost control of the country. The shah returned and Roosevelt's brilliant plan worked.

The Mossadegh affair was a watershed in the modern history of Iran. It consolidated the shah's power for the next quarter century and increased Western influence in Iran. But it also led to the creation of a new breed of revolutionaries, including Mahmoud Ahmadinejad, who wanted Iran to control its oil and its oil money for the development of Iran's economy. They didn't want Iran to turn into a market for Western consumer goods but, rather, for Iranian companies to develop their own expertise while adhering to the country's religious traditions. The Islamic revolutionaries, like Mossadegh, want to use the oil money to build a better future for the Iranian people and like him they are ready to take advantage of Western technology. Unlike him, however, they are guided by religious fanatics.

The events of 1951–53 are used now as a model. The combination of oil, street demonstrations, conspiracy, and the likelihood of a regime change are precedents that every participant in the Iranian game is reconsidering. Neo-conservatives in the Bush administration and a special unit in the Israeli defense ministry led by Uri Lobrani, the former Israeli ambassador to Tehran, believe the process could be repeated.

In Washington, the Pentagon also set up a special secret group to assess the chances of a regime change in Iran. Some of its members held the same attitudes that pushed the administration to launch the war against Iraq—that regime change is a valid instrument of state policy that can be implemented by force and punishment. The Bush administration was hoping that they could rally enough Iranians inside the country to destabilize the ayatollah's regime and eventuality to bring it down. The basic modus operandi was to repeat the tricks of Kermit Roosevelt.

In fact, this was mostly wishful thinking. It depended largely on information from three sources: the Iranian monarchists around Reza Cyrus Pahlavi, known as Baby Shah, the son of the late shah, now in his late forties; the Mujahedeen Khalq, which the State Department calls a terrorist group; and a disparate group, some of them conmen and charlatans, who either had no real contacts inside Iran or were motivated by personal interests and vendettas.[8] The dependence on unreliable sources and the bad analysis that derives from them is reminiscent of at least two colossal failures of U.S. intelligence and foreign policy: the failed invasion of Fidel Castro's Cuba in 1961 and the invasion of Iraq in 2003, which was encouraged by exiled Iraqis including Ahmad Chalabi of the Iraqi National Congress, who claimed to have a base inside his homeland. Burned in Iraq, the CIA has no faith in the neoconservatives' ability to lift their grandiose scheme off the Iranian ground, and in Iran expects a bitter failure, even bigger than in Iraq.

The Israeli analysis is less ambitious and more realistic. It evolved less around personas and more around processes. In the early 1980s, the Israeli government assigned Lobrani, a former ambassador to Iran and an expert on the Shiites, to create a special office to coordinate Israeli policy in Lebanon. He quickly recognized the growing influence of revolutionary Iran there and convened a special team of experts inside the ministry of defense to analyze the political landscape of Iran and the probability of regime change.

"I had no doubts that the opposition to the regime is weak," Lobrani said. "Change would not take place from outside. Neither the Iranian exile community in Los Angeles nor the Mujahedeen Khalq *is* capable of doing it. They have no constituency inside Iran."[9] Lobrani is a strong believer in propaganda and disinformation. His plan is to establish radio and television stations that would broadcast directly to Iran and provide accurate information interspersed with antigovernment propaganda. He pointed to the fact that despite the autocratic nature of the regime, Iran is a relatively free society. There are 100,000 Iranian Web sites. Farsi is the fourth most popular language on the

Internet. This means that spreading information and exchanging ideas are possible. Israel is already doing it with the Farsi language service of the Voice of Israel. However, Lobrani is disappointed that the Bush administration hasn't done more in this area. There are several radio stations—Radio Farda and Voice of America—and several television channels broadcasting in Farsi from America. "It's not enough," said Lobrani. "They could have done much more. Especially since Congress had allocated sufficient funds for this purpose."[10]

Lobrani also points to history. Iranians know how to protest in the streets. "Mossadegh brought them out into the streets and against the shah, and I witnessed Khomeini doing exactly the same, also against the shah. So why not, after proper preparations laying the seeds of discontent, turn the masses against the ayatollahs? What they did to others can be done to them."[11]

Lastly, Lobrani and his experts point out that Iran is not a homogenous society. Its 70 million people are divided into smaller and larger minorities. The most prominent, and to a certain degree the most discontented, are 17 million Azeris in the northwest, 5 million Kurds in the west, two million Arabs in the southwest and nearly 2 million Baluchis in the southeast. Although Lobrani and his small unit might have dreams of splitting up Iran, they know it's almost impossible to achieve alone. Israel does not have the financial and human resources. If the United States spent billions of dollars over several years to turn the ethnic minority groups against the central government, perhaps it could happen. Instead, Lobrani has a much more limited aim in mind. He wishes to create unrest among the minority groups that they would turn against the central government. Rather than promoting a regime change, this is an effort to destabilize the country.

Iran offers fertile ground for such plans. Unemployment is very high, with the unofficial rate being 20 percent. Every year 1.5 million professionals graduate from universities but have difficulties finding suitable jobs. Four million Iranians live outside the country. One hundred and fifty thousand leave Iran each year. In 1979 Tehran had 1.5 million inhabitants; now 15 million people live there. According to the figures of the World Bank, there are several hundred thousand prostitutes in Iran. Many young girls are sold into white slavery to become prostitutes in the Persian Gulf emirates. Despite Iran's large revenues from oil, 40 percent of the population earn $1 a day. Inside the establishment, there is confusion and rivalry. Iran effectively has three military organizations: the official army, the IRGC, and the Basij militia. It has fifteen different intelligence and security agencies, which are not only watching the opposition and enemies within and without, but also spying on each other.

With all these facts in mind, the small Lobrani team believes Iran is not beyond the reach of destabilization. "It will take time, conviction and solid preparation, yet it's doable," he added. Discontent, according to Lobrani, can lead to unrest and eventually to demonstrations in the streets. Another idea is to offer financial incentives to the workers of the oil industry to go on strike, as happened during the Mossadegh affair and the early days of the Islamic revolution. "We know from these precedents that the Iranian public has experience in demonstrating in the streets. Then the police and the army move in. This is the stuff that makes revolutions and eventually regime change," concluded the energetic eighty-year-old, who still vividly remembers his days in Iran and speaks fondly about its people.

Other experts, however, dismiss both the American and the Israeli ideas regarding destabilization and regime change. They suggest that the majority of Iranians, even those who dislike Ahmadinejad and his messianic allies, draw different lessons from the Mossadegh affair; they see instead the evils of foreign intervention and conspiracy against their country. Many people, however twisted their logic might be, blame foreigners for some of the misery they have suffered under the ayatollahs. Take, for example, Mrs. Fateme S.

"As soon as we landed, my shivering stopped. Until then I was shaking like a leaf. I must have recited prayers twenty times during the damn flight. Thank God we made it back," Fateme S. said after her flight in a Russian-made Tupolev 154 landed in Tehran from Tabriz. "This is the last time I am sitting in one of these flying Russian death traps." Having lived in England for many years, she was used to taking flights to places as far as Australia without any problem. "I used to enjoy flying. It was a wonderful experience, but not any more."

But flying in Iran can make you feel you're gambling with your life. Old Russian aircraft are everywhere, and most passengers recount similar experiences—horrifying tales of how the whole plane sometimes shakes violently during flight. Some passengers fear the wings are going to fall off. These experiences are made scarier by reports about air crashes; Iran has one of the worst air safety records anywhere in the world. Russian airlines have stopped using these planes, or are in the process of getting rid of their locally produced planes in favor of brand-new Airbuses and Boeings. But instead of mothballing them, the Russians found desperate customers for the old fleet—the Iranians.

Fateme S.'s flying difficulties were a result of the poor maintenance and mismanagement of the Iranian airline industry. The inability to purchase advanced, safe aircraft is due to the Islamic Republic's poor relations with the countries that are producing good airplanes. One would have expected an educated Iranian like Fateme S., a former MBA student from London City University who went back to Iran to get married, to reach the logical conclusion. But for her the culprit is elsewhere. "You know who I blame? The Americans," she said. "They are doing everything they can to make our lives as difficult as possible. It's not safe to fly in Iran anymore because they don't allow us to buy new U.S. or European passenger jets. Do they think we are going to turn them into F-16 fighter planes?"[12]

Iran was offered to purchase new, Western-made airplanes.[13] If the Ahmadinejad government stopped enriching uranium, even Boeing was allowed and ready to sell them new aircraft. Ahmadinejad chose to continue the uranium enrichment program, and to use the offer to turn his people against the West. He is spreading the argument, so well absorbed by Fateme, that the Americans are at fault, not his government.

To rub salt in the wound, proud Iranians have to endure national disgrace and embarrassment. Iran Air, the national airline, was one of the most modern airlines in the Middle East during the days of the shah. With its blue-and-white color scheme and its *homa*, a creature from Persian mythology, the airline was the pride of Iranians. Now Iranian passengers sigh in disappointment when they see brand-new commercial jets operated by poorer, third-world countries park next to their almost ancient Iran Air planes. For them it's a depressing sign of how Iran is falling behind. Yet they don't wish to be rewarded if they have to be "punished" for the opportunities offered to them. Most Iranians would like to have nuclear technology and a thriving nuclear enrichment program simultaneously with brand-new Boeings and Airbuses. They don't see the choice that the Western world is offering them: "if you want our technology to modernize your economy, you need to accommodate some of our demands. You are asking to have your cake and eat it, too." However, many Iranians perceive that as their national right. They don't think they have to compromise.

Instead, they raise another argument: Why are you picking on us? Why are we discriminated against? Iranian representatives to the IAEA point out that Israel has nuclear weapons, but Iran doesn't. Why then are the Americans providing financial and military assistance to Israel instead of sanctioning her? Many Iranians compare their situation to Pakistan, which has nuclear weapons that it has tested near the Iranian border. Yet President Pervez Musharraf is America's ally while Iran is accused of sponsoring terrorism because Iranians were involved in the bombing of the Jewish Community Center and the Israeli embassy in Buenos Aires, and the U.S. base in Saudi Arabia. If Iran supports Lebanese Hezbollah and Palestinian Hamas and Islamic Jihad, so does Pakistan support extremist causes. Pakistan supported and installed the Taliban in Afghanistan, and it was the Taliban that sponsored Osama bin Laden's al Qaeda, which killed 3,000 Americans on September 11, 2001. The Pakistani secret service is nurturing Muslim terrorists fighting India. And Pakistan, too, is undemocratic: General Musharraf took power from a democratically elected government in a coup d'état in 1999. Iran, with presidential and parliamentary elections every four years, is far more democratic than Pakistan.

Many Iranians, not only government officials and not only the paranoid, argue that the West discriminates against Iranians merely because they are Iranians. They cannot see any other reason why the West is playing a hypocritical double game. Support for their argument is available today, in Zardeh, where Iraq used chemical weapons in 1988, (as described in chapter 6). According to the United Nations, during the eight-year war between Iraq and Iran, Saddam Hussein's forces dropped more than 2,000 tons of chemical weapons on civilian and military targets in Iran.

One of the few perceptions shared by the majority of Iranians and the government regards Western behavior in regard to chemical weapons. The West, especially America, was aware of Iraq's use of chemical weapons, but did nothing to stop it. In the 1980s, Saddam Hussein was a U.S. ally. The Reagan administration provided him with loans and intelligence to enhance the efficiency of his war machine against Iran. By flagrantly using WMD, Saddam Hussein broke every international law. However, to the anger of millions of Iranians, no sanctions were imposed against his regime as a result. The Iranians claim that the Western bias against Iran reached a crescendo when George H. W. Bush, then U.S. ambassador to the UN, said that Iran might have used these weapons against its own soldiers and citizens to gain international sympathy.

Sanctions against Iran were imposed for the second time, nearly thirty years after Mossadegh, following the Islamic revolution. In retaliation for the takeover of the U.S. embassy in Tehran and holding its inhabitants hostage, the United States embargoed the sale of civil aviation technology to Iran. These are the sanctions that are turning flying into a traumatic experience for Fateme.

Of course the embargo did not halt air traffic in Iran. People still fly. It's a daunting experience, yet they still do it. They have no other choice. Iran is 2,200 miles from northwest to southeast and 1,200 miles from northeast to southwest. The old Tupolevs may be an embarrassment and a flying hazard, but they nevertheless offer a solution of some kind. They also send a message to the West that the civil aviation sanctions have been a failure and that the West should think twice before believing that economic sanctions will make Iran capitulate. Even Secretary of State Madeline Albright openly admitted, "It is easy to see now why many Iranians continue to resent this intervention by America in their internal affairs."[14]

The Iranian government has another persuasive argument, at least for domestic consumption. As in Iraq, no smoking gun has been found to substantiate claims that Iran is in fact making a bomb. This has been repeatedly stated by Muhammad el-Baradei and his IAEA reports.[15] Even senior Israeli military officials agree.[16] This acknowledgement, along with Iranian claims that its nuclear program is for peaceful purposes only, are working in the government's favor. The Iranian people are not very happy with their government, especially when it comes to issues such as democracy, human rights, and the dismal performance of the economy. In fact, many of them loathe the current system. However, because of Western embargoes that have hurt Iran's population, some Iranians have come to view Western governments, especially the United States, as responsible—or worse, as their enemy.

The national sentiment is enabling the Iranian regime to justify its stance in the nuclear negotiations. In fact, this is one area where even people who did not vote for Ahmadinejad support his policy. Although the reformists disagree with his negotiation tactic, Ahmadinejad's cry of "Why them and not us?" has brought out nationalistic fervor in many Iranians. Therefore if broad economic sanctions are imposed against Iran, it is extremely probable that they would bring the regime and the public closer. They will not convince the Iranian regime to give up its nuclear program and they will make it easy for Ahmadinejad to blame the West for the stresses that they will bring to Iran's economy. This in turn will make it much easier for the Iranian regime to deflect internal criticism. In fact, in a way sanctions may help Ahmadinejad escape responsibility for the failures of his economic policies.

The West is faced with a serious dilemma. If Ahmadinejad is left to his own devices, his popularity may be more likely to drop, because of the defects of his economic policies. This was already manifested in the December 2006 local elections. Ahmadinejad's ultraconservative camp suffered heavy losses to its rivals, the moderate conservatives. In some cities, his supporters did not win any seats at all. Even in Tehran they barely won 20 percent of the city council. If this trend continues, he will not have the luxury of blaming the West, and the Iranian people might show him the door in the next presidential election. But does the international community have the luxury of resting its hopes on the wisdom and judgment of the Iranian people? There is also the risk that nothing might happen. Ahmadinejad would be left in power and allowed to realize his nuclear aspirations.

CHAPTER ELEVEN

Preventive Strike

THE TWIST OF history couldn't escape Major General Eitan Ben Eliyahu. He was reviewing some top-secret intelligence reports and files of potential targets of Israel's enemies when his eyes suddenly focused on the name of Khorramashahr—his father's birthplace in Iran. In 1922, seventy-two years earlier, his father had immigrated to the land that was then still officially called Eretz Israel—Palestine, a mandate of the British Empire. Ben Eliyahu was born in 1944 in Jerusalem, four years before the end of British rule and the birth of the state of Israel. Now, at the age of fifty-two, he was the newly appointed eleventh commander of the highly regarded Israeli Air Force.[1] He was sitting behind his desk at his office in Hakirya, Israel's Pentagon—a complex of buildings at the heart of Tel Aviv home to several military and ministry of defense offices. "I thought to myself," he recalled, "who knows, one day, I might have to take the tough and unpleasant decision of sending my boys to launch air strikes against Iranian missile sites and military installations, including Khoramshahr."[2]

Battles and air strikes were familiar to Major General Ben Eliyahu. As a young F-4 squadron commander during the October 1973 Yom Kippur War he downed two Egyptian fighter planes. Eight years later he flew in the attack on Iraq's nuclear reactor located near Baghdad. Eight F-16s supported by eight F-15s left on June 7, 1981, from an IAF air base near the Red Sea resort of Eilat, penetrated Jordanian and Saudi Arabian air spaces without permission and without being noticed, and reached the reactor from an unexpected direction. Ben Eliyahu was not among the eight leading F-16 pilots who dropped bombs in two waves. He was an escort to repel enemy planes if the attackers were discovered.[3] The raid on the French-made reactor (which the French called Osirak and the Iraqis Tammuz) lasted two minutes. It was a classic preventive strike, aiming to prevent Saddam Hussein from making nuclear bombs.[4] The daring, internationally praised operation, which completely destroyed the reactor, was so successful that voices in Israel and elsewhere are now calling for a similar strike against Iran's nuclear sites.

Premier Menachem Begin, a man deeply influenced by the Holocaust, ordered the raid. He frequently used the words "never again." Never again in the history of mankind would the Jewish people face an existential threat. The Begin doctrine essentially asserted that Israel would never allow any country in the Middle East to possess nuclear weapons that could threaten its existence.[5] An Israeli government that decided to attack Iran to prevent it from having nuclear weapons would be implementing the Begin doctrine.

During his four-year tenure as air force commander, Eitan Ben Eliyahu was not required to face his dilemma. Yet more than any of his predecessors he is to be credited with preparing Israel for the Iranian nuclear challenge. If Israel attacks Iran's military or nuclear sites in the near future, squadrons of fighters and bombers purchased because of Ben Eliyahu will carry out the strikes. His decisions also reformed the IAF and turned it into Israel's long-distance strategic arm. A few months after he took office in 1996, despite criticism by many of his colleagues, he ordered the purchase of twenty-five McDonnell-Douglas (now Boeing) F-15I advanced planes, the first Israeli purchase of the weapon. Israel had received its first batch of F-15s in 1977, but they were inferior and had a limited range. Although they had been used in the raid on Iraq, they were incapable of reaching Iran.

The $2.1 billion purchase of F-15Is was a very expensive and controver-
sial one. Each plane cost $84 million. Many of Israel's strategic planners
thought the planes were a waste of money. Why should Israel need a long-
range fighter-bomber? Why deviate from past strategic patterns in which
Israel equipped its air force with planes capable of reaching its immediate
enemies—Egypt, Syria, and Iraq? These targets only required a flying range
of approximately 1,000 miles. Major General Ben Eliyahu was adamant. "I
realized that Israel's future challenges were extending. I felt that the next
threat was emerging from Iran and thought it appropriate that we have
planes capable of flying long distances, 2,000 miles and more."[6] In the Israel
military parlance this is called "threats beyond the horizon." Ben Eliyahu
decided that the F-15I, nicknamed in Israel "Raam" (Thunder), was the
right answer. From that moment on, the IAF has had a "mixed" capability
of longer-range F-15s fighter-bombers, together with shorter-range F-16s,
which would serve as escorts to fend off enemy fighters. Both planes enable
the IAF to conduct long-range strategic operations.

Ben Eliyahu's thinking was unconventional for other reasons, too. The
IAF had always characterized itself with phrases like "we are the best in the
world," "we don't need anyone," "we can do it better" or "no one can teach
us." Other air forces were viewed with contempt and any notion of cooperation with them was heresy. Ben Eliyahu broke these taboos. During his
four-year tenure he developed an extensive program of collaboration with
foreign air forces. Israeli pilots started joint exercises with American air force
and navy pilots. Over the Israeli Negev desert and the Mediterranean, they
practiced joint flight formations and simulated dog-fights.[7] Under Ben
Eliyahu's command, extensive exchange programs with NATO air forces
were established as well.[8] "I was already then thinking," Ben Eliyahu
explained, "about the possibility that one day we might be involved in joint
operations against a common enemy and of course what I had in mind above
all was Iran."

Nevertheless even the visionary Ben Eliyahu couldn't change some old
habits of his macho troops. Almost every IAF commander made some

inflammatory remark about Iran at some time—"We are capable of reaching any place in Middle East—Iran included" or "Israel's long arm will reach our enemies."[9] The remarks were intended to boost the morale of the Israeli public and to increase the self-confidence of the pilots. Ben Eliyahu, who mixes soft speech and good manners with arrogance and overconfidence, was not an exception. Twice during his tenure he made such statements, and repeated them when he was out of active service.

This kind of Israeli rhetoric has always angered the Iranians. Each time an Israeli leader or military commander hinted about a possibility of "dealing with Iran," Iranian leaders perceived it as a threat and replied with counter-threats. For example, in an unambiguous message, commander of the Iranian Army Muhammad Salimi stated in spring 2006, "We will deal seriously with all threats (made by) the Israelis and the Americans. The people behind these threats are playing with fire. We warn them against becoming involved in a war of aggression against us."[10]

The Israeli attitude was shaped by the successful attack on the Iraqi nuclear reactor, which created the belief that IAF could do anything it decided to do and that Israeli leaders were ready to take bold and risky decisions. Their military planners gained an image of conceiving imaginative ideas, thinking "outside the box," and the invincible Israeli pilots translated those ideas into daring operations. The Israeli leadership and military commanders became prisoners of their own myth. For nearly two decades the Iraqi nuclear reactor strike had a life of its own, a legacy with no relevance to reality. But in recent years Israeli commanders and security chiefs have come to terms with the reality. Their language is cautious, modest, and less bombastic.

No one better reflects the new spirit than Brigadier General Relik Shafir. The fifty-three-year-old tall and heavily built pilot (now turned high-tech entrepreneur) is, like Ben Eliyahu, a veteran of Israel's wars. He left the military in 2003, after realizing that he would never become the IAF commander. In his thirty years of experience he served in a range of assignments that makes him an astute observer. He flew both F-15 and F-16 planes. Between 1979 and 1982 he shot down five Syrian MiGs and Sukhois in aerial dogfights. He commanded Tel Nof, Israel's biggest air base, which according to foreign intelligence assessments houses Israel's nuclear squadron. He also participated in the raid on Iraq's Osirak reactor. He was no. 7 in the formation. His partner was Ilan Ramon, the Israeli astronaut who died in the Columbia Shuttle disaster in 2004. "The planning and the practicing for the Iraqi mission were very meticulous. The execution was relatively very easy," he recalled. "It was a piece of cake. We flew at a very low altitude, a few meters above the desert ground. No one saw us. There was no resistance on our way there. Only when we reached the target were we fired at. It was scattered antiaircraft fire, nothing serious. I was more excited by the historic and national significance and symbolism of the raid rather its operational aspects, which weren't that dangerous. I saw the reactor dome and dropped my bombs from two miles. It was a clear and big target. Nothing of that sort is expected if Iran is attacked."[11]

Brigadier General Shafir's favorable assessment of Iran is based on his professional experience and knowledge. "The Iranians drew the lessons from our attack on the Iraqi nuclear reactor. Unlike Iraq, whose whole nuclear program was concentrated in the reactor, the Iranians spread their nuclear facilities around the country. Some of them are located in the eastern parts of Iran, beyond the reach of Israel. They 'hardened' their facilities by building them in underground bunkers." Iran realized it should not to put all its eggs in one basket, a conclusion Saddam Hussein also reached after the attack. He ordered an alternative nuclear program, larger and concealed in underground bunkers.[12]

There are two major challenges to an air strike against Iran. The first one is gathering precise information, if not about all the sites, at least about the most important ones. Although the intelligence has improved a great deal in recent years (as discussed in chapter 9), it is still incomplete. The second, even more urgent, hurdle is the "hardening" of Iran's major nuclear sites. *Hardening* is a cold war term that means to conceal a nuclear arsenal from the enemy by building and storing the arsenal underground, making it difficult to detect, penetrate or destroy.[13]

Some, but not all, of Iran's nuclear sites are built in underground halls and tunnels. The uranium conversion plant in Esfahan and the Arak reactor are aboveground and relatively exposed. But the uranium enrichment facilities in Natanz are apparently housed in two large halls, each roughly 30,000 square feet dug 8 to 23 feet below ground level and covered by multiple tiers of hardened concrete supported by metal structures. Each of the halls is 170 feet wide by 190 feet long with walls roughly two feet thick. The entrances to these underground structures are also protected against an aerial attack either by a "gliding" bomb or a direct hit.[14] In discussing a military strike against Iran's nuclear sites, no one, either in the United States or Israel, speaks of using nuclear weapons.

"Frankly the IAF doesn't have real strategic capability to bomb distant targets for a prolonged period of time with the required intensity and firepower," Brigadier General Shafir calculated. "To accomplish that, there is a need for long-range bombers that can carry a heavy load of bombs, the bunker-buster type, and the capability to execute what is called carpet bombing," which means to drop many bombs of up to forty tons on a single target.[15]

The Israeli political and military leadership has slowly but gradually accepted this harsh reality. For this reason, combative premier Ariel Sharon suddenly started talking in 2003 about an international effort to tackle the Iranian nuclear threat. Sharon ordered his cabinet ministers and generals to lower the Israeli profile by eschewing provocative declarations. Sharon realized, based on analysis provided to him by Israeli intelligence, that Israel alone does not have sufficient military capability to destroy Iran's nuclear sites.[16]

Sharon and his successor, Ehud Olmert, have high expectations for what they refer to as comprehensive package of "coercive" or punitive measures against Iran.[17] They advocate gradual sanctions leading eventually to full-fledged economic sanctions, including on Iran's oil industry. These would be supplemented by covert operations inside Iran against some nuclear sites as well as by scientists and engineers working for the nuclear program. As a last resort, they envision military operations. The United States and some of its allies—the United Kingdom, France, Germany, and Italy, according to Israeli thinking—should carry out these operations. Iran has reached the same conclusion that Israeli military options are very limited. One of the proponents of such a thinking is Ali Larijani, the secretary of the Supreme National Security Council (SNSC).

Larijani is considered to be one of the most rigid, highly politicized civil servants of the regime. This is despite the fact that he studied during the early 1970s at the University of California at Berkeley. During his studies he met with Menachem Megidor, an Israeli professor. "I met him," recalled Megidor, now president of the Hebrew University of Jerusalem, "through his brother," Muhammad Javad Ardashir Larijani. The Larijani brothers were born to Ayatollah Hashem Amoli, a religious scholar of Iraqi descent. The brothers were raised in a religious tradition, but their family sent them to acquire secular education in sciences. In the early 1970s they arrived at Berkeley. Muhammad Javad enrolled in the PhD program in mathematics, while Ali from switched to philosophy and political science. "Muhammad Javad attended some of my classes," added Professor Megidor. "He was a good student and we became friends. We went out together for dinner and had long conversations about life in general and politics. He and Ali were quite open. I never realized that they came from a religious background. They never mentioned it or gave the impression that one day they would be prominent members of a hard-line Islamic regime. They were very critical of the American support for the shah, but they sounded to me like more of leftists using the usual terminology of American imperialism and anticapitalist slogans. In this context they also talked very critically of Israel, because of its alliance with the shah regime. However, in their talks with me they never questioned the right of Israel to exist." The brothers returned to Iran before the Revolution. Muhammad Javad served as the director of the Institute for Studies in Theoretical Physics and Mathematics in Tehran, was a member of the Majlis and the director of its research center, and a vice minister of foreign affairs. In March 2006, the Supreme Leader brought him back to the fold and appointed him "diplomat at large," in order to improve Iran's diplomatic standing in the international arena. Professor Megidor continued to maintain some contacts with the brothers: "Occasionally I would receive regards from them via mutual professional friends."[18]

That was in the past. However it is extremely difficult to contemplate that the Larijani brothers of today would dare deal with their Israeli acquaintances when they are preparing their nation for a future conflict with the Jewish state. "Israel was not in a position to attack Iran," asserted Ali Larijani, who is also the chief Iranian nuclear negotiator.[19]

The natural conclusion from such assessments is that realistically only the Americans have the military capability to do the job. After President George W. Bush labeled Iran one of three countries—together with North Korea and Iraq—in an "axis of evil" in his 2002 State of the Union address, contingency plans were drawn up in the Pentagon, in the White House, by the Joint Chiefs of Staff and by the CIA. This is a routine procedure for military and defense planners, who are professionally required to draw up plans based upon every eventuality, including a worst-case scenario. It doesn't necessarily mean that an attack is imminent.

Although military planners should not fight past wars, the U.S. wars against Iraq in 1991 and 2003 could be used as a precedent. The support of states neighboring Iraq enabled the United States to deploy its forces there. From air and naval bases in Saudi Arabia, United Arab Emirates, Qatar, Kuwait, Oman, and Turkey, its military launched air and maritime strikes. The United States already has bases in Afghanistan, Turkey, Iraq, and some of the Arab Emirates along the Persian Gulf. Other countries may offer additional bases upon request. The United States already has aircraft carriers of its Fifth Fleet, the naval component of Central Command, in the Persian Gulf.

Once the support of the neighboring countries is guaranteed, the United States can deploy large numbers of aircraft, ships, and submarines in the theater of operation. They can launch multiple strikes of cruise missiles fired from submarines and ships sailing in the Indian Ocean and even as far away as the Mediterranean. Most important would be air strikes. Unlike Israel, or any other nation, the United States can launch hundreds of thousands of sorties over a period of several weeks, involving hundreds of bombers and fighters simultaneously, without exhausting its resources. Another important tool is the midair refueling capability, which is unmatched by any other country.

Most of Iran's nuclear sites—even if it has dozens of them—can be attacked. It won't be an easy assignment, however. Not only because the sites have been hardened, but also because Iran has protected them with anti-aircraft missiles that are not very advanced. "The Iranian military is an odd amalgamation of high and low tech. At present, Iranian air defense appears nontrivial, but certainly not incredibly potent." said a research study by MIT.[20] Iran has three layers of defense run separately by the air force and the IRGC. Cooperation between them is not the best in the world, to say the least, placing a severe handicap on Iran's efforts to defend itself.

The first line of defense is combat aircraft. Half of them are outdated American and French planes bought in the days of the shah. The other half, mostly Russian- and some Chinese-made MiGs and Sukhois, are lower quality than U.S. planes. Iran has fewer than two hundred planes, outnumbered by both the Israeli and the American air capabilities. The Iranian pilots are not considered to be of high quality for a variety of reasons, mainly lack of training and because their selection leans heavily on ideological affinity rather than professional skills.

The second line of Iran's defense is surface-to-air missiles (SAMs) supplied by the Russians in the last two years, and with more promised, despite American and Israeli protests. Iran has deployed them around its nuclear sites, and already has placed them on high alert, as if an attack were imminent. However, their inventory of SAMs "has numerous limitations," according to the MIT research.[21] Some of them are old and lack spare parts. But some of the anti-aircraft missiles that have been recently purchased—especially the SA 15, known as the "Gauntlet"—are considered to be good quality and can pose a serious threat to any air attack. The third layer is the anti-aircraft artillery, which defends the sites against low-altitude attacks.

In an American attack on Iran, the primary force would be the big bombers, mainly B1s and B2s, equipped with state-of-the-art munitions.

The attack would be characterized by precision and weight. The precision is provided by laser-guided bombs and missiles. The weight is delivered by the guided bomb unit-28 (GBU), nicknamed the "bunker buster."[22] This special weapon designed to penetrate hardened targets was originally developed to penetrate Iraqi command centers located deep underground. These bombs would be mainly used against Iran's underground nuclear sites, especially Natanz, but even before knocking out nuclear sites, the first waves of the attack would have to focus simultaneously on three additional sets of targets, according to the contingency plans. These include:

- Iran's layers of defense—airbases, aircraft, anti-aircraft missiles and anti-aircraft artillery
- Centers of command and communication, to disrupt the leadership's ability to control and coordinate the war efforts
- Iran's long-range ground-to-ground missiles, especially the Shahab, to paralyze or at least reduce Iran's ability to retaliate

The crucial question, however, is not the capability, but the will. Is the U.S. administration ready to attack Iran over its nuclear program? Before the invasion of Iraq, the American administration would not have hesitated to deal militarily with Iran, if necessary. Even after the invasion of Iraq, the neocons, led by Vice President Dick Cheney, entertained the notion. They were focusing on the "coming wars."[23] More than a year after toppling Saddam Hussein, when it was already clear that things had not turned out as desired, the U.S. House of Representatives, in a 376–3 vote, passed a resolution calling on the U.S. government "to use all appropriate means to deter, dissuade, and prevent Iran from acquiring nuclear weapons."[24] Had the Senate passed a similar resolution, it would have given President Bush or any future administration the authority to launch a preventive strike on Iran's nuclear facilities.[25]

Since mid-2005, however, and especially after the Republican defeat in the November 2006 elections, the picture has vastly changed. The Bush administration will not only have a difficult time making a decision to attack Iran, but also to receive the backing of Congress, where the Democratic Party has renewed strength, and that of the public. Even beyond political will or public opinion, there will be military limitations as long as the American troops are stuck in Iraq and helping to put down a growing threat from the Taliban in Afghanistan. It is very unlikely that the United States would have the sufficient military resources to take on three fronts at the same time.

Yet Israeli leaders hinted that they have a guarantee from President Bush that he would not allow Iran to have nuclear weapons. Israeli prime minister Ehud Olmert claimed that he had received such a guarantee to Israeli reporters during a trip to Germany in the second week of December 2006. If indeed such a promise was made, it can be interpreted in two ways. One is that eventually President Bush's strong commitment to Israel's security and existence, nurtured by his deep religious faith, would impel him, against the odds, to attack Iran. The second is that Israel would have to do the job itself after all, but with either public support or tacit encouragement from the administration. Indeed there are growing voices inside Israel in favor of such a decision, even if the results would be limited and partial.[26] "Assuming that a military strike is ordered, Israel cannot hope to destroy Iran's entire nuclear infrastructure and would have settle for a strategy of "narrowing the target set."[27]

Israel would face obstacles in several areas, even assuming it has the intelligence required to make such an attack effective and viable.

- Training: Israeli pilots would have to train (they may already be doing so) repeatedly on models, as they did with Osirak.
- Planning: Israeli planners would have to concentrate on a limited number of sites. One can assume that the most essential sites are those directly involved in manufacturing nuclear material itself—the fissile material production. This means Esfahan's conversion plant, the starting point for the uranium enrichment process; the Natanz enrichment facilities; Arak's heavy-water plant and the

nearby construction on the nuclear reactor. It can be assumed that an attack would also try to destroy sites that, according to precise intelligence, are involved with weaponization and parallel uranium enrichment. (The Bushehr power plant, for instance, is not essential to Iran's nuclear weapons program).[28]

- Execution: "Israeli deep-strike capability remains centered on F15s and F16s," according to the MIT research study.[29] The hundred or so fighters and bombers that would be participating in an attack would need midair refueling and on-board early warning and communication centers. Israel may also use its submarines to launch missile attacks.[30]

- Munitions: The IAF has an Israeli-made penetrating bomb, known as the PB500A1, and recently Israel has purchased GBUs from the United States. Major General Eitan Ben Eliyahu said, "Even if one bomb would not suffice to penetrate, we could guide other bombs directly to the hole created by the previous ones and eventually destroy any target."[31]

- Target designation: Israel has at least two Special Forces units dedicated to locating targets. One is Sayeret Shaldag, specializing in laser-marking the targets. The other one is responsible for post-strike damage assessment.[32]

- Routes: Israel has three theoretically possible routes. One is to approach Iran via the Turkish-Syrian border. The second is directly, via Jordan and Iraq. The third is from the south via Saudi Arabia across the Gulf. The big question is whether the countries whose air space is being used—Turkey, Jordan, Saudi Arabia, Iraq—will allow Israel, even clandestinely, to cross. If not, IAF would have to fly to their targets and back without being detected. Answers to this question affect the planes' payload, gasoline, and bomb capacity.

Any military action, by any country's armed forces, can be supplemented by covert operations carried out by intelligence agents and Special Forces.

The main goal would be to sabotage some nuclear sites or to create conditions that would prevent scientists from reaching the sites, either physically or by intimidation. This area offers potential for joint operations between the various intelligence organizations. When it comes to covert operations, imagination and daring play a central role. The CIA has already planned a joint operation with the Mossad to sabotage electricity supplies to a number of Iranian nuclear sites.[33]

Real acts of sabotage are not even necessary and are always difficult, requiring agents in the field and equipment. Such an operation can fail, and endanger the life of the agents. On the other hand, spreading rumors would have a powerful psychological effect while achieving almost similar results. In a country already infested with conspiracy theories and paranoia, increasing the sense of the enemy's invincibility will cause fear of the unknown among Iranians. Any normal electricity blackout could be interpreted as sabotage. Indeed Tehran was full of rumors in the summer of 2006, when parts of the capital were crippled by electricity cuts. Many Iranians believed that someone caused the failure.

The CIA considered three other scenarios in the area of sabotage and black warfare. One is to "poison" the computer networks used for the nuclear program. The second is to actually poison people who work for the program, and to make sure that their peers are aware of it. A few deaths would be sufficient to make others leave the nuclear program. If this didn't work, exposing workers to high levels of radiation would show that the site is unsafe.

Finally the option of leadership elimination is being considered, too. Since the 1970s, this has been the specialty of Israeli intelligence. The Mossad and military intelligence have liquidated leaders of Palestinian groups. In 1979 Israeli intelligence agents assassinated Zohair Mohsen, the leader of the pro-Syrian al-Saiqa group, in the French Riviera. In 1988 they killed Abu Jihad, Yasser Arafat's deputy, in his villa in Tunisia, and in 1995, Mossad operatives gunned down Fathi Shqaqi, the founder and leader of the Palestinian Islamic Jihad, on the island of Malta. In 1991, Israel's most prestigious Special

Forces unit, Sayeret Matkal, was practicing for the elimination of Saddam Hussein. Defense Minister Yitzhak Rabin and Chief of Staff Ehud Barak had conditionally approved the plan, but it was eventually scrapped because of a training accident in which five combatants were killed while testing the missile that was to be used in the operation.

But since September 11, targeted killing is not only an Israeli trademark. The U.S. military and intelligence has been empowered by presidential directives to follow the Israeli example. Since Ahmadinejad's election, and especially since his inflammatory statements about Israel and the Holocaust, some Western officials are talking about the need to get rid of him. The counterargument is that he is not in charge of the nuclear program, so it would be useless to eliminate him. In any event, it is clear to those who are thoroughly following Iranian affairs that even killing the Supreme Leader, who is in charge of the nuclear program, would not dramatically change Iran's nuclear course. This is a national project supported by the majority of the political spectrum and the public.

Assuming that the United States will not launch a military strike against Iran and concluding that a full-fledged military strike by Israel is not a real option, the real card left for Israel to play is a limited military attack, destroying or causing severe damage to three or four of Iran's nuclear sites to partially disrupt and delay Iran's capability. Pushing the nuclear program back by a couple of years would be satisfactory to Israel, the United States, and most Western European countries. However, it is also clear that Iran would retaliate severely.

CHAPTER TWELVE

The Riddle of the Sphinx

BRIGADIER GENERAL QASSEM Soleimani, commander of the Iranian al-Quds force, part of the Islamic Revolutionary Guards Corp, was furious. It was mid-July 2006, a few days after the outbreak of Israel's second war in Lebanon, but the Israelis were not the cause of his anger. During a stormy meeting with his Shiite allies, the leaders of the pro-Iranian Lebanese Hezbollah, Soleimani denounced their decision to engage Israel saying that Hezbollah had miscalculated the Israeli reaction and thereby revealed one of Iran's most important strategic assets. One of the most influential and powerful people in Iran, Brigadier General Soleimani was appointed commander of al-Quds in 2002, after a long career in the IRGC. He reports directly to the Supreme Leader and serves as his special advisor on sensitive intelligence operations conducted abroad. In January 2006, Soleimani had been reported dead in an air crash of an IRGC plane, but the report proved to be wrong. He was alive and at this moment kicking very hard.

The meeting took place at a secure room at the basement of the Iranian embassy, located in the Bear Hassan, a Shiite stronghold in the western part of Beirut. Bombs dropped by Israeli warplanes were heard in the distance. Many parts of the neighborhood, including Dahia, Hezbollah headquarters, were devastated by the heavy and precise bombardment of the Israeli Air Force.

The Iranian Embassy occupies a massive structure in the Lebanese capital. The most frenetic part, the nerve center of the building, are the floors built underground, off-limits to most of the embassy employees. They house the clandestine side of Iran's foreign relations, multifaceted special secret units. The people in the basement spearhead Iran's global efforts to disseminate its Islamic revolution, to cement Shiite solidarity and to fight political enemies. There are intelligence officers from the ministry of intelligence and security, officials from the ministry of defense, uniformed officers from the armed forces, and intelligence officials and experts from al-Quds.[1]

Brigadier General's Soleimani was angry about the rockets. Since 1996 intelligence officers from al-Quds had provided Hezbollah with Katyusha rockets and missiles and trained its artillery and rocket personal. The shipments arrived in Lebanon either by road via Syria, another ally of Iran, or by air, without the approval of the legitimate government of Lebanon. Under Iranian and Syria patronage Hezbollah had created a state within state in Lebanon with an impressive presence in the South. By 2006, they had amassed a large quantity of Iranian-made rockets and missiles, and stored them in bunkers and safe houses. The long-range heavy missiles were ingeniously stored in the private houses of trusted Shiite families in South Lebanon, who were handsomely paid for their trouble. The homes were specially equipped with hidden sliding doors in the floors of living rooms and bedrooms, and convertible roofs supported by double walls that could open to the sky.

Israeli intelligence experts assumed that the weapons were to be used by surprise only when Iran would find it appropriate. One such moment would come if Iran's nuclear sites were attacked by Israel, the United States or an international coalition. Hezbollah, with approximately twelve thousand rockets and missiles, was prepared to serve as Iran's extended strategic arm. But in July 2006 Iran's strategic plans were impulsively exposed. Hezbollah kidnapped two Israeli soldiers, hoping that that the Israelis would follow past patterns of soft responses. Charismatic Hezbollah secretary-general Hassan Nasrallah had miscalculated, however, and Israel launched an all-out war, severely crippling Hezbollah's capabilities. To defend itself, Hezbollah hurried the Iranian missiles and rockets into position, especially the heavy long-range ones.

But Israel had prepared a surprise for the overconfident Nasrallah and al-Quds units. When a special courier brought the bad news, Nasrallah's face turned pale. He handed the note to Fuad Shukur, one of his chief commanders, who stared at it in disbelief. "It is wrong information," he murmured. "This is a psychological trick of the enemy. It can't be." Before long, however, the astonishing truth was confirmed. In three and a half hours, 80 percent of Hezbollah long-range arsenal had been destroyed by precision surgical strikes by the Israeli Air Force. Not a single house was missed. The information gathered by the Israeli intelligence about Hezbollah's hidden installations proved to be astonishingly accurate. Hassan Nasrallah was furious and embarrassed at the same time. He realized that his organization had been penetrated, and its secrets exposed. He and his field security officers would have to answer a lot of questions posed in the same tone as Brigadier General Soleimani's.[2]

Still, Nasrallah claimed that Allah was with the believers of the Party of God. Four months after the war, he met in Beirut with Ayatollah Mesbah Yazdi, the messianic visionary and mentor of President Mahmoud Ahmadinejad. Mesbah Yazdi was visiting to show support for the Shiite struggle, and Nasrallah tried to impress him with a divine experience shared by some of his fighters, a story that also explained why Hezbollah was losing battles at night. Nasrallah complained that that Israel had played two winning cards in the war. One was infrared equipment, which enabled it to target Hezbollah forces easily in the dark. The second was Israel's use of helicopters to land forces behind Hezbollah lines.

His trusted fighters told him that one night they had seen Israeli forces landing in their rear. However, he explained to the eager cleric from Qom, the fighters had had very exciting dreams in which they met the prophet

Zahra, the wife of Imam Ali and Imam Hussein's mother. When they told her about their inability to deal with the helicopters, she said to be calm and reassured them that she was praying for their success. Soon after the dream, according to the tale, an Israeli helicopter crashed. Nasrallah said that the Israelis had thought that the crash had occurred because Hezbollah was equipped with night-vision goggles. The lesson that Nasrallah wanted his visiting ayatollah to see was that the Messiah was with the believers. That could only have pleased Mesbah Yazdi.[3]

The fairy tale served Nasrallah's goal well. Even if some al-Quds or IRGC commanders were not pleased with his performance, the ayatollahs saw him as the hero of the Shiites, the man who had stood up to the almighty Israeli forces supported by the Great Satan. Despite their disappointment about Hezbollah's adventurism, the Iranian leaders were not going to abandon their ally. On the contrary, after their initial surprise and anger, they pondered how to reap dividends out of the quagmire. The IRGC and al-Quds launched a campaign in Iran to mobilize volunteers, offering reservists good wages if they agreed to rush to Lebanon to help Hezbollah. It was of more of a public relations effort than a noble sacrifice, since the war ended after thirty-three days of fighting, before the Iranian volunteers were needed. Hezbollah managed without them.

Victory or defeat in the war lay in the eye of the beholder. Hezbollah lost nearly 40 percent of its rockets, including its precious long-range missiles capable of hitting Tel Aviv, the symbol of modern Israel's existence. Many hundreds of its best combatants were dead. Most of its headquarters, communication and command centers, underground bunkers, and aboveground fortifications were destroyed. Its proud headquarters in Beirut was erased from the face of earth. Yet, despite its heavy losses, the movement claimed victory. It boasted that it had held the mighty Israeli forces for thirty-three days while continuously shelling Israel's northern cities, towns, and villages. The Israeli public and the media tended to accept the Hezbollah-Iranian narrative.

The 2006 July-August war is called Israel's Second Lebanon War. The first had been twenty-four years earlier, in June 1982. Premier Menachem

Begin and defense minister Ariel Sharon devised a strategy to root out Yasser Arafat's PLO, which had turned south Lebanon into a launching pad for attacks against Israeli territory. The successful Israeli campaign forced the PLO into an inglorious exile in Tunisia, but Israeli troops were stuck in the Lebanese mud for eighteen years. Only in 2000 did Israel finally withdraw its troops fully from Lebanese soil.

Iran has had a long tradition of interest in the Shiite communities around the globe, including in Lebanon. The connection goes back to the nine-teenth century and increased during the reign of the shah. Young Lebanese students studied theology at Iranian and Shiite Iraqi seminaries. Upon their return to Lebanon, they became agents for Shiite-Iranian culture. An increasingly important part of the imported tradition after its arrival in 1918 was the bloody self-flagellation ritual of Ashura, commemorating the martyrdom of Imam Hussein.[4]

Hezbollah, meaning "the Party of God," was created after the Israeli invasion of 1982, but that was purely an historical coincidence. The establishment of the party had nothing to do with Israel. On the contrary, at the early stages of that first war, the Shiites of south Lebanon welcomed the Israeli troops. Like their brethren around the Middle East, Lebanese Shiites were oppressed by the Sunnis, who constitute a majority in the Muslim world and consequently rule much of it. The Shiites in Lebanon were economically, socially, and politically at the bottom of society, subjugated by the Christians, the Sunni Muslims, and the Palestinians.

Thus they initially perceived Israel as their savior, but as Israel's stay in Lebanon lengthened, Israeli soldiers came to be seen by the Shiite community as simply another oppressor. Hezbollah was formed gradually in late 1982 by Lebanese religious scholars, such as Subhi Tofaili and Abbas al-Mussavi, who became the first secretary-general of the movement and was assassinated by Israel a decade after its formation. In retrospect many top Israeli intelligence officers regret the assassination. Al-Mussavi was replaced by Nasrallah, a more daring and charismatic leader who has influenced the whole region for two decades.

The first spiritual leader of Hezbollah was Muhammad Hussein Fadlalah, a respected religious authority. Among his first young followers was Hassan Nasrallah, the twenty-two-year-old son of a Shiite grocer who had nine children. Al-Mussavi sent Nasrahllah to a religious seminary in Najaf in Iraq and upon his return Nasrallah rose steadily in the movement hierarchy and eventually replaced the slain al-Mussavi.

The movement took energy from the euphoria all over the Shiite world, especially in Lebanon, that attended the Islamic revolution in Iran. It was further strengthened by Iran's zeal to export its revolution and to form an international Shiite fraternity. Ironically, the Iranian feeling of responsibility for their Shiite brethren is similar to Israel's perception of itself as a haven for Jews all over the world. Israel, too, has established secret intelligence units responsible for helping of Jewish communities in distress to organize their own defense, and for helping Jews to immigrate to Israel.

Soon Hezbollah turned from a religious movement into a social and political force, becoming the representative of the majority of Shiites in Lebanon. Its phenomenal expansion went hand-in-hand with the creation of a military wing. Hezbollah refers to its military posture as "resistance," but for the rest of the world it is terrorism. The first targets of the "resistance" were the Israeli troops and the multinational peacekeeping forces, mainly American and French, sent to Lebanon following the expulsion of the PLO. Inspired by the Iranian revolutionary fever and hatred of America, Hezbollah formed a strategy to expel the foreigners. Taking advantage of the chaos and instability, Iran sent military advisors and instructors from the IRGC and especially from al-Quds. They trained the enthusiastic young Hezbollah fighters in guerrilla tactics at secret camps and bases in the Bekaa valley, a Shiite stronghold in eastern Lebanon.

More significantly they introduced suicide bombers into the Middle East. Suicide bombing was first used by the Tamil Tigers fighting against the Singhalese majority in Sri Lanka in the 1970s, but Hezbollah perfected the method. It is relatively easy for Iranian-sponsored terrorist groups to recruit candidates for suicidal operations among poor and religiously devout Shiites, whose tradition of martyrdom goes back to Imam Hussein in the seventh century A.D.

In April 1983 a suicide bomber blew up a truck loaded with explosives in front of the American embassy in Beirut. The blast destroyed the front of the embassy, killing sixty-three people. Seventeen of them were Americans— among them were eight CIA operatives, including the CIA's Near East director, Robert Ames.

Six months later Hezbollah repeated its successful suicide tactics by crashing another truck filled with explosives through the gate of the U.S. Marine base in Beirut. 241 marines were killed and 80 seriously wounded. On the same day, in a similar way, the headquarters of the French contingent was attacked, killing 58 people. The attacks and abductions of American and Western nationals in Lebanon pushed the Reagan administration to take two contradictory measures. One was to pull the forces out of Lebanon and the other was to retaliate. The thirst to settle scores with America's enemies in Lebanon increased after Lieutenant Colonel William Buckley, a CIA opera- tive under diplomatic cover as a political officer in the U.S. embassy, was abducted in Beirut in March 1984. He was held for fifteen months, probably for a while in Teheran, severely tortured, and eventually murdered. Therefore on March 1985, a car packed with explosives exploded near Fadlalah's resi- dence in a Beirut suburb, killing 80 people and wounding 200. Anyone who had happened to be in the vicinity was killed or injured, but the target escaped without injury. Fadlalah's disciples hung in front of the destroyed building a banner that said "Made in USA." The attack was ordered by CIA director William Casey, using information from Lebanese informers paid from a secret bank account opened by Prince Bandar al-Sultan, the Saudi ambassador in Washington.[5]

The CIA, however, attacked the wrong target. Fadlalah was the spiritual mentor of the newly established Hezbollah, but the strategic decision to attack the Americans was made in Tehran, and it was planned with the sup- port of Syrian intelligence and executed by a newly recruited and talented young operative, Imad Fayez Mughniyah. Hezbollah's chief of military and special operations, Mughniyah is on the U.S. list of the most wanted terror-ists, for "conspiracy to commit aircraft piracy, and placing explosives aboard aircraft." This refers to his involvement in the June 1985 hijacking of TWA Flight 847 from Athens to Rome. The plane, with the crew and passengers aboard, was forced to land at Beirut airport and one passenger, a navy diver, was beaten and shot fatally in the head. His body was dumped on the tarmac. The bounty on Mughniyah, $5 million, reflects not only the TWA incident but his long history as the mastermind of Hezbollah terrorist attacks in Lebanon and abroad. These attacks, including the bombing of the American embassy and the marines barracks in Lebanon, have always been coordinated with Iran's intelligence units.

Mughniyah is on everybody's lips if a new conflict with Iran erupts.[6] Born in 1962 either in a poor village in southern Lebanon or a poor neighbor-hood in South Beirut, Mughniyah joined the PLO at fifteen during the civil war in Lebanon, a very unusual step for a Shiite, since the PLO is dominated by Sunnis.[7] A few years later, he returned to his Shiite roots when he joined Hezbollah. Already an experienced guerrilla fighter, Mughniyah was embraced by the inexperienced leaders of Hezbollah, who trusted his advice, relied on his schemes, and basically gave him a free hand. The early to mid-1980s were formative years for the young Shiite terrorist and the period that cemented his fraternity with al-Quds. Mughniyah became the go-between for Hezbollah with Iran's masters of special operations. He gained notoriety after leading terrorist attacks in Argentina in 1992 and 1994, following which the Argentine government issued an arrest warrant for him and added him to their most wanted list.

Information about Mughniyah is sketchy; he is elusive and has several passports under different assumed names. Israeli intelligence believes that he underwent cosmetic surgery. He barely dares to travel outside the seemingly safe route of Beirut-Damascus-Tehran. His relations with Iran have not been without friction and occasionally he has found himself in contentious dis-putes with Iran's intelligence officials. He doesn't particularly like VAVAK and didn't hesitate to show his disrespect for it. He trusts al-Quds operatives much more, and has good relations with them. Despite his reliance on Iran it would wrong to depict him as puppet of the Iranian regime. Overall Mughniyah has skillfully managed to maintain a certain degree of independence from Iran to enhance his and the Hezbollah agenda.

The closest he came to death was in 1994, when, according to international reports, Lebanese agents of the Mossad planted a car bomb next to the garage in southern Beirut owned by his brother Fouad. The bomb detonated a few minutes after he had left the area, but it killed his brother and some passersby. This miraculous escape added to his legend as an invincible, invisible terrorist. The media depicts him as being behind almost every terrorist attack in every corner of the world. The truth is that Imad Mughinyah has become the face of a long list of Hezbollah senior operatives who have gained experience, self-confidence and pride in their skill during their quarter century of struggle. Mughniyah only epitomizes the empire of terror that Iran has been building since the revolution.

This empire is run by primarily by al-Quds and VAVAK. Their activities are typified by three major features: worldwide range, sanction by the Iranian government and the religious leaders and reliance on the support of Shiite communities. They have three goals, of which the first is to spread the Islamic revolution—a permanent revolution—for which enthusiasm has subsided in recent years among Iran's population. The major tool for this was sending preachers, religious artifacts and financial support to build mosques and religious community centers in Europe, Africa, Asia and South America. This is carried out mainly by religious foundations, Islamic cultural centers, and charities that the Iranian government established and financed with hundreds of millions of dollars.

The second goal is to build bases and infrastructure among Shiite communities to enhance Iranian interests. This is one of the main functions of Hezbollah and similar organizations sponsored by Iran in Palestine, Iraq, Bahrain, Pakistan, Azerbaijan, and in South America. These groups serve as Iran's extended arm. The third aim is to use such infrastructures and to pursue and attack political enemies and dissidents.

Al-Quds is a special force within the IRGC, which was formally established by Khomeini in May 1979 to guard the revolution and help the clerics
enforce Islamic codes and ethics. One of the major reasons for its creation
was that Khomeini and the ayatollahs suspected the army of not being pure
enough. The Iranian constitution subsequently empowered the military to
defend Iran's territorial integrity, sovereignty and political independence,
while giving the IRGC the responsibility of guarding the revolution itself.

This division of responsibility is confusing and each organization's work
often blurs into the other's. Both organizations have naval, air, land, Special
Forces, and intelligence units. Yet, in due course, a modus operandi based on
precedent and experience took shape and although their responsibilities still
overlap, the two organizations have managed to live side by side. Al-Quds has
been assigned to conduct secret foreign operations, especially to train Islamic
fundamentalist groups and maintain contacts with them. Consequently, al-
Quds has special relations with organizations like the Lebanese Hezbollah, the
Palestinian Hamas and Islamic Jihad, the Mahdi Army in Iraq, and many other
smaller groups. Funds are provided through IRGC front companies, which are
very active in the Persian Gulf area, as well as through Iranian exiles and their
business enterprises and the charitable foundations.[8]

The other major intelligence and special operations arm of the regime is
VAVAK. It is difficult to know the exact division of labor between VAVAK
and al-Quds. VAVAK, established in 1984, is Iran's main intelligence organization, built out of the ashes of the shah's security services, SAVAK. It is
headed by a cabinet minister who is always a trusted confidant of the
supreme leader. In the last decade, even under the reformist president
Muhammad Khatami, messianic followers of Ayatollah Mesbah Yazdi have
occupied the office, including the current minister, Ali Akbar Mohseni Ejehi.
VAVAK is responsible for conducting operations domestically and abroad.
Domestically, it monitors groups, individuals and organizations that are perceived to be out of step with the government's policies and thus a threat. In
many cases VAVAK arrests, questions, and tortures suspects. In some cases it
simply kills them, without due legal process.

One of the most famous and intriguing stories illustrating the dark, cruel, and mysterious face of VAVAK was about Saeed Emami. He was born in 1961 in the city of Shiraz in central Iran. He studied mechanical engineering in America, and worked part-time at the Pakistani embassy in Washington, D.C., which represented Iranian interests in the United States in the absence of diplomatic relations between Iran and the United States. Later he was transferred to the Iranian Permanent Mission to the UN in New York. It is not clear how and when he became an intelligence operative. Most of the information about him comes from opposition sources, either the Mujahedeen Khalq or groups supporting the Baby Shah. At a certain point in the mid-1980s, Emami returned to Iran and became a senior official at VAVAK. In 1989, newly appointed minister of VAVAK Ali Fallahian appointed Emami to be his deputy. Fallahian served the longest of any minister, eight years, and Emami assisted him throughout them, a typically shadowy figure of the cloak-and-dagger world, unknown to the public.

A decade later, however, Emami found himself in jail. In the spring of 1998, the bodies of a couple working for a small reformist group were found cut in pieces at their home, a murder that became known as the "serial killings." The Khatami reformist administration demanded answers from VAVAK, and under pressure the intelligence organization delivered an explanation. Ali Fallahian had to resign and fingers were also pointed at Emami, who was arrested and accused of organizing the killings. Sometime later, a VAVAK "internal investigation" declared that Emami had committed suicide in his cell, using arsenic that he extracted from a hair-removal product. No one believed this explanation, either in Iran or abroad.

It is clear that someone in VAVAK wanted to see him dead. He had probably become privy to too many secrets that could compromise members of the organization if they were made public. Probably one such secret was about the true culprit behind the "serial killings" and thousands of other killings—Fallahian. After Emami's mysterious death, it was claimed that he was actually born Daniel Ghavami, to a Jewish family.[9]

Most of the outrageous international terrorist operations that the Islamic

Republic has carried out are associated with Emami and Ali Fallahian. The first incident that captured world attention was the Mykonos affair, named for a Greek restaurant in Berlin where, in September 1992, two gunmen burst in and opened fire, killing three Iranian Kurd political activists, members of a political group calling for the independence of Iranian Kurdistan. Their murders bore similarities to the operation three years earlier in Vienna in which President Ahmadinejad may have participated.

In 1996, four years after the Mykonos murders, a German investigation concluded that Ali Fallahian had masterminded the killings and a German court issued an international arrest warrant for Fallahian. (Fallahian is also wanted by the Swiss government for the assassination of another Iranian dissident.) The court ruled in April 1997 that the killings were ordered by the "highest state levels" in Iran's capital. The judges convicted two Lebanese of murder and sentenced them to life in prison. Two others were given lighter sentences as accessories to murder. A fifth was acquitted. The presiding judge said in his verdict that the men had no personal motive but were following orders. Without naming names, he said the gangland-style murders had been ordered by what he referred to as "Iran's Committee for Special Operations," to which Iran's president and supreme leader belonged.

Prosecutors contended that Supreme Leader Ayatollah Ali Khamenei and Iranian president Hashemi Rafsanjani had personally ordered the killings.

The exiled Abdul Hassan Bani Sadr, Iran's first postrevolution president, testified that all the killings of the regime's "enemies" had to be approved by the supreme leader.[10] Germany implicated some Iranian diplomats and expelled four of them. "The participation of Iranian state agencies, as found in the court verdict, represents a flagrant violation of international law," the German foreign ministry said in a statement. The relations between the two countries were soured and both recalled their ambassadors.[11]

The Mykonos operation had the modus operandi characteristic of Iran's operations. The intelligence bureau at the presidency drew up a list of potential targets, which were sent to the president. Once approved by the president, the names were sent back to the intelligence bureau with the instruction to check the feasibility of the operation and start initial planning. The intelligence bureau designed a tentative plan that was sent for further discussion and confirmation by the Supreme National Security Council (SNSC).[12] The decision by SNSC required the approval of the supreme leader. Once he confirmed it, the intelligence bureau assigned either VAVAK or al-Quds to execute the plan and provided additional instructions to relevant embassies to help the operation and cover its expenses. Using diplomatic pouches, special couriers would carry weapons or explosives to the nearest intelligence station based in an Iranian embassy. The intelligence officers in charge at the embassy would activate a "sleeper cell" usually consisting of Iranian exiles living abroad or trusted Shiites of other nationalities. These cells have a very clear division of labor. Some shadow the target and collect data on it, others provide logistical support for the "hit team."

This is exactly how another mission was carried out in the same year, on the other side of the world. In March 1992, a van loaded with explosives blew up outside the Israeli embassy in Buenos Aires. Twenty-two people, including seven Israeli diplomats and one Mossad operative, were killed and a few dozen injured. Twenty-eight months later, an even bigger calamity forced Argentine president Carlos Menem to open an official inquiry. In July 1994, a bomb destroyed AMIA (Asociación Mutual Israelita Argentina), the Jewish community centre in the Argentine capital, killing 85 and injuring more than 200.

The several investigating judges and committees dragged their feet. Accusations of bribes paid to judges, investigators, and government officials including President Menem tainted the process. Eventually, in 2003, Miguel Angel Toma, the director of Secretaría de Inteligencia del Estado (Secretariat for State Intelligence, or SIDE), the Argentine intelligence organization, came to Israel. He met with his Israeli counterpart, Meir Dagan, the head of Mossad, and presented him with a secret report of thousands of pages containing transcripts of interrogations of suspects, interception of telephone call and records of border control document among other evidence.

The SIDE report relied heavily on the Mossad, FBI, and CIA investigations that had already been completed and reached the same conclusions. Though the SIDE report only investigated the AMIA bombing, that attack was similar to the bombing of the Israeli embassy and both were classic VAVAK–al-Quds operations. An important contributor was Abdul Ghasem Mesbahi, a senior VAVAK intelligence officer who defected in 1996 to Germany and provided detailed testimony to the German BND, the Mossad, the CIA, and SIDE.

The SIDE report revealed that the decision to attack the Israeli embassy and subsequently AMIA was revenge for the Israeli assassination of Abbas Mussavi, the first Hezbollah leader, in March 1992. Both attacks were approved, supervised and financed by Ali Khamenei and President Rafsanjani. The preparation and planning was quick, using sleeper cells that al-Quds and VAVAK had established years before. Minister Ali Fallahian administered the operation, helped by Hezbollah, which sent a suicide bomber who detonated the truck. One can understand the Iranian logic to sanction a Hezbollah revenge operation against the Israeli embassy. But why did Iran allow to bomb AMIA? It is doubtful wjhether Iran's leaders would have approved such an operation on a friendly soil. But Argentina was no longer a friend of Iran. Under U.S. pressure, President Carlos Menem stopped a deal to provide Iran with 20 percent enriched uranim.

It would take Argentina ten years and a change of president to find the courage to follow the German government precedent and issue an international warrant against twenty-three Iranians implicated in the AMIA attack. Most of them were Iranian intelligence officers posing as diplomats or clergymen. Topping the list are Ayatollah Rafsanjani; former Foreign Minister Ali Akbar Velayati, for the role played by his ministry; General Mohsen Rezai, the former head of IRGC; and Ali Fallahian.[13] Difficulties in providing a solid piece of information about Khamenei excluded the supreme leader from the wanted list. After the warrants issued by Argentina, the Iranian government threatened in 2004 to retaliate as it had done against the German government. But in both cases, nothing happened.

As a by-product, the investigation exposed the power struggle and the widespread conspiracy fears among the top echelon of the Iranian regime. Rafsanjani's supporters believed that the IRGC tipped off SIDE and provided information to implicate the former president. Without the IRGC's inside information, they thought, it would have been impossible to issue the international warrant. Rafsanjani disciples believed the IRGC's top echelon hated Rafsanjani because it saw him as corrupt and pro-Western.

The hatred is mutual. Rafsanjani perceived the IRGC leadership as an ungrateful group of ignorant people. He and Khomeini helped them during the early years after the revolution to consolidate their power, to build their empire, and to benefit financially, but they didn't reciprocate the favour. Insulted, Rafsanjani retaliated when he became president in 1989. He expelled the IRGC's intelligence body from the Supreme National Security Council and gave the seat to their archrival VAVAK. Thus, Rafsanjani provided the reasons for the IRGC to take their revenge on him.

In June 1996 another Iranian-sponsored terrorist operation parked a fuel tanker laden with explosives next to the Khobar Towers in Dharan, Saudi Arabia. The building served a compound for the members of the 404th Wing of the U.S. Air Force, who were assigned to enforce the no-fly zone in Saddam Hussein's Iraq. The blast wave destroyed Building 131, killing nineteen U.S. airmen and an unknown number of Saudi civilians and injuring hundreds. The ferocity of the explosion was unprecedented among terrorist acts. It created a crater 10 feet deep and 30 feet wide.

Initially the attack was attributed to Osama bin Laden. It was assumed that only this Saudi fundamentalist who had been expelled by his government would conspire on such an act, perceived as a challenge to get rid of the Americans from holy Saudi land. The group that claimed responsibility for the attack called itself Hezbollah al-Hijaz," Hezbollah in Saudi Arabia. But Saudi Arabian security services discovered the group was the offspring of a joint venture run by al-Quds, VAVAK, and Hezbollah. After interrogating some suspects, the Saudi Arabians found out that the lethal truck was assembled in a terrorist compound of Hezbollah and al-Quds in the Bekaa

Valley in Lebanon. The truck was smuggled into Saudi Arabia and the operation was carried out by Lebanese, Saudi Arabians, and Iranians.

Initially the American media accused Saudi Arabia of being unwilling to share information and to thoroughly investigate the case, but in 2005 former FBI director Louis Freeh revealed that it was the Clinton administration that was reluctant to pursue the case. He accused Bill Clinton and his national security advisor, Sandy Berger, of trying to appease the reformist camp in Iran led by President Khatami. Only after Freeh asked former president George H. W. Bush, whose Saudi connections are very strong, to intervene, did the FBI have access to the terrorists.[14] The FBI agents interrogated them in a Saudi jail and filed a complete report on this case that reiterated the Saudi findings and detected the pattern of an Iranian terrorist operation.

The terrorists were recruited by General Ahmad Sharifi of al-Quds, who briefed them about the operation at the Iranian Embassy in Damascus, Syria. Supreme Leader Khamenei approved the Khobar Towers carnage. In December 2006 a U.S. Federal Court judge ordered Iran to pay $254 million. "The totality of the evidence at trial, combined with the findings and conclusions entered by this court . . . firmly establishes that the Khobar Towers bombing was planned, funded and sponsored by senior leadership in the government of the Islamic Republic of Iran," Judge Royce Lamberth wrote.[15]

The Argentine, German, and Saudi cases helped to uncover several distinct trends in the Iranian global strategy. One can be found in Foz do Iguaçu (Iguazu Waterfalls), a town in an area shared by Brazil, Argentina, and Paraguay. To Shabtai Shavit, who visited this town, it looked like "a typical Shiite Lebanese city." It has mosques, *moazens* (Muslim prayer leaders), local inhabitants wearing traditional Muslim dress, women covering their heads with scarves, and shopkeepers playing with prayer beads. Shavit recalled a meeting he had with James Woolsey, the director of the CIA, and some of his associates in Washington. Over lunch he asked Woolsey if he knew what was happening in Foz do Iguaçu. "From their looks I realized that they didn't know what I was talking about. I said, 'It's in your backyard and you don't know.'"[16]

In fact, Israeli intelligence was not fully aware of the extensive reach of Iran's international networks until the bombing of the Israeli Embassy in Buenos Aires. Since then, both Israeli and American intelligence communities have opened their eyes. The Muslim Triangle, as the area is known in the Israeli intelligence jargon, is now on their radar screens as well as many other parts of South America that are considered fertile ground for spreading Iran and Hezbollah's support groups. They take advantage of the large Shiite emigré communities in Latin America to plant networks of supporters, agents and operatives. Venezuela is a prime example. Since the election of leftist Hugo Chávez in 1998, Venezuela has become increasingly anti-Israeli. Chávez, who visited Iran when Ahmadinejad was the mayor, has said that he is a personal friend of Mahmoud Ahmadinejad. In honor of the visit, Mahmoud Ahmadinejad named a Tehran square after Chavez's hero, South American liberator Simón Bolívar.

In early 2000 a group openly calling itself Hezbollah Venezuela was established, despite the negative association the name carries in the West. This small group, whose members are mainly Venezuelans of indigenous origin, calls for the establishment of an anti-Western Islamic state in Venezuela. To prove that it means business, the group tried to set off a small explosion near the U.S. embassy in 2006.[17] Hezbollah Venezuela does not yet pose a serious challenge to American, Israeli, or other Western interests and it is smaller than other groups and organizations flourishing in the Foz do Iguaçu district. "The spreading of 'Hezbollah Latin America' does not permit a clear picture of the real character and goal of the group," says Ely Karmon of the Institute for Counter Terrorism. However, he says, "there is a growing trend of solidarity between Islamists and leftists, Marxists and even rightist elements. There is the possibility that Lebanese Hezbollah or al Qaeda would recruit 'converted' Latin American terrorists for their operational international activity."[18]

Iran's efforts in South America exemplify how the Islamic regime is spreading its influence and message abroad, building networks that might be called on when Iran decides that the Day of Judgment arrived. Israeli,

American, and other Western intelligence organizations are preparing them-selves for such an eventuality. They estimate that Iran may have placed sleeper cells in South America, Europe, and Asia, which might be activated to hit Amer-ican or Israeli targets.

Another tool available to Iran's masters of terrorism and special opera-tions are the networks of what is called Global Jihad. These are usually cells or groups of Sunni fundamentalists who adhere to the anti-American and anti-Western preaching of Osama bin Laden. They don't share the religious beliefs of Iran, but might agree to serve as Iran's "subcontractors" in its terror schemes in return for financial support, documentation, and shelter.

This pattern was revealed initially after 9/11 and the U.S. occupation of Afghanistan. U.S. intelligence discovered that al-Quds allowed senior al Qaeda operatives to infiltrate Iran from Afghanistan, and provided them shelter and financial support. Among them was Saad bin Laden, the son of the master terrorist.[19] The special relations between al Qaeda remnants, newly emerged Jihad groups, and Iran is certainly an possibility that Amer-ican, Israeli, and Western intelligence organizations are considering.

Still, the most lethal weapon available to Iran for its worldwide terrorist campaign is the Lebanese Hezbollah and its cadre of professional terrorists led by Imad Mughinya. Under him are a few more important operatives, including his deputy Fouad Shukor, number two in the military hierarchy, as well as Tallal Hamya and Hassan Ghossan. Tallal Hamya and other high-ranking Hezbollah officers have been commuting between Lebanon, Iran, and Iraq since the American occupation of Iraq. Some of Hezbollah's best and most experienced military minds were summoned to al-Quds headquar-ters in Iran for a brainstorming session to discuss how to mobilize the Shiite community of Iraq and to turn it into a fighting force against the American occupation. Hamya and some of his associates volunteered their experience and were instrumental in organizing the al-Quds–sponsored military factions in Iraq.

Iran has several militia forces at its disposal in Iraq, but the most important is the Mahdi Army, established by Muqtada al-Sadr, a young firebrand Shiite cleric. Born in 1973 in Najaf, al-Sadr is a member of a well-established Shiite family of clerics. His father was the grand ayatollah Muhammad Sadeq al-Sadr, who knew the founding fathers of Iran's Islamic revolution, including Ayatollah Khomeini. His father and his two brothers were murdered by assassins of Saddam Hussein's security service. With such a prominent background, it is no wonder that the young al-Sadr rose to fame among Iraqi Shiites and almost automatically got the attention of the Iranian regime.

The Iranian game in Iraq is not clear. One can argue that it's not even clear to the Iranian ayatollahs. Do they want to turn Iraq into a Shiite fiefdom? Is it possible? Or do they want to split Iraq up and create a small Shiite state on their border? Another possibility is a grand old Iranian dream now dressed up in a new name. This is the Shiite Crescent (or as Israeli intelligence calls it, the Shiite Banana)—one big Shiite caliphate extending from the Persian Gulf and the Indian Ocean to the Mediterranean. It would contain Iran, parts of Iraq, parts of Syria (ruled since 1970 by the Assad family, members of an Alawite clan related to the Shia), and Lebanon. Alternatively, the regime in Teheran may simply wish to bleed America on Iraqi soil.

For any one or more of these ideas, Muqtada al-Sadr is exactly right. In the spring of 2004, a year after the invasion, al-Sadr mobilized his disciples, mainly seminary students, called them the Mahdi Army, and tried to attack the American forces. The rebellion neither succeeded nor was quashed. The U.S.-sponsored administration had to reconcile with him, recognizing his power and popularity. The Mahdi Army became a fixture in Iraq's political landscape. It is not clear whether Muqtada al-Sadr is an admirer of Iran's ayatollahs, but clearly an army of believers named for the Mahdi appeals to many messianic Ayatollahs in Iran. Tehran also considers al-Sadr an important pawn in their regional and global chess game against the West. Al-Quds and VAVAK operatives have a strong direct and indirect presence in Iraq. They maintain contact with al-Sadr and other more or less radical Shiite organizations. They mingle in Iraq's domestic policies. Any solution to the Iraqi civil war that would enable U.S. troops to return home has to coordinated with the regime in Tehran.

Both sides are is preparing for the worst. Iran is mobilizing its allies in Iraq, Lebanon, South America, and most important, the IRGC, al-Quds, and VAVAK. At the same time, the Pentagon, European military forces, and Israel's defense forces are bracing for an assault. U.S. and Israeli intelligence estimate that Iran would use everything in its possession, from the terror networks to its ballistic missile capabilities, to hit back if it is attacked. Iran has already proven that its Shahab missiles, with a range of 1,300 kilometers, can hit every place in Israel. But it has bigger ambitions. During last year's military maneuvers, Western intelligence services detected that some war games proposed missile formations directed not only at Israel but also at Saudi Arabia and the Persian Gulf states. Experts assume that in a worst-case scenario Iran would use its missile arsenal to set the entire region on fire. "With the Shahab family of ballistic missiles, Iran has already projected its power over the entire Middle East," says Uzi Rubin, a specialist at the Institute for National Security Studies in Tel Aviv University. "Every major city and military installation between the western shores of Turkey and the eastern border of Pakistan and between the Black Sea in the north and in the southern narrows of the Red Sea are within range of Shahab missiles."[20] By the end of this decade Iran should have missiles capable of 2,500 to 3,500 kilometers. "At this rate, Iranian missiles will dominate the entire continent of Europe."[21]

The terror networks and the missile capabilities are Iran's most serious threats to the region and the world. But Iran could also be bluffing. "Such threats are not automatically credible," says Gerald Steinberg of the Begin-Sadat Center for Strategic Studies at Bar Ilan University near Tel Aviv. "The Iranian leaders from President Ahmadinejad to the Supreme Leader Khamenei appear to be overplaying a weak hand. For now the threat of advanced weapons delivering crushing blows to anyone who would attack the installations being built for the nuclear weapons program appear to be overstated."[22]

CHAPTER THIRTEEN

Living in the Shadow of the Nuclear Sphinx

FOR DR. MUHAMMAD el-Baradei, Christmas 2006 turned bleak. Ministers of the Gulf Cooperation Council (GCC) met in November 2006 in the Saudi Arabian capital of Riyadh and voted to develop nuclear technology. The member states of the GCC are the oil-rich states: Saudi Arabia, Oman, Qatar, Kuwait, Bahrain, and the United Arab Emirates. All of them are scared of the day Iran develops nuclear weapons. Though they declared that their intention is to develop a peaceful nuclear program, that is Iran's claim as well. India, Pakistan, and, it is generally assumed, Israel used the same excuse to justify their nuclear programs, all of which ended up being both civilian and military in nature.

Saudi Arabia and the Persian Gulf States will join Egypt, which announced in autumn 2006 that it was renewing its nuclear program, which had been frozen after the Chernobyl disaster. Turkey, too, has made it clear that it will build nuclear power reactors for electricity. Morocco, Algeria, and Syria all have nuclear infrastructures and technology of one kind or another and the capability of expanding them.

The Middle East is moving faster toward nuclearization—precisely the nightmare that el-Baradei has been warning about. The IAEA director-general has urged for years that the Middle East should be turned into a nuclear weapon–free zone, a call that has been directed first and foremost at Israel. Israel is not opposed to the idea in principle, if all countries in the region recognize Israel's right to exist and sign peace and security agreements with Israel.

However, el-Baradei himself must carry the most blame for the danger of the spread of nuclear weapons. His organization fell asleep on the job. It woke up only in 2002 when it learned that Iran was violating its commitments to the IAEA and the Non-Proliferation Treaty. But even after Iran's deceptions were exposed, the IAEA was indecisive. According to the IAEA statute, the agency must report any and every violation of the agreements immediately to the UN. The agency is not directed to understand or justify why a state may be "noncompliant." El-Baradei, however, produced mild reports and held a dialogue with Tehran, thus giving the Iranian regime time to fend off international pressure while it continued to upgrade its nuclear capability secretly. This is why Iran is very close to what Israeli intelligence defines as the "technological threshold," after which Iran will be able to produce an atom bomb in two or three years. Had el-Baradei referred Iran's nuclear file to the UN Security Council in 2003 rather than February 2006, it might have been easier to formulate broad international consensus to impose effective sanctions on Iran.

The soft sanctions that were imposed at the end of 2006 are not going to cripple Iran's efforts to obtain nuclear weapons, but they come better late than never. The resolution is a warning to Iran that it risks retribution unless it acts in accordance with international rules and desires. More sanctions are in the making and it will be up to the new secretary-general of the United Nations, Ban Ki-moon, to lead the international community through 2007 and 2008 when crucial decisions on Iran's nuclear program must be made. There will be clear-cut choices about Iran's nuclear program: either to stop it by coercive diplomacy and/or military action or to persuade Iran to abandon it voluntarily. Ban Ki-moon is the right person at the right time in the right place. As a South Korean, he knows what it feels like to live in the shadow of a nuclear threat—a volcano that may erupt at any moment—but he also can serve as a living example that such a life is bearable.

Iran's efforts to develop nuclear weapons are anchored in its history. The Shah's dream prepared the infrastructure for the nuclear plan, which would probably have reached fruition had he remained in power. Nuclear power will lift national pride, enhance Iran's scientific and technological infrastructure, and turn Iran into a regional and global power. No wonder the majority of the population supports the plan. In that sense, Mahmoud Ahmadinejad is no different from the shah, or his presidential predecessors Khatami and Rafsanjani, whom the West regards as moderates. Rafsanjani said in 2001, "If one day, the Islamic world is also equipped with weapons like those that Israel possesses now, then the imperialists' strategy will reach a standstill because the use of even one nuclear bomb inside Israel will destroy everything. However, it will only harm the Islamic world. It is not irrational to contemplate such an eventuality."[1]

Not even Ahmadinejad dares to go that far. He has never explicitly said that Iran, or any other entity, should use nuclear weapons against Israel. He has talked of wiping Israel off the face of the earth, but in the sense of requiring Jews to leave Palestine and return to their countries of origin. Nonetheless Israelis, Jews—everyone—has to worry that he will take the next step. When Rafsanjani openly discussed Israel's destruction, he was not speaking as an official of the state. He was chairman of the Expediency Council and still an ambitious and influential politician, but no longer president. Ahmadinejad however, is officially, second in command of the country after the Supreme Leader. His statements consequently hold more power and more threat.

Some experts argue that Ahmadinejad is not particularly important in regard to the nuclear program because the Supreme Leader holds ultimate authority and has the final word. Yet the fact that Ali Khamenei allows Ahmadinejad to speak his mind is significant. There are three possible interpretations for this license. One is that Khamenei doesn't care, because ultimately he has the final word on Iran's nuclear program. Two, what Ahmadinejad is saying is to his liking, because he, too, believes that Iran should take a tough negotiating stance on the nuclear issue. Three, that he doesn't have enough power to restrain Ahmadinejad, or reining him in would come at the price of compromise on other issues that are more important for him than Ahmadinejad's rhetoric.

Ironically, Israeli intelligence is quite pleased with the "Ahmadinejad factor." Its top officials admitted in private conversation, "If he did not exist, we should have invented someone like him." For years Israeli intelligence tried to draw the world's attention to Iran's nuclear drive forward with no success. After Ahmadinejad's election and his inflammatory verbal assaults, Israel finds it easier to convince the world that Iran poses a threat to the existence of the Jewish state, as well as the stability of the region and the world. This is in itself a great success for Israel. The Mossad, the CIA, MI6, and Western and Arab governments will persevere in their efforts to prevent Iran from attaining nuclear weapons.

Some experts believe that the world should stop Iran and that threats, additional sanctions, and international demands will succeed in doing so. These efforts can be supplemented by covert intelligence operations, for instance by sabotaging critical equipment and facilities without leaving a trace. Unable to determine who did it, Iran would also be unable to point fingers. These experts suggest that a "culture of lies" exists in Iran, a society in which there is a tendency to lie and not to report the truth, especially to the authorities. This could mean that the top political leaders are not really informed about the real scientific and technological development of the nuclear program. In Iraq, in the '80s, scientists were afraid to tell Saddam Hussein that they were not able to produce a nuclear bomb. They were afraid that he would kill them. Up to the very last moment before the American invasion, Saddam Hussein received reports that his scientists were on the right track. Iran is certainly not as rotten as Iraq was, but clearly, there is room to assume that a certain gap exists between scientific reality on the ground and what the political leaders hear from their scientists. In other words, Iran might be in a less developed stage than it boasts.

Other experts tend to believe that nothing will stop Iran but military action. It is widely agreed that America has the capability to do so, but whether the Bush administration or the next administration has the will to order such an attack is an open question. If the United States doesn't act, Israeli leaders will have to decide whether, as a last resort, they have no other option to secure Israel's future. To instruct the Israeli Air force to strike, given its limited capabilities, is a decision of existential proportions that will in any case have to be coordinated with the U.S. administration and gain its support. The support may be tacit or more explicit, but it will have to be granted in advance.

After being elected in March 2006, Israeli prime minister Ehud Olmert formed a "consultative body," consisting of former prime ministers of Israel, to advise him on how to deal with Iran. They recommended that he should talk to the U.S. president face to face, with no else one in the room, to look him straight in the eye, and have his word, that if worst comes to worst and Israel has to strike Iran, the United States will fully support it. Olmert hinted at various opportunities at the last months of 2006 that he indeed had gained such a commitment from President Bush. This is in addition to already the existing commitment to Israeli prime ministers that the United States is committed to the defense of Israel and would help Israel to maintain its "qualitative edge." In 1999, Israel and the United States signed a memorandum of understanding that deals with questions regarding Israel's defense. "Qualitative edge" in this context usually refers to the strategic sphere—meaning Israel's nuclear superiority, according to international media and experts. The agreement contains a secret appendix of four clauses that have never been published.

There is another question, however. What would the aftereffects of a military attack be? Most experts believe that a military attack could severely cripple Iran's nuclear program but not fully destroy it. Facilities, materials, and equipment can be destroyed, but not knowledge of the technology. With its community of skillful scientists and engineers, Iran has almost accumulated the know-how to produce a nuclear bomb and would do so eventually. Moreover, a military attack could mobilize Iranians to rally around the regime, further fueling the government's desire for the bomb. It will also undermine any hope for a regime change, which is what the Western world and its allies want to see—a moderate, more accommodating regime.

Those experts who doubt the wisdom of a military attack argue that it would be better to engage in dialogue and negotiation with any Iranian government, including Ahmadinejad's. They point out that Iran has a long tradition of suspicion about foreign interference, with some justification. Iran was occupied by foreign powers and heavily influenced by the United States during the shah's reign. It is now surrounded by American troops.

However, even if negotiation is a valid way forward, how to do it remains the stumbling block. Some would suggest that negotiations should be without any preconditions. Others, not only in the United States but in most of the European Union, claim that straightforward negotiations would be interpreted by Iran as a weakness, stiffening their will against compromise and concessions. This school of thought supports the idea of opening a dialogue with Iran only after it agrees to suspend its uranium enrichment program and the construction of the Arak reactor.

In analyzing the issues surrounding Iran's nuclear program and its president, the following point about Iran's politics, economy and nuclear policies should not be ignored:

- The country has been in a deep economic crisis for two decades and it is not going to end soon.
- Iran's oil industry, the main source of its livelihood, is facing severe difficulties. Iran's oil companies are calling for tens of billions of dollars in investments to replace old, crumbling equipment. Estimates projects that if Iran does not invest soon in its oil industry, its oil exports may disappear within a decade.[2]
- Despite its one-party system and the ayatollahs' tight grip on the reins of power, Iran has a lively political system. Dissenting voices find a way to express themselves despite the authoritarian nature of the regime. Ahmadinejad's policies are constantly being challenged domestically.
- Sanctions, especially tough economic sanctions such as an oil embargo, may work. However unlikely they are, they would put

Iran's leadership under tremendous pressure. But sanctions can backfire, as the events of the 1950s showed.

- Iran's nuclear facilities are spread in dozens of hidden sites, some of which are located in residential areas or inside hardened bunkers. A military strike in these areas might increase hatred of the West and the rally the Iranian people.
- Iran will retaliate if it is attacked and it has the ability to cause extensive damage to countries in the region and to U.S. forces stationed in neighboring countries, and to launch terrorist attacks against Israeli, Jewish, U.S., and European targets.
- Regime change is a long process that, based on the Iraqi precedent, seems beyond the ability of an American administration for some time to come.
- Even if Iran possesses nuclear weapons, it may not necessarily use them. Furthermore, the likelihood that Iran would hand over nuclear weapons to terrorists is even slimmer. On the surface, Iran's leaders show no mercy and have no inhibitions, but they have occasionally proved to be responsible and even restrained.
- Even if Iran has nuclear weapons, sanctions and regime change can still take place.

Nuclear Iran may create a new strategic reality in the Middle East not unlike the "balance of terror" model created between the United States and the Soviet Union during the cold war. Each side had nuclear weapons, a parity that neutralized the will and the ability of the other to use them. Actually, according to international experts, Israel is heading into a situation also modelled on the nuclear relations between the two superpowers: the nuclear arms race. After the two superpowers had nuclear warheads, they had to develop a second-strike capability in order to maintain their supremacy. That is, if one side is attacked, with nuclear weapons, the other needed to maintain the ability to strike back with nuclear weapons. That second strike would be carried out mainly with nuclear submarines, which are undetectable. In the last fifteen years, Israel has replaced its two outdated submarines with three new ones made in Germany, and it is now purchasing two more. According to the international media, the new Israeli submarines are capable of carrying missiles with nuclear warheads.

In conclusion, without dialogue and without a viable military solution, the world might simply accept a nuclear Iran and live in the shadow of a nuclear sphinx.

In Greek mythology, the sphinx had the head of a woman and the body of a lion. It killed anyone it encountered who could not answer its riddle. Because of the statute at the Giza pyramid in Cairo, in Western culture the sphinx has symbolized a mysterious, enigmatic person. On the surface, Iran's president seems the opposite of a sphinx. He is so talkative, it is nearly impossible to stop him. He expresses his views very clearly and honestly. World leaders, analysts, and Iranian observers believe that the world has to listen to and believe Ahmadinejad—he says what he means and means what he says.

Whether that is true or not, his words are troubling. He says that he doesn't want to see Israel among the world's nations and the world believes him. But he also claims that Iran doesn't want nuclear weapons. Can the world believe him again? Can we take the risk of believing him? Can the world live in peace and tranquility with a nuclear Iran and trust that its leaders would never push the button? Or will the nuclear sphinx kill anyone who cannot figure out its riddle?

Appendix A

NUCLEAR ABBREVIATIONS AND TERMS

AEOI	Atomic Energy Organisation of Iran
AUC	Ammonium Uranyl Carbonate
AVLIS	Atomic Vapour Laser Isotope Separation
BNPP	Bushehr Nuclear Power Plant, Bushehr
CO	Carbon Monoxide
CSL	Comprehensive Separation Laboratory, TNRC and Lashkar Ab'ad
CVL	Copper Vapour Laser
DIV	Design Information Verification
ENTC	Esfahan Nuclear Technology Centre
FEP	Fuel Enrichment Plant, Natanz
FFL	Fuel Fabrication Laboratory, ENTC
FMP	Fuel Manufacturing Plant, ENTC
GSCR	Graphite, Sub-Critical Reactor, ENTC
HEU	High Enriched Uranium
HWPP	Heavy Water Production Plant, Arak
HWSPR	Heavy Water Zero Power Reactor, ENTC
ICR	Inventory Change Report
IR-40	Iran Nuclear Research Reactor, Arak
JHL	Jabr Ibn Hayan Multipurpose Laboratories, TNRC

LEU	Low Enriched Uranium
LSL	Laser Separation Laboratory, TNRC and Lashkar Ab'ad
LWSCR	Light Water Sub-Critical Reactor, ENTC
MBR	Material Balance Report
MIX	Facility Molybdenum, Iodine and Xenon Radioisotope Facility, TNRC
MLIS	Molecular Laser Isotope Separation
MNSR	Miniature Neutron Source Reactor, ENTC
PFEP	Pilot Fuel Enrichment Plant, Natanz
PIL	Physical Inventory Listing
SF6	Sulphur Hexafluoride
TNRC	Tehran Nuclear Research Centre
TRR	Tehran Research Reactor, Tehran
UCF	Uranium Conversion Facility, ENTC
UCL	Uranium Chemistry Laboratory, ENTC
UF4	Uranium Tetrachloride
UF6	Uranium Hexafluoride
UO2	Uranium Dioxide
UO3	Uranium Trioxide
U3O8	Urano-Uranic Oxide
UOC	Uranium Ore Concentrate
WHF	Waste Handling Facility, TNRC
WSF	Waste Storage Facility, Karaj

Source: IAEA

GENERAL ABBREVIATIONS AND TERMS

Title	Full name
Abadegaran	Abadegarane Iran-e-Islami, Developers of Islamic Iran, A Political Coalition
AEOI	Atomic Energy Organization of Iran
Aman	Israeli Military Intelligence
AMIA	Asociación Mutual Israelita Argentina – Main Jewish Organization of Argentina
AIO	Aerospace Industries Organization – Iran
Ayatollah	Title meaning "Sign of God"
Baseej	People's militia – Iran
BND	Bundesnachrichtendienst – German Foreign Intelligence
Bonyad	Government controlled charity organization – Iran
CIA	Central Intelligence Agency
DG	Director General at the IAEA
DGSE	French Foreign Intelligence
ENTC	Esfahan Nuclear Technology Centre
EU	European Union
FBI	Federal Bureau of Investigation
FEP	Fuel Enrichment Plant
GBU	Guided Bomb Unit
GCC	Gulf Cooperation Council
GTI	Gulf Technical Industries Co
HEU	Highly Enriched Uranium
Hezbe Jomhouriye Eslami	The Islamic Republic Party – Iran
Hezbollah	Party of God – Lebanon
Hojatol Eslam	Full Title: Hojatalislam Wa-l-Muslemin meaning "authority on Islam"
HUMINT	Human Intelligence
IAEA	International Atomic Energy Agency

Title	Full name
IAF	Israeli Air Force
IRGC	Islamic Revolutionary Guards Corp
Isargaran	Jame'eye Isargarane Enqhelabe Eslami – The Islamic Revolution Devotees Society Political Coalition
Jame'e Roohaniyoone Mobarez	Association of Combatant Clerics
Kalaye Electric Co.	AIO cover for producing and testing centrifuges
Maktab	Religious primary school
MI6	Britain's Foreign Intelligence
MIT	Massachusetts Institute of Technology
MKM – MKO	Mojahedeen Khalq Movement – People's Mujahedeen Movement – Also known as Mojahedeen Khalq Organization
Mossad	Ha Mosad le Modi'in ve le Tafkidim Meyukhadim – The Institute for Intelligence and Special Tasks, referred to as Mossad, meaning the Institute Israel's Foreign Intelligence.
NATO	North Atlantic Treaty Organization
NCRI	National Council of Resistance of Iran
NIOC	National Iranian Oil Company
NPT	Non-Proliferation Treaty
NRO	National Reconnaissance Office – U.S.
NSA	National Security Agency – U.S.
NYU	New York University
OSU	Office for Strengthening and Unity – Daftare Tahkim va Vahdat
PDKI	Democratic Party of Iranian Kurdistan
PFEP	Pilot Fuel Enrichment Plant

Title	Full name
PLO	Palestine Liberation Organization
R&D	Research and Development
SIG	Sanam Industrial Group – a subsidiary of Iran's Aerospace Industries Organization (AIO)
SAVAK	Sazemane Ettelaat va Amniyate Keshvar, Organization for Intelligence and National Security – Pre-Revolution – Iran
Seyyed Alshohada	Lord of the Martyrs
SHABAK	Shirut Bitakhon Klali General Security Services – Israel's Domestic Service
Shahadat	Martyrdom
SIDE	Secretaría de Inteligencia del Estado – Argentinean Secret Service
SIGINT	Signal Intelligence
SNSC	Supreme National Security Council – Iran
SVR	Russian Foreign Intelligence Service
Tudeh	Iranian Communist Party
UAE	United Arab Emirates
UCF	Uranium Conversation Facility
UF4	Uranium Tetrachloride
UF6	Uranium Hexafloride
UK	United Kingdom of Great Britain
UN	United Nations
UNSC	United Nations Security Council
UOC	Uranium Ore Concentrate
VAVAK	Vezarate Etelaat Va Aminiyate Keshvar – Ministry of Information and Security – Iran
Velayete Faghih	The Supremacy of the Islamic Jurist Consul

LIST OF IRAN'S MAJOR AND KNOWN NUCLEAR SITES

LOCATION	Facility and Purpose	STATUS
TEHRAN NUCLEAR RESEARCH CENTRE	Tehran Research Reactor (TRR)	Operating
	Molybdenum, Iodine and Xenon Radioisotope Production Facility (MIX Facility)	Constructed, but not operating
	Jabr Ibn Hayan Multipurpose Laboratories (JHL)	Operating
	Waste Handling Facility (WHF)	Operating
TEHRAN	Kalaye Electric Company	Dismantled pilot enrichment facility
BUSHEHR	Bushehr Nuclear Power Plant (BNPP)	Under construction
ESFAHAN NUCLEAR TECHNOLOGY CENTRE	Miniature Neutron Source Reactor (MNSR)	Operating
	Light Water Sub-Critical Reactor (LWSCR)	Operating
	Heavy Water Zero Power Reactor (HWSPR)	Operating

LOCATION	Facility and Purpose	STATUS
	Fuel Fabrication Laboratory (FFL)	Operating
	Uranium Chemistry Laboratory (UCL)	Closed down
	Uranium Conversion Facility (UCF)	Operating
	Graphite Sub-Critical Reactor (GSCR)	Decommissioned
	Fuel Manufacturing Plant (FMP)	In detailed design stage, construction begun in 2004
NATANZ	Pilot Fuel Enrichment Plant (PFEP)	Operating
	Fuel Enrichment Plant (FEP)	Under construction
KARAJ	Radioactive Waste Storage	Under construction, but partially operating
LASHKAR AB'AD	Pilot Uranium Laser Enrichment Plant	Dismantled
ARAK	Iran Nuclear Research Reactor (IR-40)	Under construction

LOCATION	Facility and Purpose	STATUS
	Hot cell facility for production of radioisotopes	In design stage
	Heavy Water Production Plant (HWPP)	Under construction, not subject to inspection
ANARAK	Waste storage site	Waste to be transferred to JHL

Source: IAEA

Appendix B

LIST OF IRANIAN COMPANIES AND INDIVIDUALS BANNED
BY THE UNITED NATIONS SECURITY COUNCIL UNDER
RESOLUTION 1737

A. Entities involved in the nuclear programme

1. Atomic Energy Organisation of Iran
2. Mesbah Energy Company (provider for A 40 research reactor—Arak)
3. Kala-Electric (aka Kalaye Electric) (provider for PFEP—Natanz)
4. Pars Trash Company (involved in centrifuge programme, identified in IAEA reports)
5. Farayand Technique (involved in centrifuge programme, identified in IAEA reports)
6. Defence Industries Organisation (overarching MODAFL-controlled entity, some of whose subordinates have been involved in the centrifuge programme making components, and in the missile programme)
7. 7th of Tir (subordinate of DIO, widely recognized as being directly involved in the nuclear programme)

B. Entities involved in the ballistic missile programme

1. Shahid Hemmat Industrial Group (SHIG) (subordinate entity of AIO)
2. Shahid Bagheri Industrial Group (SBIG) (subordinate entity of AIO)

3. Fajr Industrial Group (formerly Instrumentation Factory Plant, subordinate entity of AIO)

C. Persons involved in the nuclear programme

1. Muhammad Qannadi, AEOI Vice President for Research & Development
2. Behman Asgarpour, Operational Manager (Arak)
3. Dawood Agha-Jani, Head of the PFEP (Natanz)
4. Ehsan Monajemi, Construction Project Manager, Natanz
5. Jafar Muhammadi, Technical Adviser to the AEOI (in charge of managing the production of valves for centrifuges)
6. Ali Hajinia Leilabadi, Director General of Mesbah Energy Company
7. Lt. Gen. Muhammad Mehdi Nejad Nouri, Rector of Malek Ashtar University of Defence Technology (chemistry dept, affiliated to MODALF, has conducted experiments on beryllium)

D. Persons involved in the ballistic missile programme

1. Gen Hosein Salimi, Commander of the Air Force, IRGC (Pasdaran)
2. Ahmad Vahid Dastjerdi, Head of the AIO
3. Reza-Gholi Esmaeli, Head of Trade & International Affairs Dept, AIO
4. Bahmanyar Morteza Bahmanyar, Head of Finance & Budget Dept, AIO

E. Persons involved in both the nuclear and ballistic missile programmes

1. Maj. Gen. Yahya Rahim Safavi, Commander, IRGC (Pasdaran)

Appendix C

Nuclear Fuel Cycle

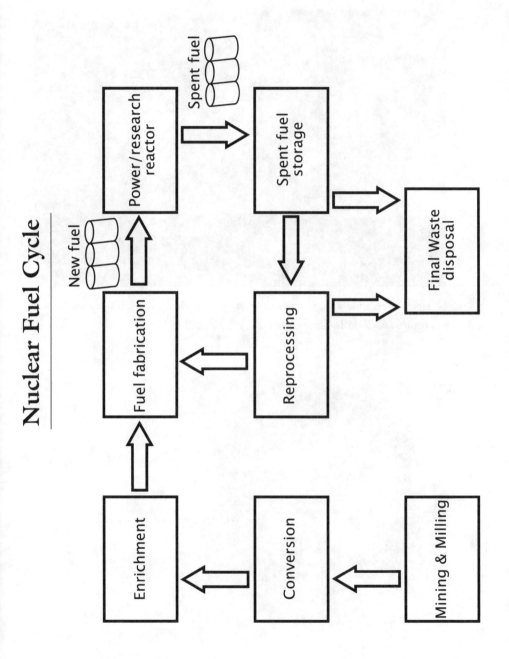

Appendix D

An Israeli submarine which is capable of carrying nuclear warheads and may be used in a future attack on Iran's nuclear sites.

An electric clock from Kalaya's uranium centrifuge workshop.

Underground structure, under construction, intended as a support building for the two cascade buildings

Underground structures, under construction, intended to house gas centrifuge cascades

Thick Wall

3

6

4   2   1

1

6   6

5

Centrifuge Assembly Area

Underground Truck Road

Tunnel Entrance

Administration Building

Photo credit: AP Images

A prime target for a future attack on Iran's nuclear sites. In this heavily fortified site, built underground, Iran is enriching uranium for what is believed to be the development of nuclear arsenal. (AP Photo/National Council of Resistance in Iran/HO)

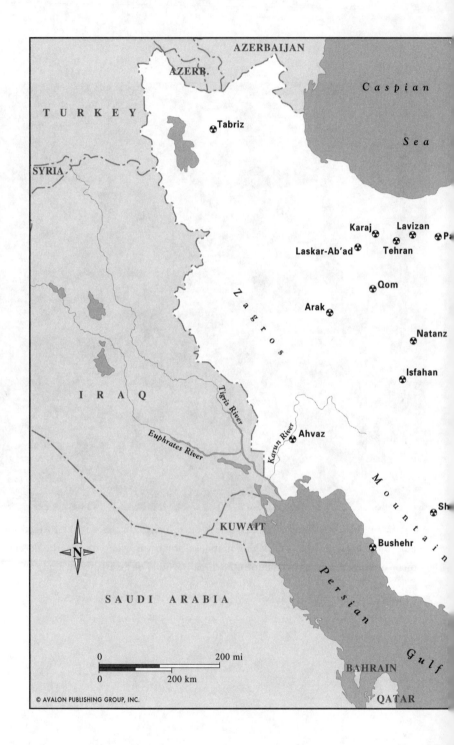

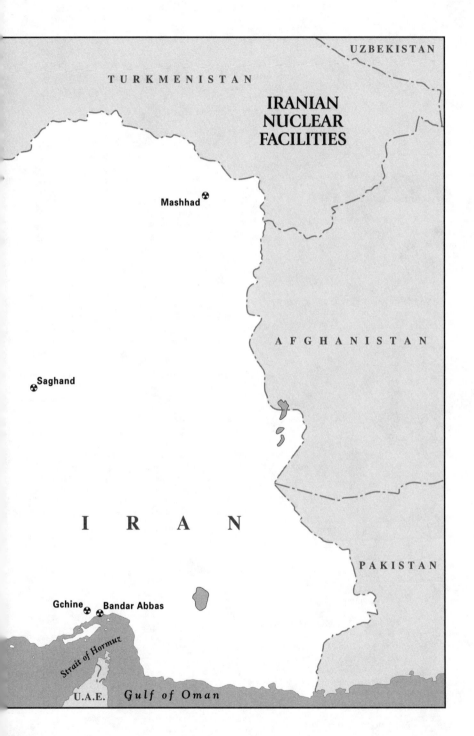

Bibliography

THIS BOOK IS based on around one hundred interviews with government officials and experts. They included intelligence officers, military commanders, and nuclear specialists from numerous countries and organizations: The United States, Israel, Britain, Germany, France, Italy, Poland, Egypt, the International Atomic Energy Agency (IAEA), to name a few. Most of them provided very important information and insights, but asked not to be named. Although we believe in the principle of "on the record," we have to respect their wish. Thus we can only provide a very limited list of interviewees and sources. The same rule applies to many Iranians. Many Iranians, including religious officials who live in Iran, were interviewed by phone, or e-mail messages.

Interviews
- Arad, Uzi
- Asculai, Ephraim
- Barak, Ehud
- Ben Eliyahu, Eitan
- Ben Peretz, Opher
- El-Baradei, Muhammad
- Einhorn, Robert
- Etemad, Akbar
- Halevy, Ephraim
- Lobrani, Uri

- Malka, Amos
- Megidor, Menachem
- Olmert, Ehud
- Perle, Richard
- Tantar, Raymond
- Rubin, Uzi
- Samore, Gary
- Saguy, Uri
- Segev, Yitzhak
- Shafir, Relik
- Shavit, Shabtai
- Sneh, Ephraim
- Steinitz, Yuval
- Tsafrir, Eliezer
- Ze'evi Farkash, Aharon

Research and reports
- Boureston, Jack, and Charles Ferguson. "Schooling Iran's Atom Squad," in *Bulletin of the Atomic Scientists,* 60, no. 3 (May/June 2004): 31–35.
- Einhorn, Robert, and Gary Samore, "Heading off Iran's Bomb: the Need for Renewed U.S-Russian Cooperation," *Yederny Control Digest 7*, no. 3, PIR Center, Moscow, 2002.
- Federation of American Scientists; for information about Iran's Special Weapons Program, go to http://www.fas.org/nuke/guide/iran/index.html.
- Global Security has also produced extensive reports on Iran, which can be found at http://www.globalsecurity.org/military/ops/iran-timeline.htm#070201.
- IAEA has produced several reports, almost on quarterly basis on Iran. These can be found at http://www.iaea.org/NewsCenter/Focus/IaeaIran/index.shtml.

- Inbar, Efraim, "The Need to Block a nuclear Iran." *Mid East Security and Policy Studies,* no. 67. The Begin-Sadat Center for Strategic Studies, Bar Ilan University, April 2006.
- Lerner, Jonathan. "Iran's Threat to Israel's Security. Present Dangers and Future Risks" The American Jewish Committee New York 1993.
- NTI (Nuclear Threat Initiative). Extensive information on Iran's Chemical, Biological and Nuclear Weapons program. Go to http://www.nti.org/e_research/profiles/Iran/index.html.
- Raas, Whitney, and Austin Long. "Osirak Redux? Assessing Israeli Capabilities to Destroy Iranian Nuclear Facilities." Working paper for Security Studies Program (SSP) at MIT, April 2006.
- Rubin, Uzi. "The Global Reach of Iran's Ballistic Missiles" Institute for National Security Studies" at Tel Aviv University, November 2006.
- Squassoni, Sharon. "Iran's Nuclear Program: Recent Developments." Congressional Record Service, Foreign Affairs, Defense and Trade Division, 2006.
- Steinberg, Gerald. "Iran Is Bluffing When It Threatens Massive Retaliation." The Begin Sadat Center for Strategic Studies Bulletin no. Bar Ilan University, May 20, 2006.
- Zak, Chen. "Iran's Nuclear Policy and the IAEA—An Evaluation of Program, 93+2." The Washington Institute for Near East Policy, Military Research Paper no. 3, Washington DC 2002.
- Zarif, M. Javad and Saeid Mirzaee. "U.S. Unilateral Sanctions against Iran." *The Iranian Journal of International Affairs* 9, no.1 (Spring 1997).

An important source for this book has been Iranian and Farsi language Web sites. These include

- Advar News
- Aftab News
- Ali Reza Nourizadeh
- Ansar Hezbollah
- Asr Daily
- Baztab
- BBC Persian
- Bourse News
- Entekhab News
- Ettelaat
- Farda News
- Fars News
- Gooya News
- Hadaf News
- Hamshahri
- Iran Focus
- Iran Mania
- Iran News
- Iran Press Service
- Iranian Labour News Agency
- Iranian Students News Agency–ISNA
- Islamic Republic News Agency–IRNA
- Keyhan
- Khedmat
- Mehr News
- Peik Net
- Raja News
- Rooz
- Shabestan News Agency
- Shargh Online
- Sharif News

- Student News Network–SNN
- Voice of America–Persian Service

Books

1. Afrasiabi, Kaveh. *Iran's Nuclear Program: Debating Facts Versus Fiction*. Book Surge Publishing, 2006.
2. Ajami, Fouad. *The Vanished Imam, Musa al Sadr and the Shi'a of Lebanon*. Cornell University Press, 1986..
3. Al-Suwaidi, Jamal. *Iran and the Gulf: A Search for Stability*. I.B. Tauris Publishing 1996.
4. Alam, Asadollah. *The Shah and I: The Confidential Diary of Iran's Royal Court 969–1977*. London: I.B. Tauris, 1988.
5. Alikhani, Hossein. *Sanctioning Iran: Anatomy of a Failed Policy*. I.B. Tauris Publishing 2001.
6. Alizadeh, Parvin. *The Economy of Iran: dilemmas of an Islamic state*. I.B.Tauris Publishing 2001.
7. Ansari, Ali. Confronting Iran: *The Failure of American Foreign Policy and the Next Great Crisis in the Middle East*. Perseus Books Group, 2006.
8. Baer, Robert. *See No Evil: A True Story of a ground soldier in the CIA's War on Terrorism*. New York: Three Rivers Press, 2002.
9. Beaton, Leonard, and John Maddox. *The Spread of Nuclear Weapons*. (Hebrew) Ministry of Defense Publishing House, August 1963.
10. Clawson, Patrick, Henry Sokolsky. *Getting Ready for a Nuclear-Ready Iran*. The Strategic Studies Institute of the US Army War College, 2005.
11. Cohen, Avner. *Israel and the Bomb*. New York: Columbia University Press, 1998.
12. Cole, Juan. *Conversations with History*. Institute of International Studies at the University of California–Berkeley.
13. Gheissari, Ali, Vali Nasr. *Democracy in Iran: History and the Quest for Liberty* Oxford University Press, 2006.
14. Hiro, Dilip. *The Longest War: The Iran-Iraq Military Conflict*. Routledge Publishing, 1991.
15. Hitchcock, Mark. *Iran: The Coming Crisis: Radical Islam, Oil, and the Nuclear Threat*. Multnomah Publishing, 2006.
16. Kam, Ephraim. *From Terror to Nuclear Bombs, The Significance of the Iranian Threat*. (Hebrew) Tel Aviv University, Tel Aviv: Ministry of Defense Publishing House, Jaffee Centre for Strategic Studies, 2004.
17. Keddie, Nikkie. *Modern Iran: Roots and Results of Revolution*. Yale University Press, 2003.
18. Menashri, David. *Post-Revolutionary Politics in Iran: Religion, Society and Power* Routledg, Publishing, 2001.
19. Moin, Baqer. *Khomeini Life of the Ayatollah*. St. Martin's Press, 1999.

20. Nafisi, Azar. *Reading Lolita in Tehran*. (Hebrew) Yeduot Aharonot Publishing, 2006.
21. Nakdimon, Shlomo. *First Strike: The Exclusive Story of How Israel Foiled Iraq's attempt to get the Bomb*. New York: Summit Books, 1987.
22. Ram, Haggai. *Reading Iran in Israel: The Self and the Other, Religion and Modernity*. (Hebrew). The Van Leer Jerusalem Institute, Hakibbutz Hameuchad Publishing House, 2006.
23. Richelson, Jeffrey. S*pying on the Bomb: American Nuclear Intelligence from Nazi Germany to Iran and North Korea*. New York: W. W. Norton 2006.
24. Risen, James. *The Secret History of the CIA and the Bush Administration*. Free Press, 2006.
25. Ritter, Scott. *Target Iran: The Truth About the White House's Plans for Regime Change*. Nation Books, 2006.
26. Segev, Samuel. *The Iranian Triangle*. New York: The Free Press, 1988. (Based on the Hebrew version.)
27. Shapira, Shimshon. "Hezbollah between Iran and Lebanon" (Hebrew) Hakkibutz Hameuchad Tel Aviv 2000.
28. Shyam, Bhatia. *Nuclear Rivals in the Middle East* New York: Routledge, 1988.
29. Takeyh, Ray. *Hidden Iran: Paradox and Power in the Islamic Republic*. Times Books, 2006.
30. Wilber, Donald. *Regime Change in Iran: Overthrow of Premier Mossadeq of Iran November 1952–August 1953*. Spokesman Books, 2006.
31. Woodward, Bob. *Veil: The Secret Wars of the CIA, 1981–1987*. Headline Book Publishing, UK 1987.
32. Yaghmaian, Behzad. *Social Change in Iran: An Eyewitness Account of Dissent, Defiance, and New movements for Rights*. SUNY Press, 2002.

Notes

Prologue

1. Previously unpublished transcripts of conversation with Mahmoud Ahmadinejad prior to the Presidential elections, Mehr News 04/08/2005.

2. "Ill Health of Ahmadinejad's Father, Cause of Speech Cancellation," Baztab News, 14/11/2005.

3. Imam Hussein's murder is remembered by ritual chest-beating to express pain and anguish every year in the Ashura ceremony.

4. "7th Day Mourning Ceremony is Held for the President's Father," Mehr News 05/06/2006.

5. Robert Tait, "A Humble Beginning Helped to Form Iran's New Hard Man," *The Guardian*, 02/07/05.

6. "My Father Loved Imam Khomeini and the People," IRNA 31/05/2006.

Chapter One

1. Robert Tait, "A Humble Beginning Helped to Form Iran's New Hard Man," *The Guardian*, 7/2/05.

2. G. Shams, "Ahmadinejad: It's Possible, and We Can Do It," *The Green Family Magazine*, no. 137, www.ksabz.net.

3. Robert Tait.

4. G. Shams.

5. Mahmoud Ahmadinejad official blog, www.Ahmadinejad.ir.

6. G. Shams.

7. Ibid.

8. Ibid.

9. F. Ghazizadeh, "Don't Have Much Hope from Students of Science and Technology University," *Rooz* online 8/2/2005.

10. Barbara Slavin "In Iran, Revolution is a Presidential Priority," *USA Today* 3/13/2006.

11. Robert Tait.

12. Bob Woodruff, "Profile: Mahmoud Ahmadinejad," ABC news 1/4/2006.

13. Mahmoud Ahmadinejad official blog, www.Ahmadinejad.ir.

14. Ibid.

15. "My Father Loved Imam Khomeini and the People," IRNA 5/31/05.

16. Ibid.

17. Mahmoud Ahmadinejad official blog, www.Ahmadinejad.ir.

18. Ibid.

19. "Biography of Mayor Turned President Ahmadinejad," Islamic Republic News Agency 8/3/2005.

20. Robert Tait.

21. "Ahmadinejad? Who's He?" Iran Focus 6/25/05.

22. Robert Tait.

23. Ibid.

24. "Exclusive: Photo Shows Iran's Ahmadinejad as Hostage-Taker of U.S. Diplomats," Iran Focus 6/29/05.

25. "Iran's New President Has a Past Mired in Controversy," Iran Focus 6/25/2005.

26. "Profile: Mahmoud Ahmadinejad," Al Jazeera 6/19/2005.

27. David Gollust, "U.S. Considers Visa Request from New Iranian President" Voice of America News 8/8/2005.

28. "U.S. Looking into Iranian Leader" *China Daily,* 7/1/2005.

29. Nevertheless, in a report on CNN on August 12, 2005, the CIA stated that its investigation into Ahmadinejad's involvement "is not final." "U.S. Looking into Iranian Leader," *China Daily* 7/1/2005.

30. Previously unpublished transcripts of conversation with Mahmoud Ahmadinejad prior to the Presidential elections, Mehr News 8/4/05.

31. Ibid.

32. Blog—the three-year-old girl (named after one of Imam Hussein's martyred daughters who was three years old when she was killed).

33. "Ahmadinejad Won't Become a Palace Dweller," Islamic Republic of Iran News Agency 7/30/2005.

34. "Simple Life of a President," Farda News 1/18/2006.

35. "Apostle of the Apocalypse," *The Sunday Times Magazine* 6/18/06.

36. "135,000 Letters from the People of Golestan to Ahmadinejad," Baztab News 3/2/06.

37. A. Zagorin, "10 Questions for Mahmoud Ahmadinedjad," *Time* 09/26/2005.

38. "Ahmadinejad's Son Becomes Member of Central Committee of Islamic Students Union," Farda News 8/14/2005.

39. Maryam Sobhani "Removal of Ahmadinejad's Son from a Student Organization," *Rooz Daily* 11/22/2005.

40. "Rumours of Ahmadinejad and the Northern Bride," Baztab News 5/28/2006.

41. "During the Mourning Ceremony of Ahmad Ahmadinejad, a Man in Black Had a Smile on His Face," *Hamshahri* 6/12/2006.

42. "Ahmadinejad's Election Biography—from His Election Website," Gooya News 6/25/2005.

43. "French Daily: Iran's Ahmadinejad Was Key U.S. Embassy Hostage-Taker," Iran Focus 6/29/2005.

44. Previously unpublished transcripts of conversation with Mahmoud Ahmadinejad prior to the Presidential elections, Mehr News 8/4/2005.

45. "Ahmadinejad's Election Biography—from His Election Website," Gooya News 6/25/05.

46. Ibid.

47. The involvement of Ahmadinejad in this operation was also mentioned by the Austrian newspaper *Der Standard*, "Iran President-Elect's Role in 1989 Attack 'Part of Pattern'" Iran Focus 7/2/05. See also "Iran Revolutionary Guards Expect Key Changes in High Command," Iran Focus 8/4/05.

48. Interview with Dr. Peter Pilz, leader of the Austrian Green Party, July 20, 2005. Published in *Ha'aretz* (Hebrew) 7/26/2005.

49. Ibid.

50. Ibid.

51. Pilz claimed that the Austrian government at that time did not want to launch a detailed and comprehensive investigation. Upon the election of Ahmadinejad, Pilz demanded the case be reopened, this time focusing on the role of the newly elected president. However, "there was strong

pressure from Iran on my government not to reopen the investigation," Pilz says, insisting nonetheless that his sources pointing to Ahmadinejad's involvement are solid.

52. "Apostle of the Apocalypse," *The Sunday Times Magazine* 6/18/2006.

53. "End of Vote Counting—Winner Has Been Declared," Entekhabat News Agency 6/25/2005.

54. "Dr Ahmadinejad, in the 9th Presidential Elections, Has Won the Highest Number of Votes," ISNA 6/25/2005.

55. "Points of View of Mahmoud Ahmadinejad," BBC Persian News 6/26/2005.

56. Ibid.

57. John Moody, "Iranian President's Got Game. But Which Game?" Fox News 6/15/06.

58. "Iran's Borders Are Protected By 10 million Basijis," Mehr News 11/27/05.

59. Mahan Abedin, "Ahmadinejad May End Up Being the Clerics' Bane," *Daily Star,* Thursday, June 30, 2005.

60. "The Threat from Tehran," *Der Spiegel,* October 31, 2005.

61. "Postcard from Tehran, Traffic Chaos," BBC News 2/13/04.

62. Previously unpublished transcripts of conversation with Mahmoud Ahmadinejad prior to the Presidential elections, Mehr News 04/08/2005.

63. Ibid.

64. Ibid.

65. Barbara Slavin, "In Iran, Revolution is a Presidential Priority," *USA Today* 3/9/06.

66. Ibid.

67. Report of Tehran Municipality activities for the last 23 months is presented to members of town council, Mehr News 4/20/05.

68. "Ahmadinejad in Final Round of World's Best Mayor Contest," *Tehran Times,* August 13, 2005.

69. F. Ghazizadeh, "The Mayor Who Does Not Like Criticism," *Rooz Daily* 6/20/05.

70. Ibid.

71. Samane Ghadar Khan, Tehran reporter, specializing in Tehran Municipality affairs, interview with BBC Persian News, May 30, 2005.

72. Ghasem Khorammi, interview with BBC Persian News, May 30, 2005.

73. Behnam Majid Zadeh, "Record of Financial Cheating Was Broken During Ahmadinejad's Tenure as Mayor," *Rooz Daily* 18/10/2005.

74. Ibid.

75. "Iran Hardliner to Contest Run-off," BBC News 6/18/05.

76. "Iran Hardliner Sweeps to Victory," BBC News 6/25/05.

Chapter Two

1. "Ahmadinejad: By Eliminating Waste We Will Resolve Issues Facing the Youth," Baztab News 25/06/2005.

2. "Ahmadinejad Expresses His Views After Casting His Vote," ISNA 24/06/2004.

3. Mahan Abedin, "Ahmadinejad May End Up Being the Clerics' Bane," *Daily Star*, Thursday, June 30, 2005.

4. Bill Samii, "Iran: A Rising Star in Party Politics," Radio Free Europe 07/11/2005.

5. Bill Samii, "Iran: Abundance of Candidates Worries Hard-Liners," Radio Free Europe 15/06/2005.

6. Ibid.

7. Bill Samii, "Iran: A Rising Star in Party Politics," Radio Free Europe 07/11/2005.

8. "Exit of Ahmadinejad from the List of the Council for the Co-ordination of Islamic Forces," *Shargh* 03/02/2005.

9. "Ahmadinejad: I was Under a Lot of Pressure to Pull Out of the Elections. Will Declare the Name of Those Pressuring Me in Eight Days," IRNA 30/05/2005.

10. Ibid.

11. Bill Samii, "Iran: Abundance of Candidates Worries Hard-Liners," Radio Free Europe 15/06/2005.

12. Ibid.

13. "Iran's Ex-Revolutionary Guards Chief Abandons Race," Iran Focus 15/06/2005.

14. John Snow, "Podcast from Tehran," Channel 4.

15. "Postcards from Iran: Traffic Chaos," BBC News 13/02/2004.

16. "What Can Be Done to Combat Air Pollution in Tehran?" BBC Persian News, 07/01/2005.

17. "Noise Pollution in Tehran is Twice the Global Standards," Mehr News 20/05/2005.

18. "Smuggling of Illegal Weapons into the Country Increased by 10 Fold," Fars News 17/05/2006.

19. "Aircraft Problems Are Completely Ordinary," Aftab News 18/04/2005.

20. "Iranian Postcards: Wrapped in Red Tape," BBC News 13/02/2004.

21. "Every Day Two Women Die Under the Plastic Surgeon's Knife," Baztab News 11/05/2005.

22. Barbara Slavin, "Iran's Ex-President: U.S. Should Show Goodwill," *USA Today* 02/06/2005.

23. "Iran—Who Holds the Power?" BBC News.

24. "Pictures of Rollerblading Boys and Girls in Support of Rafsanjani," Mehr News 17/06/2005.

25. David Menashri, *Post-Revolution Politics in Iran*, 2001.

26. "Rafsanjanis Are Iran's Power Brokers for Investors," Bloomberg News Service 21/04/2004.

27. Paul Klebnikov, "Millionaire Mullahs," *Forbes Magazine* 21/07/2003.

28. "Scandal Puts Top Statoil Jobs on the Line," *Aftenposten* (Norway), 15/9/2003.

29. Interview with Ali K., former reporter with a Tehran-based Reformist newspaper (surname hidden), 15/07/2006.

30. "Pictorial Report of Disturbances at Rafsanjani Rally," Aftab News 06/06/2006.

31. "At a Glance—Iran," UNICEF.

32. "90 Percent of Iran Population Under Poverty Line: MP," Iran Focus 21/01/2005.

33. "Gap Widens Between Iran's Rich and Poor," BBC News 11/06/2005.

34. Ibid.

35. "Ahmadinejad: Iran Needs a Third Revolution for the Establishment of Islamic Government, Based on Velayete Faghih," IRNA 03/06/1384.

36. Ibid.

37. Marie Colvin, "Iran's Man of Iron Vows to Turn Back Clock," *The Times* 26/06/2005.

38. "Ahmadinejad: Behind the Scenes Dealings of a Few Wont Affect Election Results," Mehr News 03/05/2005.

39. " Ahmadinejad: As Long As We Are Alive, We Are Fighters," ISNA 07/05/2005.

40. "Ahmadinejad's Complaint to Islamic Republic Broadcasting," IRNA 29/05/2005.

41. Mathias Kuntzel, "Ahmadinejad's Demons," *The New Republic* 24/04/2006.

42. Ibid.

43. Ibid.

44. Ibid.

45. Ibid.

46. Ahmadinejad's election Web site, www.mardomyar.com.

47. "Conversations with Atrianfar About the Defeat of Rafsanjani," Farda News 01/7/2006.

48. "Nirouye Moghavamate Basij—Mobilisation Resistance Force," Globalsecurity.org.

49. Conversations with a Esfahani native living in Tel Aviv, Israel.

50. "Photo Report of Ahmadinejad's Trip to Esfahan Province," Mehr News 13/6/2005.

51. Ibid.

52. "Ahmadinejad: We Didn't Have a Revolution So That We Rule in Turns," Ansar News 20/06/2005.

53. "Overcrowding of People Waiting to Greet Ahmadinejad Left One Dead," Mehr News 13/06/05.

54. "Ahmadinejad Welcoming Ceremony Ends in Tragedy," Shabestan News 14/06/2005.

55. "Photo Editorial—Burial of Behnam Karimian," Mehr News 14/06/05.

56. These included www.ahmadinejad.blogfa.com, www.entekhabe27.parsiblog.com, www.yardarkhaneh.blogfa.com.

57. "Ahmadinejad: If Instead of Missiles We Imported Citroens, Our Enemies Would Not Feel Hurt," IRNA 10/06/2005.

58. Karl Vick, "Hard-Line Figure in Iran Runoff," *Washington Post* 19/06/2005.

59. "List of Ahmadinejad's Wealth," Baztab News 31/12/2005.

60. "Apostle of the Apocalypse," *The Sunday Times Magazine* 18/06/2006.

61. "Iran's President Nominates Fourth Oilman," Iran Focus 04/12/2005.

62. "Nuclear Capabilities Aside: The Trickle-Up Politics of Ahmadinejad," *Bidoun*, Issue 6, 2005.

63. "Iran's Presidential Race Hinges on Class," NPR Report 23/06/2005.

64. David Menashri, *Post-Revolutionary Politics in Iran*, 2001.

65. "Rafsanjanis Are Iran's Power Brokers for Investors," Bloomberg News Service 21/04/2004.

66. "Iran Hardliner to Contest Run-off," BBC News 18/06/2005.

67. Robin Wright, "In Iran, Students Urge Citizens Not to Vote," *Washington Post* 19/11/2004.

68. "Iran Hardliner to Contest Run-off," BBC News 18/06/2005.

69. Bagher Zadeh, "A Palace Coup in the Making," Iran Press Service 17/06/2006.

70. "National Trust Party Authorized," *Iran Daily* 8/14/05.

71. "Conversations with Atrianfar About the Defeat of Rafsanjani," Farda News 01/7/2006.

72. Tait, "Fraud Claims Mar Iranian Poll Run-off," *The Guardian* 25/06/2005.

73. "Behind the Scenes Decision by Rafsanjani to Participate in Second Round of Elections," Baztab News 6/20/05.

74. "People Want Rafsanjani Without the People Who Surround Him," Mehr News, 6/20/05.

75. "Iran's Presidential Race Hinges on Class," NPR Report 6/23/05.

76. "The 'Address' of Hezbollah in Esfahan Has Been Discovered," Sharif News 31 Khord 1384.

77. "What Happened in Za'afariye on Saturday Night?" Sharif News 31 Khord 1384.

78. Islamic Republic of Iran TV interview with Tehran Mayor Mahmoud Ahmadinejad, 6/10/05.

79. "Conversations with Atrianfar About the Defeat of Rafsanjani," Farda News 7/1/06.

80. Flynt L. Leverett, "Iran: The Gulf between U.S." *The New York Times* 1/4/06.

81. Ibid.

82. "Iran Is Behind the Badr Brigade in Iraq—Report," Iran Focus 11/17/05.

83. Lioneel Behner, "U.S. Intervention in Iraqi Politics," Council on Foreign Relations 3/30/06.

84. "Jalal Talebani Hails Iranian Support for Iraqi Opposition," Iran Press Service 1/7/06.

85. Massoume Price, "Meeting Faezeh the Rise and Fall of a Talented Woman," *The Iranian* 10/5/00.

86. "IRAN: Presidential Candidates," Council for Foreign Relations 6/15/06.

87. Barbara Slavin, "Iran's New President Walks a Hard Line," *USA Today* 6/27/05.

88. Amir Taheri, "Behind the Scenes in Tehran," *Jerusalem Post* 8/15/05.

Chapter Three

1. "Iran President Says Celestial Light Protected Him at the UN," *The Scotsman* 02/12/2005—video of Ahmadinejad's meeting with Ayatollah Amoli, supplied by Baztab News Agency.

2. Anton Laguardia, "Divine Mission Driving New Iranian Leader," *Daily Telegraph* 14/01/2006.

3. Matthias Küntzel, "A Child of the Revolution Takes Over," *The New Republic* 14/04/2006.

4. Interview with Bright Futures Organisation, Qom, Iran.

5. Amir Taheri, "The Frightening Truth of Why Iran Wants a Bomb," *Daily Telegraph* 06/04/2006.

6. "Suspicious Activities of a Clergy, and the Misuse of Religious Text," Baztab News Agency 17/05/2006.

7. Interview with Yaghoub Ja'afari, Koranic analyst and interpreter, "The Holy Koran Has Many Interpretations About the Mahdi's Return," Mehr News 09/04/2006.

8. Ibid.

9. Amir Taheri, "The Frightening Truth of Why Iran Wants a Bomb," *Daily Telegraph* 06/04/2006.

10. Ali Nazeri, "Mesbah Yazdi's Connections with the Presidential Elections—Who Is Mesbah Yazdi? Part 2," *Rooz* online 20/09/2005.

11. Ibid.

12. Mehdi Khalji, "New Wave of Messianic Ideologies (Mahdaviat) in Iran; Its Roots," *Rooz* online 22/11/2005.

13. Ibid.

14. Arash Motamed, "The Sanctity of a President," *Rooz* online 21/07/2005.

15. "Claims of Communication with Imam Mahdi," *Emrouz* 05/12/2005 (attributed to Fars News report, published 11/11/2005).

16. "Claims of Communication with Imam Mahdi," *Emrouz* 05/12/2005.

17. Scott Peterson, "Waiting for the Rapture in Iran," *Christian Science Monitor* 21/12/2005.

18. Arash Mahdavi, "The Man Behind the President," *Rooz Daily* 06/11/2005.

19. "Special Order from the Presidential Office," Aftab News 23/11/2006.

20. "Reformist, Fundamentalist Candidates Ruled Out of Assembly Election," Radio Free Europe 04/12/2006.

21. "The $3.5 Million Assistance to Mesbah Yazdi's Institution, Allocated in Ahmadinejad's Budget," Aftab News 04/02/2006.

22. "Claims of Communication with Imam Mahdi," *Emrouz* 05/12/2005 (attributed to report in ILNA 29/11/2005).

23. "Claims of Communication with Imam Mahdi," *Emrouz* 05/12/2005 (attributed to Rooydad News 25/09/2005).

24. Anton Laguardia, "Divine Mission Driving New Iranian Leader," *Daily Telegraph* 14/01/2006.

25. "Ahmadinejad: The Islamic Revolution Can Only be Analysed in the Framework of Holy Figures," Mehr News 03/07/2005.

26. "Ahmadinejad: Victory Belongs to Hezbollah," Ansar News 20/06/2005.

27. "International Exhibition Area is Turned into Ladies Only Garden," *Keyhan* 18/07/04.

28. "Ahmadinejad: The First Governmental Meeting Will Start at the Tomb of Imam Reza," President Ahmadinejad Web site (www.president.ir) 25/08/2006.

29. Matthias Küntzel, "A Child of the Revolution Takes Over," *The New Republic* 14/04/2006.

30. Dilip Hiro, "It's Not Just Iran's Leaders Who Think it Better to Fight and Die Than Compromise with America," *Daily Telegraph* 12/03/2006.

31. "Ahmadinejad: The Spirit of Martyrdom Seeking Is Our Secret of Invincibility," IRNA 27/03/2006.

32. "Ahmadinejad: The Fate of the Enemies of Islam Is Nothing Short of Destruction," ISNA 09/02/2006.

33. "Ahmadinejad: Liberalism, the Founding Philosophy of Zionism Have Also Been Sacrificed," Mehr News 08/07/2006.

34. "Ahmadinejad Claims Holocaust Invented to Embarrass the German People," *Deutsche Welle* 28/08/2006.

35. "Iranian Leader Denies Holocaust," BBC News 14/12/2005.

36. "Ahmadinejad: Wipe Israel Off Map," Al Jazeera 28/10/2005.

37. Sardar Salehi, ed., *Az Pass-e Shanaiy-e Shah: Seyri dar Safar Farangestan-e Nasser ed-Din Shah* (Rotterdam: Dena Publishing Center), 1997, p. 208–09.

38. "Ahmadinejad: Very Soon We Will See the Demise of the Zionist Regime," Farda News 23/07/2006.

39. Speech by Mahmoud Ahmadinejad, Iranian News Network (IRINN) 02/08/2006.

40. "Ahmadinejad: Lebanon Was the Scene of the Victory of Believers in God," ISNA 15/08/2006.

41. Mahmoud Ahmadinejad blog, www.Ahmadinejad.ir.

42. Interview with Mike Wallace, *60 Minutes* 14/08/2006.

43. Mahmoud Ahmadinejad blog, www.Ahmadinejad.ir.

44. "Ahmadinejad's Letter to Bush," *Washington Post* 09/05/2006.

45. Interview with Mike Wallace, *60 Minutes* 14/08/2006.

46. "Ahmadinejad's Strange Words During the Breaking of His Ramadan Fast," Aftab News 15/10/2006.

47. "Ahmadinejad's Letter to Americans," CNN 29/11/2006.

48. Safa Haeri, "Tehran's Demons Revisited," *Asia Times* 26/07/2004.

49. "The Atomic Energy Crisis and the Islamic Republic," Student News Network (SNN) 04/03/2006.

50. "Claims of Communication with Imam Mahdi," *Emrouz* 05/12/2005.

51. Arash Motamed, "The Appearance of Imam Mahdi in 2 Years," *Rooz* online 18/10/2005.

52. "People of Iran Have Imam Hussein," Ansar Hezbollah News 16/01/2006.

53. Shervin Omidvar, "The U.S. Fears the Mahdi's Return," *Rooz* online 25/03/2006.

Chapter Four

1. Sami Moubayed, "Iran and the Art of Crisis Management," *Asia Times* 1/19/05.

2. Frances Harrison, "Iranian MPs Reject Oil Minister," BBC News 11/23/05.

3. Ibid.

4. "What is Driving Oil Prices So High?" BBC News 4/2/06.

5. U.S. Department of Energy—Energy Information Administration—Iran country profile 2006. "Iran's Oil Reserves Among the World's Most Lasting," *Tehran Times* 2/7/05.

6. U.S. Department of Energy—Energy Information Administration—Iran country profile, 2006.

7. Andy Critchlow and Marc Wolfensberger, "Iran's Navy Attacks and Boards Romanian Rig in Gulf," Bloomberg News Service 8/22/06.

8. Simon Tidsall, "Iran Threatens to Use Oil Weapon in Nuclear Standoff," *The Guardian* 07/08/2006.

9. "China's Oil Import from Iran Up 25%" *China Daily* 6/7/06.

10. "Shell & Repsol Sign 4 Billion Dollar Natural Gas Deal with Iran," Islamic Republic News Agency 24/09/2004.

11. This was confirmed by Zogby International/Reader's Digest poll, conducted by telephone from outside Iran in 2006, in which 41 percent of the respondents said that making the economy more efficient was more important than nuclear capabilities or regional issues, with 27 percent disagreeing. Simon Tidsall, "Nuclear Row Boosts Iranian President," *The Guardian* 8/11/06.

12. Interview with a number of Iranian citizens visiting London, March 2006.

13. "30% Rise in Government Wages for Nurses," Baztab News Agency 4/9/06.

14. "Analysis Report from Mehr News—Provision of Financial Assistance to 1.2 million Pensioners," Mehr News 9/24/05.

15. Nader Habibi "Iran's 2006–07 Budget Puts More Emphasis on Economic Justice," Global Insight 2006.

16. Marc Wolfensberger, "Iran's Threat to Cut Oil Flow in Nuclear Dispute May Backfire," Bloomberg News Service 8/2/06.

17. "Government Doubles Its Withdrawal from Its Reserve," Baztab News 9/16/06.

18. "What Are the Goals and Motivations of Ahmadinejad Regarding His Change of the Monetary System?" BBC Persian News 11/13/05.

19. Kave Omidvar, "Enthusiasts for Cheap Loans Apply in Droves," BBC Persian News 9/17/06.

20. "Ahmadinejad and Rafsanjani, Start of the Second Round," Bourse News 8/17/05.

21. "Former Communications Minister: Return of $50 million from the Previous Government has Commenced" Baztab News Agency, 11/19/06.

22. "Dark Sun Glasses of Mr. Bodyguard" Alef News, 9/3/06.

23. "Ayatollah Khomeini's Grandson: 'Iran Needs Democracy and Separation of Religion and State;' 'The Iranian Regime Is the World's Worst Dictatorship" Middle East Media Research Institute, 8/6/03.

24. H. Ahdi, "Billions Missing in Tehran Municipality," *Rooz* online 6/23/06.

25. "The Village of Mr. President," Ansar Hezbollah News, October 2006.

26. AzadarNews.com.

27. "The Argument Between Chief Inspector Davood Ahmadinejad and Zaribafan," Farda News 11/30/05.

28. "The New in Law of the Government Team," Aref News 4/13/06.

29. "Ahmadinejad Complains About Rafsanjani," Aftab News 10/2/06.

30. This was confirmed in interviews with Iranian residents living in Iran and abroad.

31. "Ahmadinejad Promises Single Digit Inflation Rate," IRNA 8/29/06.

32. This view was confirmed during interviews with a number of Tehran citizens.

33. Roger Stern of Johns Hopkins University wrote the study whose findings were published by the AP, 12/25/2006.

Chapter Five

1. An interview with Dr. Etemad, the founder of Iran Atomic Energy Organization (IAEO) 6/2/06.

2. Ibid.

3. Interview with Ambassador Uri Lobrani, 11/12/06.

4. Asadollah Alam, *The Shah and I—The Confidential Diary of Iran's Royal Court, 1969–1977* (London: I. B. Tauris, 1988), 453.

5. Samuel Segev, *The Iranian Triangle* (New York: The Free Press, 1988), 30–31 (based on the Hebrew version).

6. An interview with Eliezer Tsafrir, February 20, 2006.

7. General Freidon Jam wrote an introduction in 1999 from his exile in London to a book published in Hebrew. The book, *Írangate—A Hope Shattered*, written by Jacob Nimrodi, a former Israeli military attaché in Tehran during the Shah's reign, was published in 2004 by Maariv, Tel Aviv.

8. An interview with General Yitzhak Segev, May 23, 2006.

9. Ibid.

10. Ibid. Toufanian went several times, secretly, to Tel Aviv and received several top-level Israeli delegations in Tehran. "Toufanian was a very ambitious and self-centered man," recalled General Segev. "His main and sometimes only interest was how much he would personally gain from this deal or that agreement." The new understanding held great potential for General Toufanian.

11. Ibid.

12. For more about Israel's nuclear development read Avner Cohen, *Israel and the Bomb* (New York: Columbia University Press, 1998).

13. An interview with Uri Lobrani, 5/30/06.

14. Ibid.

15. www.nti.org—NTI Profile, Iran, Nuclear Chronology and Muhammad Sahimi, Iran's Nuclear Program: Part 1: Its History in http://www.payvand.com/news.

16. Ibid.

17. Ibid.

18. An interview given by Dr. Etemad to *Berliner Zeitung*, 3/31/2006.

19. Ibid.

20. The diplomat asked not to be named.

21. Dr. Etemad, *The Iranian Nuclear Program*, Abadan Publishing Company.

Chapter Six

1. See Juan Cole, *Conversations with History* (Berkeley: University of California Institute of International Studies, 2006).

2. See www.nti.org.

3. "Bushehr in the Budget," *Nuclear News*, October 1985, p. 76.

4. See Amir Taheri, *Jerusalem Post*, 5 October 2006. Taheri claimed that Khomeini actually dismantled in March 1979 Etemad's Atomic Energy Organization of Iran.

5. The students published in 1981–2 a series of 13 volumes based on documents they captured at the U.S. embassy. The volumes were titled *Documents from the Den of Spies.*

6. See Baqer Moin, *Khomeini: Life of the Ayatollah* (New York: St. Martin's Press, 1999), chap. 1.

7. Baqer Moin.

8. See Nikki R. Keddie, *Modern Iran: Roots and Results of Revolution* (New Haven: Yale University Press, 2003), 191.

9. Ibid.

10. Hojatol eslam (proof of God) is a title of religious honor only somewhat less respectful than ayatollah (miraculous sign of God).

11. Baqer Moin.

12. Keddie, 193.

13. From an interview with Lobrani, July 2006.

14. This phrase first appeared in the *Washington Post.* See David Segal, "Atomic Ayatollahs: Just What the Mideast Needs—An Iranian Bomb," 12 April 1987.

15. This information was obtained from senior Western intelligence officials who asked not to be named. The officials said they gleaned the information from interviewing Iranian exiles who worked for Iranian government in the mid-1980s.

16. The first invasion of Iraq by the United States, in 1991, following Saddam Hussein's conquest of Kuwait, is called the second Gulf War and the 2003 invasion of Iraq by the United States can be defined as the third Gulf War.

17. Francis Harrison, "Waiting for Justice in Iran," BBC 15/10/2005.

18. Phone interview with Afshin Ramezani, March 2006.

19. See "Communication Dated 12 September 2005 from the Permanent Mission of the Islamic Republic of Iran to IAEA," 121. The Iranian ambassador delivered this statement to the IAEA Ali Asghar Soltanieh. www.iaea.org.

20. In 2006 General Mohsen Rezai was the deputy head of the Expediency Council; the owner of Baztab, a leading news Web site; and a candidate in the 2005 presidential election.

21. See Shyam Bhatia, *Nuclear Rivals in the Middle East* (London and New York: Routledge, 1988), 83.

22. See Jack Boureston and Charles D. Ferguson, "Schooling Iran's Atom Squad," *Bulletin of the Atomic Scientists* 60, no. 3 (May/June 2004): 31–35.

23. Ibid., based on a 1991 *Nucleonics Week* report.

24. Iran filed a lawsuit in August 1986 with the International Commerce Commission asking for $5.5 billion in compensation for Germany's violation of its contractual obligations. By 2006 the matter was still unsettled. See Muhammad Sahimi, Iran's Nuclear Program: Part I: Its History, 10 February 2003.

25. See Robert Thomson, "China Denies Nuclear Weapons Allegations," *Financial Times,* 25 October 1985, 4.

26. See IAEA report, "Implementation of the NPT Safeguards Agreement in the Islamic Republic of Iran," November 2004.

27. See IAEA report, "Implementations of the NPT Safeguards Agreement in the Islamic Republic of Iran," November 2003. In the report the IAEA director general revealed that "practically all of the materials important to uranium conversion had been produced in laboratory and bench scale experiments between 1981 and 1993 without having been reported to the Agency."

28. See Jeffrey T. Richelson, *Spying on the Bomb: American Nuclear Intelligence from Nazi Germany to Iran and North Korea* (New York: W.W. Norton, 2006), 504.

29. See Elaine Sciolino, "China Will Build a Plant for Iran," *New York Times* 9/11/92.

30. The information about Khan's visits was obtained from American and Israeli intelligence officials and from IAEA officials who asked not to be named in conversations held in Vienna, Washington, and Tel Aviv between 2004 and 2006.

31. See Bill Gertz, "U.S. Defuses Effort by Iran to Get Nukes," *The Washington Times* 10/24/94.

32. From interviews with IAEA senior officials with Western intelligence officers and researchers; see Al J. Venter, *Iran's Nuclear Option: Teheran's Quest for the Atom Bomb* (Philadelphia: Casemate, 2005), 145–46.

Chapter Seven

1. The exchange at Natanz is based on interviews with IAEA officials who are privy to the events that took place there. The interviews were conducted at IAEA headquarters in Vienna in February 2006.

2. All dates and figures in this chapter are based on IAEA official records and information, which can be found at www.iaea.org, and interviews with IAEA public affairs and press officers.

3. See the Atoms for Peace speech, at www.iaea.org.

4. Ibid.

5. See David Fischer, *History of the International Atomic Energy Agency: The First Forty Years* (Vienna: IAEA Publications, 1997).

6. See Dan Raviv and Yossi Melman, *Every Spy a Prince: The Complete of Israel's Intelligence Community* (Boston: Houghton Mifflin Company, 1990), 67–73.

7. See Jeffrey T. Richelson, *Spying on the Bomb*, 222–21.

8. Ibid., 328–29.

9. See William Broad and David Sanger, "Restrains Fray and Risks Grow as Nuclear Club Gains Members," *New York Times*, 10/15/2006. In December 2006 the board of governors approved several Iranian requests for technical assistance but refused to comply with Iran's request to monitor the safety of the reactor built in Arak. Tehran has rejected the board's demand that Iran suspend the construction of the plant.

10. From the official El-Baradei biography released by the IAEA.

11. From interviews with senior officials of Israeli Atomic Commission, 2006.

12. From conversations with senior State Department officials, 2006.

13. See the IAEA report "Implementation of the NPT Safeguards Agreement in the Islamic Republic of Iran," August 2003.

14. From conversations with senior State Department officials and Israeli government ministers who asked not to be named, 2006.

15. From interviews with Muhammad El-Baradei in Vienna, December 2003, and in Israel, July 2004.

16. The IAEA senior official asked to remain anonymous.

17. From conversation with Western intelligence officers who asked not to be named.

18. From conversations with IAEA inspectors, 2006.

19. From an interview with Muhammad El-Baradei in his office, Vienna, 2003.

20. This is an official reply from IAEA's Press and Public Information Office to the authors' questions.

21. See U.S. State Department, "Foreign Terrorist Organizations," report submitted to the Congress in February 2004, p. 69.

22. See Jeffrey T. Richelson, *Spying on the Bomb: American Nuclear Intelligence from Nazi Germany to Iran and North Korea* (New York: W.W. Norton, 2006), 512.

23. From interviews in late 2006 with very senior Israeli intelligence officials, who asked not to be named.

24. From conversations with IAEA inspectors, 2003–2006.

25. See Sharon Squassoni, Congressional Record Service, "Iran's Nuclear Program: Recent Developments," p. 3 by Specialist in National Defense, Foreign Affairs, Defense and Trade Division, 6 September 2006.

26. See IAEA report, November 2004.

27. Interviews with IAEA senior officials.

28. This is the description of the U.S. delegation during IAEA board of governors meeting in Vienna in September 2003.

29. BBC News, 12 February 2004, www.bbc.co.uk.

30. Ibid.

31. In a BBC story, Dr. Khan's daughter, who lives in London, hinted that before her father was put under house arrest, he relayed to her almost the full version of his testimony, which would implicate and embarrass senior Pakistani officials. 02/10/2006.

32. The Western intelligence sources asked not to be named.

33. IAEA report, November 2004.

34. Ibid.

Chapter Eight

1. The report titled "U.S. Task Force on Terrorism and Unconventional Warfare" was prepared in 1992 by the House Republican Research Committee. See also Global Security Organization at www.globalsecurity.org/wmd/world/iran/Lavisan.html.

2. The report was part of a series of alarmist articles published by the *Jerusalem Post* in April 1998. In these articles it was said that a defecting Iranian nuclear scientist and documents had revealed (probably to American and Israeli intelligence officials) details about Iran's nuclear program. The defector and the documents, according to the articles, discussed Iranian efforts to purchase nuclear warheads from the former Soviet Union republics. One of the documents dated December 1991 supposedly argued that "Iran received several nuclear warheads from a former Soviet republic in the early 1990 and Russian experts maintained them." Another document said that the deputy head of the revolutionary guards told the head of AEOI, Reza Amrollahi, that "two war materials of nuclear nature" had arrived from Russia and were being held by the guards at Lavisan.

3. See Uzi Rubin, "The Global Reach of Iran's Ballistic Missiles," November 2006, by Institute for National Security Studies at Tel Aviv University, an interview with General Uzi Rubin in July 2006. Rubin used to be the head of the Israeli defense ministry's research and development department.

4. This statement was issued on May 15, 2003, at a U.S. press conference chaired by Alireza Jafarzadeh, an Iranian consultant who is the unofficial spokesman of the NCRI in the United States.

5. This information was obtained from interviews with senior Western European intelligence officials.

6. The communication between Iran and the IAEA is based on extensive interviews with senior IAEA staff, which reconstructed for the authors the messages the two sides exchanged.

7. From an interview with senior Western intelligence officials in August 2006.

8. IAEA report, "Implementation of the NPT Safeguards Agreement in the Islamic Republic of Iran," November 2004, p. 21.

9. Ibid.

10. Ibid.

11. Ibid.

12. "Iran Denies IAEA Access to Nuclear Site," www.aljazeera.com quoting AP story 21/08/2006.

13. IAEA report "Implementation of the NPT Safeguards Agreement in the Islamic Republic of Iran," August 2006.

14. IAEA Report, November 2004.

15. Ibid.

16. IAEA report, February 2006.

17. IAEA report, April 2006.

18. IAEA report, November 2004.

19. IAEA report, November 2004.

20. Asgar Soltaneih addressed the IAEA's Board of Governors in mid-2004.

21. Polonium 210 is a radioactive material which the former Russian intelligence officer, Alexander Litvinenko, was poisoned in London in November 2006 in the famous "spy poisoning case."

22. ABC News 09/2005, read by David Albright at www.isis-online.org.

23. See Robert Tait, "Iran Claims About Nuclear Plans," *The Guardian*

14/11/2005. See also Daphna Linzer, "Strong Leads and Dead Ends in Nuclear Case Against Iran," *Washington Post* 08/02/2006.

24. See James Risen, *The Secret History of the CIA*, 194–212.

25. The authors learned about the two IAEA camps, which are still arguing about the authenticity of the laptops from interviews with several IAEA officials, Vienna, 2005 and 2006.

26. See the IAEA report, August 2006.

27. The information about the structure of Iran's nuclear program was provided to the authors in briefings with three Western intelligence organizations.

28. See Nicholas Birch, "In Iran, Clerics' Wealth Draws Ire," *Christian Science Monitor* 20/08/2003.

29. "Iran: 'Nuclear Symphony' to Open in Tehran," AKI 26/06/2006.

30. See "A Symphony from Kiev About Nuclear Ambitions in Iran," BBC World, June 2006.

31. See "Nuclear Symphony Commissioned," *Iran Daily* 17/12/2005.

Chapter Nine

1. One of the authors interviewed Shabtai Shavit on December 17, 2006.

2. Israeli intelligence focused mainly on prioritizing and ranking topics of interests in three traditional areas: to gather information on war intentions against Israel and to assess and analyze it; the struggle against Palestinian terrorism; to monitor the military capabilities of those countries which were considered enemies and carried real or potential threat to the Jewish state. They primarily included Syria, Iraq, and to a lesser degree Libya and Egypt, which were perceived as a less immediate threat.

3. Colonel Opher Ben Peretz talked about his experience and information in e-mail exchanges with one of the authors in September and October 2006.

4. Shavit.

5. Jeffrey T. Richelson, *Spying on the Bomb*, 506.

6. Ibid.

7. Ibid.

8. One of the authors interviewed Uri Saguy in May 2005.

9. Shavit.

10. See Uzi Rubin, "The Global Reach of Iran's Ballistic Missiles," Memo-

randum 86, November 2006, Institute for National Security Studies, Tel Aviv University, and Ephraim Kam, *From Terror to Nuclear Bombs: The Significance of the Iranian Threat* (in Hebrew) (Tel Aviv: Ministry of Defense Publishing House), 143–175.

11. Shavit.

12. For elaborated discussions of the Israeli campaign against the Soviet Union see Nehemiah Levanon, *"Nativ" Was the Code Name* (Tel Aviv: Am Oved, 1995).

13. The former KGB officer asked to remain anonymous. Eventually, in 1997, he cooperated with the FSB, Russia's domestic security service, which in charge of preventing the "leakage" of nuclear technology and materials abroad. He also cooperated with some foreign governments to expose Iranian purchasing networks. One of the authors interviewed him in Moscow, September 2006.

14. Shavit.

15. See Robert Einhorn and Gary Samore, "Heading off Iran's Bomb: The Need for Renewed U.S.-Russian Cooperation," *Yederny Control Digest* 17, no. 3 (Moscow: PIR Center, 2002).

16. Since we've already discussed efforts directed at China and North Korea, it sounds repetitive to include the whole world ("elsewhere") in the preface to the following discussion.

17. One of the authors interviewed General Amos Malka in June 2006.

18. One of the authors interviewed Uzi Arad in December 2006.

19. Shavit.

20. Arad.

21. See Ephraim Kam, 194.

22. Michael Gordon, "Against U.S. Wishes, Russia Will Sell Reactors to Iran," *The New York Times* 7/3/1998.

23. Shavit.

24. Ibid.

25. Interview with Saguy, December 2006.

26. The Israeli official asked not to be named.

27. All the above-mentioned developments were told to the authors by senior America, British, and Israeli intelligence and other government officials who asked not to be named or identified.

28. Interviews with several heads of Israel's intelligence agencies, including

Shavit, Saguy, Malka, and Ephraim Halevy, in December 2006, and Aaron Ze'evi Farkash in November 2006.

29. Richelson, 512.

30. Graham Allison, "How Good Is American Intelligence on Iran's Bomb?" Yale Global online, www.yaleglobal.yale.edu, 13/06/2006.

31. The Israeli official asked not to be named.

32. From an interview on National Public Radio, 18/09/2006.

33. See "Report: Britain Approved the Export of Radioactive Material to Iran," Haaretz News Service 08/01/2006, quoting a story published originally by the *London Observer.*

34. See "Iran Row Hits Belgian Spy Chief," BBC 31/1/2006.

35. Jon Swain, "Iran's Plot to Mine Uranium in Africa," *Times* online citing a *Sunday Times* story 08/06/06.

36. "Austria Probes Firm Over N-related Iran Exports," IranMania quoting Reuters 16/12/2006.

37. One of the authors interviewed Dr. Ephraim Asculai, who is currently a nuclear researcher at Tel Aviv University.

Chapter Ten

1. See "Islamic Revolutionary Guards Corp Practices Closure of the Strait of Hormuz," Rajanews 06/11/2006.

2. "Iran Warns the West," Advar News, www.advarnews.com, 23/01/2006.

3. See Simon Henderson, "Facing Iran's Challenge: Safeguarding Oil Exports from the Persian Gulf," The Washington Institute for Near East Studies, 07/06/2006.

4. Brad Foss, George Jahn, "Iran sanctions could drive oil past $100," Associated Press 22/01/2006.

5. See Bronwen Maddox, "U.S. preparing to get tough as UN dithers over Iran sanctions," *The Times* 19/09/2006.

6. "Russia, China Urge Caution in Iran Nuclear Dispute," Radio Free Europe 17/01/2006.

7. See Nikkie R. Keddie, *Modern Iran: Roots and Results of Revolution* (New Haven, CT: Yale University Press, 2003).

8. One of these people who were in touch with the neo cons was Manuchehr Ghorbanifar, an Iranian businessman in exile who was involved in the '82–'86 Írangate—a joint Israeli-American ambitious

adventure that executed the following scheme. Selling Israeli weapons to Iran, using the proceeds to finance behind the back of congress and illegally the Contras in Nicaragua, securing in return the release of some American hostages held by pro-Iranian Hezbollah in Lebanon and replenishing Israel with new weapons from American stocks. The resurfacing of Ghorbanifar was reported by Laura Rozen in *American Prospect* 26/09/2006.

9. From an interview with Uri Lobrani, 12/11/2006.

10. Ibid.

11. Ibid.

12. From a telephone interview with Fateme S. in Tehran, 15/04/2006.

13. See Jacqueline W. Shire, "U.S. Offers Iran Economic Incentives," ABC News 11/03/2005.

14. See CNN transcripts, "Secretary of State Albright Announces Easing of U.S. Trade Ban on Iran," 17/03/2000.

15. See IAEA quarterly reports prepared by the director general for the board of governors since 2003.

16. "Israel Presses West to Get Tough on Iran," *New York Times* 13/01/2006.

Chapter Eleven

1. The air force had recently changed its name to Air and Space Arm.

2. An interview with General Eitan Ben Eliyahu, November 2006.

3. For a comprehensive description on the 1981 raid, see Shlomo Nakdimon, *First Strike: The Exclusive Story of How Israel Foiled Iraq's Attempt to Get the Bomb* (New York: Summit Books, 1987).

4. The term *preemptive strike* is often confused with *preventive strike*. Preemptive strike means to spoil by surprise an imminent attack. Preventive strike is to stop or avert the adversary from achieving his goal.

5. The late Menachem Begin explained the doctrine after the raid in several newspaper interviews and in a conversation with one of the authors in October 1981.

6. Interview with Ben Eliyahu.

7. For details about the Israeli-U.S. military and intelligence cooperation and its code names, see William M. Arkin, *Code Names: Deciphering U.S. Military Plans, Programs and Operations in the 9/11 World* (Hanover, NH: Steerforth Press, 2005), 13-139. Arkin was interviewed in February 2005 by one of the authors.

8. See the Israeli daily *Yediot Aharonot* (Hebrew), 31/3/2000.

9. See the Israeli daily *Haaretz* (Hebrew), 3/6/1998.

10. www.isracast.com, 14/4/2006.

11. One of the authors interviewed Brigadier General Relik Shafir in March 2005.

12. This claim was raised by Dr. Khadir Hamze, an Iranian nuclear scientist, on CNN *Crossfire,* February 07, 2003.

13. See Leonard Beaton and John Maddox, *The Spread of Nuclear Weapons* (in Hebrew), Ministry of Defense Publishing House, August 1963, and General Yehoshafat Harkabi, *Nuclear War and Nuclear Peace,* Ministry of Defense, 102.

14. See David Albright and Corey Hinderstein, "The Iranian Gas Centrifuge Uranium Enrichment Plant at Natanz: Drawing from Commercial Satellite Images," www.isis-online.org/publications/iran/natanz. The report was supplemented by satellite photos showing how Iran has been building, hardening, and expanding the site.

15. General Shafir.

16. One of the authors had a conversation about Iran's nuclear policy with Ariel Sharon in October 2002.

17. See Efraim Inbar "The need to block a nuclear Iran," *Mid East Security and Policy Studies,* no. 67, 16–18 (The Begin-Sadat Center for Strategic Studies, Bar Ilan University, April 2006).

18. Interview with Professor Menachem Megidor, December 2006.

19. Ali Larijani talked to reporters during a November trip to Pakistan. See the Pakistani Web site www.Pakitribune.com, 25/11/2006.

20. "Osirak Redux? Assessing Israeli Capabilities to Destroy Iranian Nuclear Facilities by Whitney Raas and Austin Long," working paper for Security Studies Program (SSP) at MIT, April 2006, 17.

21. Whitney Raas and Austin Long.

22. For more details about the GBU, see Federation of American Scientists, http://www.fas.org/man/dod-101/sys/smart/gbu-28.htm The GBU-28 is a 5,000-pound laser-guided conventional munition that uses a 4,400-pound penetrating warhead. The bombs are modified Army artillery tubes, weigh 4,637 pounds, and contain 630 pounds of high explosives. They are fitted with GBU-27 LGB kits, 14.5 inches in diameter and almost 19 feet long. The operator illuminates a target with a laser designator and then the munition guides to a spot of laser energy reflected from the target.

23. Seymour N. Hersh, "The Coming Wars—What the Pentagon Can Now Do in Secret," *The New Yorker* 01/24/2005.

24. 108th Congress, 2nd Session, H.Con.Res.389, Concurrent Resolution, May 6, 2004.

25. Samy Salamah and Karen Ruster, "A Preemptive Attack on Iran's Nuclear Facilities Possible Consequences," Center for Non Proliferation Studies 09/09/2004.

26. Among the supporters of an "Israeli attack " are Deputy Defense Minster Erfraim Sneh, Head of Mossad Meir Dagan, and Minister for Strategic Affairs Avigdor Liberman.

27. Whitney Raas and Austin Long.

28. Ibid.

29. Ibid.

30. *The Sunday Times,* 5/3/2006.

31. *Janes Defence Weekly,* 04/05/2005.

32. Rass and Long.

33. See James Risen, "State of War," pp. 8–9.

Chapter Twelve

1. The authors learned of the inside developments in Hezbollah from well-informed Lebanese sources who live abroad.

2. Ibid.

3. "Mesbah Yazdi Surprised from Nasrallah Modesty," Baztab News, 05/12/2006.

4. For more detailed discussion of the historic relations between Iran and the Shiites in Lebanon, see Shimon Shapira, *Hezbollah, Between Iran and Lebanon* (Hebrew) (Tel Aviv: Hakibbutz Hameuchad Publishing House, 2000), 15–48.

5. Bob Woodward, *Veil, The secret wars of the CIA, 1981–1987* (Headline Book Publishing, 1987), 396–97.

6. www.fbi.gov/wanted/terrorist.

7. Robert Baer, a CIA operative, claims in his book, *See No Evil—A True Story of a Ground Soldier in the CIA's War on Terrorism* (New York: Three Rivers Press, 2002), 98–99, that the family was illegally residing in Beirut.

8. For more detailed explanation of IRGC and al-Quds, see www.Globalsecurity.org/intell/world/iran/qods.htm.

9. The main sources for these unconfirmed report is the government-owned English-language *Tehran Times,* which covered the story extensively in 1998. The story was later picked up by opposition Web sites such as www.iranterror.com. The main puzzle in this story is whether it would have been possible for a boy of Jewish descent, even if he or his family had converted to Islam, to rise to such a senior and sensitive position in a government so highly suspicious of Jews.

10. See Ephraim Kam, *From Terror to Nuclear Bombs: The Significance of the Iranian Threat* (in Hebrew) (Tel Aviv: Tel Aviv University, 2004), 251–215.

11. "German court implicates Iran leaders in '92 killings," CNN Interactive 10/04/1997.

12. Kam.

13. Information about the Argentine terror attacks is based on interviews with Israeli, Argentine, and American intelligence officials as well as Israeli foreign ministry officials. Sanitized portions of the SIDE report were seen by one of the authors. See also *New York Times* 09/11/2002. The article talks about Mesbahi's evidence.

14. See Luis Freeh, "Kh-obar Towers: The Clinton Administration Left Many Stones Unturned," *Wall Street Journal* 25/06/2006. Freeh was promoting in 2005 his memoir *Bringing Down the Mafia, Investigating Bill Clinton and Waging War on Terror.*

15. See "Court Blames Iran for U.S. Death," *Jerusalem Post* citing AP 22/12/2006.

16. Shabtai Shavit was interviewed by one of the authors.

17. See Ely Karmon, "Hezbollah Latin America—Queer Group or Real Threat?" Interdisciplinary Center Herzliya IDC, Institute for Counter Terrorism, 07/11/2006.

18. Ibid.

19. CBS News citing a *Washington Post* story, 17/10/2003.

20. See Uzi Rubin, "The Global Reach of Iran's Ballistic Missiles," Memorandum 86, Institute for National Security Studies, Tel Aviv University.

21. Ibid.

22. See Gerald Steinberg, "Iran Is Bluffing When It Threatens Massive Retaliation," The Begin-Sadat Center for Strategic Studied Bulletin Number 20, May 2006, Bar Ilan University.

Chapter Thirteen

1. See Rafsanjani's Qods Day speech (Jerusalem Day), Voice of the Islamic Republic of Iran, Tehran, in Farsi, translated by BBC Worldwide Monitoring, original broadcast December 14, 2001.

2. See Barry Schweid, "Report: Iran's Oil Exports May Disappear," Associated Press 25/12/2005.

Index